S0-BIN-618

# ANCIENT AMERICA
## of the "PRE~COLUMBIAN" period

1st (ed.)

7⁵⁰
R65
AA

Birthday Greetings
to Mr. Morrison
from Dorothy Vedder

December 5, 1931.

# COLUMBUS CAME LATE

E. H. Thompson and Gregory Mason at Chichen Itza, between
rear of Nunnery (right) and chapel (left)

# COLUMBUS
# CAME LATE

*By* GREGORY MASON

*With Illustrations*
*and Maps*

## THE CENTURY CO.

*New York*                    *London*

COPYRIGHT, 1931, BY THE CENTURY CO.
ALL RIGHTS RESERVED, INCLUDING THE
RIGHT TO REPRODUCE THIS BOOK, OR
PORTIONS THEREOF, IN ANY FORM

*First printing*

PRINTED IN U. S. A.

## PROLOGUE

To A certain extent this is a mystery story; but it is not one conceived in the fertile brain of a Gaboriau, a Van Dine, or a Poe. It is also a tale of great human achievement; but it is not one imagined by a Scott or a Dickens or a Conrad. However, if you like such tales as those, you should like this one. For it is true, and the hero is not a single individual but a group of nations with a high civilization composing an entire people—the people of ancient America.

No one who sees the remains of roads and bridges and aqueducts in Peru can doubt that achievement. No one who sees the immense pyramids of Mexico, the ancient irrigation canals of Arizona can doubt it. No one can possibly doubt it who has cut the thick bush of Yucatan and Guatemala from the roofs of lovely crumbled temples and palaces as I have done, who has traced one-time canals across meadows now peopled only by herons and bitterns, or followed great raised roads—crowded hundreds of years ago with a proud commerce—through the jungle which tears up their beds but has not yet, after more than

v

four centuries, succeeded in entirely destroying the traces of the beauty and the grandeur that once were there.

Archæology is not dry dust, it is frozen history. The layman who takes it up accidentally, as I did, finds it an exciting and fascinating game. It is just as exciting as watching eighteen men play baseball, and just as fascinating as working out a cross-word puzzle.

A few minutes before writing that paragraph I was reading a volume dealing with the mystery surrounding the great stone ruins of South America. A woman friend of mine—fellow-guest at the inn where I was staying—looked over my shoulder and exclaimed:

"Oh, you are reading that heavy stuff again!"

Then she went to a sofa and began to work on a cross-word puzzle.

This woman was one of three who about that time spent an entire week putting together a gigantic jig-saw puzzle. Literally, they worked at it morning, afternoon, and evening for a week. Their energy and assiduity were remarkable. But was not the choice of an object for the exercise of their energy and assiduity somewhat pitiable? It happens that all three of them are intelligent and educated women. When they had finished the jig-saw puzzle they had nothing to show for their efforts. Whereas, if they had expended

vi

the same time and energy in studying Dr. Sylvanus G. Morley's "Introduction to the Study of Maya Hieroglyphs" they would have added materially to their education and would have acquired a hobby which would stay with them for life, and which is far more absorbing than jig-saw puzzles.

But the riddle of the Maya hieroglyphs is only one of a number of fascinating enigmas American archæology offers the intelligent layman. The type of mind that is successful with chess or cross-word puzzles is just the type of mind likely to be successful in coping with the engrossing problem offered by the presence in Bolivia of great stone ruins possessing certain similarities to the ruins of Guatemala. If you can prove that in ancient times there was a connection between Bolivia and Guatemala you will be doing more for humanity than by solving a million cross-word puzzles.

Auction bridge and contract are not mere pastimes. Unquestionably they are developers of valuable mental powers. Yet if all the mental power exercised on card games to-day, by the people of the United States and Europe, could be directed to science, who knows but man might soon solve the riddle of the universe? At any rate, by such a redirection of popular mental energy we could produce in the United States an informed public opinion which would be of incalculable help to the Jeans and Lowells and Millikans and Einsteins who are doing our more advanced thinking. And that general lifting of the level of human intelligence would almost certainly lead to the more frequent birth of Jeans and Lowells and Millikans and Einsteins. Perhaps the most pitiful feature of contemporary civilization is the vast amount of mental effort wasted on trivialities. It is only fair to say that our great thinkers, our great scientists, are themselves partly responsible for this state of affairs. Since the beginning of time intellectual leaders of the human race have been lamentably incapable of explaining the results of their cerebrations, in terms understandable to the average man and woman.

Which consideration is the justification of such books as this. For the volume is not put forth as an original addition to the sum of human knowledge: it is merely an attempt to increase the circle of those who understand what that sum of knowledge already is in the field the author covers, pre-Columbian America; an attempt to induce an appreciation of the romance and satisfaction involved in the pursuit of an understanding of the achievements of our "foster-ancestors," the early Americans.

I hope I can persuade you to read on and be convinced that archæology is not dry dust, but is fascinating frozen history. It would encourage you to know how many illustrious scientists have developed from members of the lay order who took up science as a hobby. A good example of this sort of thing was provided at the 1928 Congress of the Americanists, in New York City. These Americanists are professional and amateur students of the red-skinned native of our western continents. The two outstanding sensations of the 1928 Congress were provided by two laymen: an insurance salesman from Hartford, Connecticut, and a chemist from New York City. These two men had taken up two different phases of early American culture as a hobby, just as they might have taken up cross-word puzzles, chess, or bridge. The former, Mr. B. Whorf, demonstrated his ability to read certain texts in Nahua which had "stumped" the professional students of this language of ancient Mexico. The latter, Mr. J. E. Teeple, threw new light on the significance of some of the baffling hieroglyphs of the Mayas.

As a matter of fact, more and more laymen are coming to feel the lure of these old American cultures. More books and magazine and newspaper articles concerning them are now published in the United States every year than were formerly published in one decade, as was indicated by a recent compilation of bibliography made by Professor Marshall H. Saville. By giving your spare time to this recreation instead of to bridge or chess or the movies you may become a Champollion, may discover a Rosetta Stone that will unlock the secrets of a whole race.

If you don't like hieroglyphs, perhaps you can arrange to spend your vacations among the modern Maya Indians of Central America. Many clues to the mystery may be picked up from them, for in them is the blood of the race which developed the highest of all ancient American cultures. These modern Maya Indians seem to be descended from the great slave class which survived the yellow-fever epidemics and the civil wars that killed off the aristocracy just before Columbus reached America and which never *did* know how to read the glyphs. But mixed with the Roman Catholicism given them by Spain they maintain old rites and customs that *they themselves* do not understand. If you watch them carefully you may see these pathetic rum-sodden Indians uncomprehendingly acting out, in honor of some "Christian" saint, a rite depicted for us by their glorious ancestors, in paint or sculptured stone. If you do, you will get a thrill not to be equaled elsewhere for any lover of mystery. And incidentally you will come back from your vacation equipped with what is just about the most engrossing hobby an intelligent man or woman can take up in this twentieth century.

# CONTENTS

# ILLUSTRATIONS

# ILLUSTRATIONS

# COLUMBUS CAME LATE

# CHAPTER I

## AMERICA GREW UP ALONE

IN 1492 America discovered Columbus. On the morning of October 12 of that year some fishermen who lived on an island in the outer fringe of the Bahamas saw three strange vessels at anchor off the sandy beach of their green isle. Although two of the strange ships were not much bigger than some of the largest canoes used in America, the first vessel was easily the greatest the Americans had ever seen. She was the *Santa Maria,* ninety feet long and twenty broad, and she carried the chief of an extraordinary party of men who had come out of the eastern sea. Dressed in scarlet, this chief came ashore in a small canoe propelled by paddles plied horizontally, instead of vertically in the American manner. Landing, he planted on the beach a splendid banner, whereupon he and his followers engaged in ceremonies altogether curious and bewildering to the natives, who could not guess that they were about to be robbed of their homeland.

The strangers were armed with swords of a hard, sharp material never before seen in America. It is said that a fisherman, approaching one of the new

3

arrivals, grasped the latter's sword out of curiosity and cut his fingers. In this incident we may see a tragic symbol of the whole conquest of America. Europe accomplished that conquest not by superiority in the arts of peace—which she did not possess—but merely because Europeans were more skilful than Americans in the "art" of killing men.

Those rude fishermen were not the most cultured Americans. They themselves were probably ignorant of the high achievements in art and science which had flowered on the two continents behind them. They could not have told the Spaniards of these things had they wished, and the Europeans would have been little interested to hear. The latter were rude men of action concerned with the pursuit of gold and precious stones. They came to America with a tremendous confidence in themselves which alone had made possible the crossing of an uncharted ocean. They saw that the natives' spears and arrows were no match for their swords and cannon, the very boom of which filled the Americans with terror. They were satisfied to see that they had gone much farther than these brown "barbarians" toward the mastery of mechanics, and for them the mastery of mechanics was synonymous with civilization. We, their successors, have persisted in the error of this view.

Even fourteen years later, when Columbus lay dying, the idea had not entered his head that the an-

4

Courtesy American Museum of Natural History

Peruvian pottery

Courtesy American Museum of Natural History

Fossilized ear of corn found in Peru

cestors of the people his followers were conquering in A₁ ............ l created a painting, a sculpture, a mathematics, and an astronomy worthy of comparison with the best art and science of Europe. It was obvious that stone could not cope with steel, nor bowstrings with gunpowder. So the Genoese navigator, who had thought his Bahama island was a piece of land lying off the coast of India or China, easily assumed that the civilization of Europe was superior to the civilization of the "New World" sighted by him that morning of October 12, 1492, from the high poop deck of the *Santa Maria*.

To-day we live in an age of machines. And because of that fact we are too much inclined to take it for granted that a mastery of mechanics spells civilization. Yet there may be some among us who wonder, now and then, if the age of Marconi and the Wrights actually exhibits a higher culture than the age of Socrates and Praxiteles, or the age of Dante and Leonardo da Vinci. And if not, it might be said that the early American astronomers and architects were more civilized than the rough men-at-arms who conquered them!

However, in the twentieth century Christopher Columbus is more of a hero in the Americas he accidentally "discovered" than in the Europe from which he sailed. This is because we who rule North and South America to-day are still subconsciously European. We are grateful to Christopher Columbus for having "discovered" the two vast continents on which we live, and on which millions of civilized beings had lived before Columbus was born. We are aware of a great deal of what we owe to Europe, but we appreciate very little of what we owe to America.

The very vastness and diversity of America may be partly responsible for our failure in appreciation. But the chief reason for it is that we people of North and South America, and particularly those of us who live in the United States, suffer from a hemispheric inferiority complex. We assume entirely too readily that the indigenous institutions of Europe and Asia are *ipso facto* superior to the indigenous institutions of the Americas. We cannot bear to entertain the notion that the early culture of our twin western continents may have been as high as or higher than that of the so-called "Old World." And if you suggest that "New World" may be a misnomer for our hemisphere, in the opinion of most of your hearers you are merely proving yourself a little mad.

Like a good many individual inferiority complexes, this hemispheric inferiority complex may spring from egotism. Most of the civilized people of the western hemisphere are descended from men and women who emigrated from Europe and Asia. It is naïve but natural of them to assume that there was nothing of importance in the way of civilization in this hemi-

6

sphere before their ancestors arrived in the *Santa Maria* or the *Mayflower*. It is naïve but natural of them to conclude that if there *was* any worth-while culture over here before Columbus it was brought by some earlier *Santa Maria* coming from the regions of those Holy Lands we are taught by tradition to consider the birthplace of the human race.

In a hundred amusing ways this hemispheric inferiority complex is exhibited, especially among us citizens of the United States, who with blithe arrogance have reserved to ourselves alone the title of "Americans." Many of us feel that we have achieved the pinnacle of social prominence when we have succeeded in marrying one of our daughters to the bearer of a European title, irrespective of the true worth of the man. We rush to buy the works of British novelists and crowd our halls to hear these authors lecture, while Americans who write or talk equally well are comparatively neglected. Our art galleries are crowded with the canvases of Europeans, our millionaires pay fabulous prices for the "masterpieces" of dead Frenchmen, Englishmen, or Italians; meanwhile American painters, as able artists as any wielding the brush to-day, must waste their time illustrating advertisements for our magazines—or starve. It is easy for a third-rate European musician to get his compositions played by our symphony orchestras, whose European-born leaders reject the

7

works of first-class American composers, with the approval of the rich Americans who support these orchestras and who have been taught to believe that America has no art of her own. Our millionaires establish large foundations for the pursuit of archæological investigation in Greece or Egypt, but it is like pulling teeth to get a dollar out of them for excavating the wonder and glory of ancient America.

As indicated above, there is little doubt that our Christian training is partly responsible for begetting in us the erroneous assumption that man owes everything worth while in his present culture to the Old World. It is understandable that laymen should suffer from the mistaken assumption; but the entertainment of this hemispheric inferiority complex by some of our men of science is less forgivable and is more damaging. Even yet some scientists shut their eyes to the evidence that America grew up alone, and in the recent past not a few archæologists and explorers have tried to explain the presence of a high culture in the western hemisphere before the advent of Columbus by the theory that early navigators whose names have been forgotten must have brought the rare flower of knowledge from Europe or Asia.

The very splendor of the pre-Columbian American scene has tended to discredit it. Too wonderful to be real, men thought it—that is, to be really American. The same awe, almost incredulity, felt by the

8

first European settlers when they gazed upon the crumbling vestiges of civilizations that had flourished in America when the British Isles were a wilderness, we feel to-day. But we ought to know better than the European "discoverers." It is high time that we gave the justice of a proper appreciation to those early builders of gigantic roads, lovely temples, and majestic palaces, to those geographical ancestors of ours, the first Americans. Although they had no say in the matter, we are their foster-children.

There is still a great deal of mystery about the first Americans. However, our scientists, trying to solve the riddle, may be considerably helped by the presence of an educated public opinion and a popular sympathy behind them. Let us throw away our European prejudices to the extent of trying to gain an accurate appreciation of our American antiquities.

How few of us there are who have even a sketchy acquaintance with the high lights of the early American scene! Doubtless there are Roman Catholic priests in Peru and Mexico, and Protestant clergymen in Arizona, who would be indignant if you informed them that American "Indians" of Peru, Mexico, and Arizona were settled nations subsisting on root flour and cooked cereals at a time when the inhabitants of the Holy Land were mere nomads, snatching figs from trees. Doubtless in North and South America are millions of persons who consider themselves cultivated and who have heard of the famous Gobelin tapestries of Europe. But how many of these appreciators of beautiful things do you suppose are aware that both for arrangement of color and design, and for mastery of spinning and weaving, the tapestries of ancient Peru surpass all others in the world?

How many surgeons of Montreal, New York, Mexico City, Havana, Rio de Janeiro, and Buenos Aires realize that in the Middle Ages perhaps no surgeons in the world could be compared, for skill, with the surgeons of the Inca Empire in Peru, or know that those Peruvian surgeons understood how to trepan an injured skull and that they were probably the first medical men in the world to use anesthetics in operations? How much attention do modern students of government give to the empire of the Incas? Yet in Peru several centuries before the French Revolution, concerning which hundreds of histories have been written, was carried out the most successful experiment in socialism the world has ever seen.

Every high-school boy and girl in the United States has heard of the mysterious rock ruins to be seen in Stonehenge, England. But how many have heard of the equally mysterious gigantic "seats" cut in the living rock near Lake Titicaca, in Bolivia? Or of the lovely great gateway cut from a single stone which stands at Tiahuanaco, in this same country?

Lately there has been much talk all over the world concerning the possibility of abolishing war. Would it not be worth the while of those who wish to establish perpetual peace upon earth to study two early American peoples—the Pueblos of our Southwest and the Mayas of Central America—which seem to have been organized on a very pacific basis; and to study the obscure "Archaic" culture which preceded the glory that was Maya and the grandeur that was Inca, and which likewise appears to have been little concerned with the pomp and splendor and folly of war?

If "the proper study of mankind is man," then every person of ordinary education should be familiar with such important phenomena of history as these, certainly every person who is an inhabitant of North or South America. Is it intelligent of us to be aware that the Normans were building castles in England in the twelfth century and to be unaware that a noble and unwarlike American people, the Pueblos, were building great apartment-houses in New Mexico and Arizona at about the same time? Is a man wholly educated who has heard of the aqueducts of the Romans but who has never heard of the aqueducts of the Peruvians?

Ask the next man you meet at the country club or in the smoking-car what ancient people built the largest pyramid. The chances are ten to one he will an-

11

swer, "The Egyptians." Then you will have the pleasure of telling him that at Cholula, Mexico, the Toltecs built a pyramid three times greater in bulk than the biggest one in Egypt.

Not only have we Americans a shameful ignorance of the splendid past of our own hemisphere: the further pity is that such knowledge as we have is confused and distorted. When you mention American antiquities to your friend of the country club or smoking-car, more likely than not he will say, "Oh yes, the Aztecs and the Incas." Probably he has never heard of the Mayas, much less realized that the Maya civilization was the fountainhead for the lesser cultures of the Toltecs and of the over-advertized Aztecs, and that the Maya civilization was also demonstrably superior to that of the Inca. (By the way, the first three letters of the word *Maya* are pronounced to rhyme with *buy,* not with *hay.*)

A point to notice here with a certain amount of irony is that Prescott, one of our few historians to pay any attention to pre-Columbian American civilization, knew very little of the Maya culture, which to this day has suffered lamentably for the lack of a good press-agent.

The Mayas were the Greeks of the West. And a knowledge of them is especially desirable for the modern American, particularly the American of the United States, as in many ways life among the Mayas

12

The Paramount Building, New York, showing the setback principle derived from the Mayas

Courtesy American Museum of Natural History

Model of Temple of Tikal—side view—one of the first illustrations of the setback principle

presented resemblances to life in the United States at the present time. In the Maya country, as in the United States, economic effort was fairly evenly divided among agriculture, manufacturing, and commerce. The trade routes of the Mayas compare favorably in extent and range with the trade routes of the ancient Phenicians and Sumerians. The principle of the setback, so conspicuous in the sky-scrapers of New York, was first used by the builders of the Maya temples. Moreover, whereas our modern American architects are content to copy the column of the Greeks and have originated next to nothing, the Mayas devised the serpent column, unique in the entire world. Their great elevated stone roads were stronger and have endured better than have the roads of the Romans. Their painting and sculpture were superior to the art of the Egyptians.

But it was their wonderful system of writing, their knowledge of mathematics and of astronomy that should make modern Americans particularly proud of them. The Maya system of counting time presents dates which are the number of elapsed days from a mundane era that equals October 14, 3373 B.C., in the backward projection of our present Gregorian calendar. The Mayas put this calendar into operation on August 6, 613 B.C. Dr. Herbert J. Spinden states, "The writing out of the Maya calendar involved place value 1000 years before it was known anywhere in the Old World and an eral count of days 300 years before the first eral count of years in the Old World (the Era of the Seleucidæ, October 1, 312 B.C.)" Maya mathematicians invented zero several centuries before its separate invention by the Arabs, and were able to multiply and divide ten centuries before Europeans could do so.

If it is fair to judge by the Maya calendar, we may say that when the caravels of Columbus reached the Bahamas the Americans were better astronomers than the Europeans. Certainly the Maya calendar was more accurate than the Julian calendar, which all Europe was using at that time, and which Greece and Russia used into the twentieth century.

When this embarrassing fact began to be digested, Europeans with a hemispheric superiority complex joined Americans with a hemispheric inferiority complex in asking, "How could American Indians possibly have devised so accurate a calendar as that?" Later we shall examine the arguments of those who maintain that the flower of American civilization must have been derived by contact with the Old World before the time of Columbus. In order to understand the utter absurdity of their arguments we must first familiarize ourselves with the facts of America's greatness. Suffice it to say here that it is the consensus of opinion of the most brilliant scientists that America *developed* her own culture. The first primitive Amer-

14

icans may have come from Asia or they may not. *But irrespective of where America was born, America grew up alone.*

*Once and for all, let us get it into our heads that these great early American civilizations—Maya, Inca, Toltec, Aztec, Pueblo, and others—were "Indian," that is, native American.*

It is unfortunate that that misnomer "Indian" was ever applied to Americans by the blundering European discoverers. And it is unfortunate that the "Indians" with whom the forefathers of many of us came in contact were very low in the American scale. That is, they were primitive agriculturists like the Algonquins, or bloodthirsty barbarians like the Apaches. But they belonged to the same great branch of the human family as the people of the Incas and as the Mayas.

It is bad enough to confuse the Maya with the Peruvian or the Pueblo with the Aztec. It is as bad as it would be to confuse Greece with Rome or Egypt with Etruria. But it is even worse, it is inexcusable, for any of us to go on living in the assumption that the height of American civilization before the arrival of the white man was represented by a Sioux warrior with his dripping scalps.

There was as great a gap between that Sioux warrior and a Maya astronomer as there was between an English swineherd in the seventeenth century and

15

Galileo. Yet there was a certain similarity about all American civilizations. From the Great Lakes to the mountains of Peru, maize, or "Indian corn," was a fundamental food. The cultivation of corn was dependent on an adequate supply of water. Hence the worship of rain-gods played a more or less important part in the life of all the highest of the early American peoples which were agricultural.

It is high time that Americans knew themselves. It is high time that they ceased looking backward at the continent whence their ancestors came and looked at the continents upon which they are living, the home of their foster-ancestors—those wonderful people whom, for the last time in this book, I shall refer to here as "Indians."

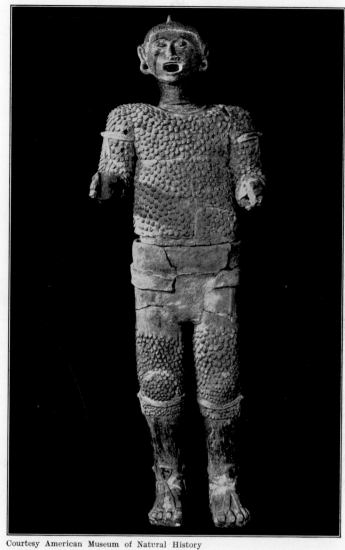

Courtesy American Museum of Natural History

Terra-cotta figure representing a Mexican warrior dressed
in quilted cotton armor—Coatlinchan, near Texcoco

# CHAPTER II

OUR HEMISPHERIC INFERIORITY COMPLEX

OUR immediate forefathers—the Britons, Spaniards, Frenchmen, and Portuguese who conquered and settled America—were too busy subduing the wilderness to indulge in philosophic speculation. Most of them were good Christians and accepted the doctrine of Biblical students, as formulated by Dr. James Usher in the seventeenth century, that the world was created in 4004 B.C. And of course according to this theory the first man was an Asiatic.

Later, when the discoveries of scientists began to force thinking laymen to revise their conceptions of the origin of the universe, the emphasis was still on Asia. The early evolutionists did most of their work in the "Old World," and the first archæologists to unearth human remains of great antiquity worked in Europe, Asia, and Africa. Champollion's deciphering of the inscription on the famous Rosetta Stone in the early nineteenth century set the whole world marveling at the antiquities of Egypt.

Of course it was known even then that the Peruvians and Mexicans had had high civilizations before the arrival of the white man. But much was made of the existence of an American myth attributing the origin of culture in the Western world to a bearded god, clad in white, who came from the east. When, about 1840, the American explorer John L. Stephens began to report the existence of magnificent stone cities and other vestiges of a very high past culture in Central America, most of the learned men of the time were inclined to attribute this Maya civilization to Old World origin.

So, both by Dr. Usher's theory of the Creation in 4004 B.C. and by the discoveries of scientists which destroyed this theory, the emphasis was put on Asia as the original place of human habitation.

It is strange how heated man can become in discussing his own genesis. Few questions have brought out more of man's hatred for man than this. And yet why? Why should one human being ever hate another? We are all in the same boat; we must sink or swim together. We do not know where we came from, we do not know where we are going; in the absence of a compass or a chart we invent our own theories, and we hate those who refuse to share them. It is all petty and sad. Instead of passing laws prohibiting the teaching of evolution, as some of the legislatures of the United States have done, would it not be better —if we must have laws—to enact statutes forcing teachers to air *all* theories? The attitude of seeking the truth is becoming to man; the attitude of running away from any bit of evidence is contemptible. But the narrow-mindedness is not all in one camp. Nor is there any greater bigot than a bigoted scientist.

However, whether you are an evolutionist or a fundamentalist, you cannot yet put your finger on any spot on the map and say, "Man originated there."

Most of the experts feel that man started either in Asia or in Europe. Very few have suggested that he may have started in America. This is largely because the evidence so far gathered points to an "Old World" origin, but there is another element in the matter which we might do well to bear in mind, although to over-emphasize it would be a great mistake. The fact is that scientists are conventional men. Now, many of the savants conspicuous in the research work of our universities and museums are Europeans. An inherited assumption of the superior antiquity and devolopment of human institutions in Europe and Asia makes it difficult for them even to *conceive* of the possibility of America's being as old as their own continent. Suffering from a hemispheric superiority complex, they are disinclined to give due acknowledgment to the fact that the evidence for the greater antiquity of "Old World" man is negative evidence. That is, it consists merely of our failure, up to now, to find any traces of anthropoid apes in America.

American scientists with a hemispheric inferiority

19

complex likewise seem inclined at times to give undue importance to this negative evidence. There is something of a vicious circle here. So long as European man and Asiatic man are assumed to be older than American man, it is likely that more work of investigation will be done on the other side of the water than over here. But until an equal amount of exploration has been done here, the careful person will not accept the dictum of any scientist that man originated in this or that definite locality.

For a number of years now it has been realized that man existed in Europe and Asia in the Pleistocene period or the last of the Tertiary, the third of the four great geological periods of the earth. That would mean that man was there at least twenty-five thousand and probably fifty thousand years ago. When a few daring scientists suggested that man was living in those European areas in the Pliocene, or period immediately before the Pleistocene, they were considered rather radical. Then evidence began to accumulate showing that man had been in America in the Pleistocene. Whereupon research in Europe was intensified and certain anthropologists rather frantically began to change their minds and to accept the theory of man's European existence in the Pliocene.

Paleontologists (from the Greek words *palaios,* ancient, and *onta,* beings; that is, students of ancient beings) have recently made a number of studies which have pushed back the horizons of human history in America. Evidence that man existed in America in the Pleistocene has now been found in thirty or forty different localities. In some cases the evidence may be questioned, owing to the fact that the relics of ancient man were discovered by laymen and may have been accidentally dislodged from their original positions before scientists arrived to study them. But in other cases there is no more reason to doubt that the relics are of the Pleistocene period than that cited by Dr. O. P. Hay, of the Carnegie Institution, who, in commenting on human bones and artifacts found in the same stratum of soil with the bones of the extinct mammoth at Vero, Florida, said, "At present I perceive no other reason for doubting this than that their presence . . . contravenes our present ideas regarding the history of the human race." Brave Dr. Hay, who dares to point out the American hemispheric inferiority complex!

In a gravel-bed at Frederick, Oklahoma, probably dating back to before the last glacial period, is alleged to have been found a few years ago a stone dart-head. Mr. Harold J. Cook, geologist, who examined the find, seems convinced that the artifact actually was encountered in that gravel by the layman who first reported the matter, and Cook has contended that the missile must have been made from three hundred and fifty thousand to four hundred thousand years ago,

21

to have been included in that geological stratum. Naturally, the farther back we go in time the more difficult it is to gage accurately the age of vestiges of human existence, and the testimony of geologists becomes of great importance where human bones or artifacts are found in undoubted association with ancient gravel-beds or rock strata. Dr. Charles N. Gould, Director of the Oklahoma Geological Survey, certified to the Washington Academy of Sciences that the missile was undoubtedly present in this old gravel. While a controversy was raging with regard to its age—the whole point being to determine whether it had actually originally lodged in the stratum where it was found or had merely got into it through erosion or other accident at a time much later than the formation of the gravel-bed—a certain scientist who had been among the most skeptical returned to Frederick and there found a second stone dart-head whose authentic position in this ancient stratum could not be questioned.

Another important item in the list of recent discoveries indicating considerable antiquity for American man was made in 1929 by Dr. Chester Stock, paleontologist. In a cavern in Bishop's Cap Mountain, New Mexico, Dr. Stock found human bones in association with remains of Pleistocene animals. It is difficult to say when these bones were clothed with human flesh. It may have been fifty thousand years ago. It may

22

have been less than that. And it may have been much more.

In 1930, in Gypsum Cave, near Las Vegas, Nevada, Mr. Mark R. Harrington found not one but nine hundred man-made articles under or in close association with fossilized remains of the extinct little ground-sloth (*Nothrotherium Shastense Sinclair*); and last, but not least in importance, under a layer of fossilized sloth manure Mr. Harrington discovered the ashes of what he and other experts are convinced was the camp-fire of the primitive men who hunted this Pleistocene animal in that cave.

Perhaps the strongest piece of evidence of man's American existence in the Pleistocene is that found at the town of Folsom, in New Mexico. Here, at a depth of from four to thirteen feet, spear-points or dart-heads of jasper and chalcedony were found in or among the skeletons of thirty bison of a species long extinct. Mr. Barnum Brown, Curator of Fossil Reptiles of the American Museum of Natural History, New York, who has made a close study of the remains, places them at the close of the Pleistocene period. That is, the bison were shot by early Americans at a time "during those climatic changes which accompanied the disappearance of the great ice caps farther north." Mr. Brown, therefore, thinks these dart-heads are from fifteen thousand to twenty thousand years old. That is much less than the age of the

Frederick darts, but it nevertheless represents a considerable antiquity for our American.

An exceedingly interesting thing about these Folsom missiles is that they are much better made than any other spear- or dart-heads ever found in America or than the arrow-heads left on the surface by the most recent aborigines. Moreover, instead of tapering the whole length to the base to form a V the missile reaches its greatest breadth a very short distance from the point. Mr. Brown declares that this means it would have had a much greater penetration than a dart or arrow-point of the ordinary type. When these Folsom darts or spear-points were shown by Mr. Brown to a very learned anthropologist who is European by birth, the latter said that they were too well made to have been manufactured fifteen thousand or twenty thousand years ago as Mr. Brown suggested. The American scientist then gently reminded the other of the fact that European artifacts of the Solutrian period, of about eighteen thousand years ago, are much better made than many European artifacts of a more recent age. The European anthropologist had never questioned the age of these excellently made European artifacts on the grounds that they were too well chipped.

There you have the European superiority complex again! This European scientist, with the best intentions in the world, no doubt, was subconsciously de-

termined to declare the Folsom atlatl (dart-thrower)
missiles to be of recent manufacture. The only reason
he could give for his conclusion was the absurd one
just cited.

The exhibit illustrating the Folsom discoveries in
the American Museum of Natural History affords
an interesting example of how uncertain our conception of early America is, and of how rapidly that conception is being revised. A panel in the back of a
show-case in the museum is taken up by a picture in
which a modern artist has imagined how the Folsom
bison-hunt took place. He depicts the aborigines as
equipped with bows and arrows, for it was at first
supposed that the Folsom missiles were arrow-points.
But already the conclusion has been reached by the
experts of this museum, as by authorities elsewhere,
that the Folsom projectiles are dart-points or spear-
points, which were hurled by the throwing-stick,
or atlatl, an older American arm than the bow.

Dr. Aleš Hrdlička is employed by the National
Museum of Washington, D.C. But he is European by
birth and point of view, and he is a leader among the
anthropologists with European superiority complexes
who attack the suggested antiquity of anything
American. Dr. Clark Wissler, distinguished Curator
of Anthropology in the American Museum of Natural History, in his excellent book "The American
Indian" makes the following very illuminating com-

25

ment on Dr. Hrdlička and his school. Says Dr. Wissler, writing even before the discoveries at Folsom, Frederick, Bishop's Cap, and Gypsum Cave were made or anlayzed:

A considerable number of fragmentary skeletons have come to light, and achieved literary fame, among which are the Lansing man, the Calaveras Skull, the Nebraska Loess Man, and the *Homo Pampæus* proposed by Ameghino. The claims of all these to a respectable age have been vigorously assailed by Hrdlička, and, consequently, placed in the doubtful column. *Nevertheless, one must suspect that where so many cases arise which exercise the utmost ingenuity of scientists to disprove, the probability of some being authentic is very great.*

The italics are mine.

Why, you may ask, must it be assumed that human life originated in some one spot? The assumption is not necessary. It is possible that human life originated in two or more widely separated spots at virtually the same time. Yet the presumption is that man did develop in one particular locality, for it has been found that many species of mammals other than man have had only one origin; and no case has yet been found where similar conditions existing far apart have produced the same species of creature.

However, it is worth bearing in mind that the mammals of America are as old as the mammals of Europe

26

and Asia. Moreover, lemuroids, supposed by evolutionists to be near the direct line of man's development, have already been found in the Western world. (The lemur, which takes its name from the Latin plural noun *lemures,* meaning ghosts, is a nocturnal arboreal animal allied to the monkey.) A creature called Tarsius, a sort of half-ape, and ancestor of the anthropoids from which evolutionists believe man developed, is believed to have originated in the region of Wyoming. (The theory is that anthropoids did not develop until some descendant of Tarsius had reached the "Old World" from America.)

Still another item for us to remember in contemplating the mystery of American man's past is that a skull has been found in Tierra del Fuego which presents striking similarities to the cranium of Neanderthal man, who was living in Europe some fifty thousand years ago. Aichel has traced Neanderthal-like traits in skeletal material found on the west coast of South America. Commenting on this matter, Dr. Bruno Oetteking, distinguished anthropologist of Columbia University and the Museum of the American Indian, Heye Foundation, remarks that if the existence of this primitive human type is established in ancient America, we must assume that he migrated here not later than the last interglacial period.

The opinion held by scientists until recently that

man reached America after the last glacial epoch is becoming more and more difficult to defend in the light of modern discoveries. Obermaier and Paul Sarasin have met recent contentions for the antiquity of American man with the assertion that geologic strata in America were formed more recently than what appear at first perhaps to be coeval strata in Asia and Europe, and that hence the age of human remains found in such American strata must be somewhat discounted. The burden of proof, however, seems to be squarely on those who make such assertions. This matter is most important, by no means so simple as it may sound offhand, and assuredly merits further study.

Meanwhile anthropologists as a body believe that America was first populated by immigrants from Asia via a land bridge across Bering Strait or across the northern Atlantic from Europe to America via Iceland and Greenland. The present orthodox form of the theory envisages two streams of immigration, one from eastern Siberia and one from western Siberia. It is thought that the western wave may have returned to Siberia from America and have been responsible for the existence of the so-called Paleo-Asiatic population groups which show marked resemblance to Americans. The eastern wave of immigration is believed to have been responsible for the existence of our Eskimo.

The Eskimo, by the way, is something of a problem to the anthropologist (as the field anthropologist with his stature-rods, spreading calipers, and everlasting measurements is a problem to the Eskimo!). In pronounced ways the Eskimo is as unlike the other inhabitants of America as he is unlike the Siberian. Some men argue that this means the Eskimo arrived here later than other Americans. It is indeed probable that if America *was* peopled from Asia there was more than one wave of migration.

Dr. Franz Boas, head of the Department of Anthropology of Columbia University, who is a believer in the Asiatic origin of Americans, nevertheless forcefully points out reasons for thinking that the peopling of the western continents occurred in extremely remote times. The development of markedly distinct types of American aborigines must have required many centuries. Furthermore, the fact that there is so great a dissimiliarity in the fundamental human traits of the eastern and western hemispheres argues that the arrival of the Americans was a decidedly ancient event. One example of such dissimilarity is the almost complete absence of the judicial function in American aboriginal government. Another example is the wide gulf between American and Asiatic agriculture, and a third is the great difference between the languages of the two hemispheres.

29

Developing the picture being pieced out by paleontologists—who are concerned with the earliest human remains when they are concerned with human materials at all—archæologists have pushed back definite knowledge of fairly high cultures in America to a mark comparable in antiquity to what Asia can offer.

In 1916, Dean Byron Cummings of the University of Arizona discovered a cone-shaped, three-storied structure at Cuicuilco, near Mexico City, estimated to be from three thousand to five thousand years old. This estimate can be made with some assurance by geologists, owing to the fact that the foundations of the temple or monument lie twenty-five feet deeper than the congealed volcanic lava surrounding them. Not very far from this spot the eminent archæologist Mrs. Zelia Nuttall found ancient potsherds and figurines and "fragments of flakes of obsidian with a dull surface and a patina which unquestionably indicate great antiquity" in an old river-bed, seventeen feet beneath the lava-bed in her orchard. Dr. S. K. Lothrop of the Museum of the American Indian, Heye Foundation, has found in Salvador remnants of the handiwork of potters who, he says, "lived there a very long time ago, when the surface of the land must have been quite different in detail from at present. He states further:

As the refuse of these people is older than that of the Maya Old Empire, it is safe to say that they flourished more than 2,000 years ago. The stylistic affinity of their handiwork to the "Archaic" art of the Valley of Mexico leads to the same conclusion. The technical merit of the early pottery indicates that we may expect to find still older cultural phases.

Since Dr. Lothrop wrote those words his prediction has been fulfilled by Dr. George Vaillant of the American Museum of Natural History. In the Valley of Mexico, Dr. Vaillant has found stratified pottery and other archæological remains of several cultures distinct from one another and from that so-called "Archaic" culture, and several of them seeming to be older than the "Archaic."

To sum up all these considerations concerning the antiquity of man and his culture in America, the prudent layman will do well to remember that it is too early to determine the age of man in America or any other continent, or to say dogmatically that man originated here or there. We cannot afford to be positive on the latter point until we have collected all the available evidence, a proceeding which may take us thousands of years.

In the meantime—always remembering that *American culture was undoubtedly developed in America* —we may accept, if we like, as a somewhat hazy work-

31

ing hypothesis, the supposition that man came to America over a land bridge from Asia thousands of years ago. But do not forget that the number of those thousands is being increased by discoveries almost every year, and it is highly desirable that as much search for remains of ancient man should be made in America as has been made in Europe and Asia. And indisputably, as the late Dr. P. E. Goddard of the American Museum of Natural History said, "The assumption that the development of American culture and the great linguistic variation of the two continents have resulted since the retreat of the last ice cap far enough to open a road across Bering Sea is untenable."

*A long upward struggle of man in America has occurred to account for the foundations of an agriculture and of languages so different from those of the other hemisphere.*

In fine, man's antiquity in this hemisphere is now so well established that it is rather academic to refer any longer to the western hemisphere as the "New World." That term, reflecting as it does the conceit of the blustering European adventurers who swarmed over America in the sixteenth century like a plague of destroying locusts, will be used by me no more in this book.

Courtesy American Museum of Natural History

Pleistocene artifacts from Folsom, N. M., fifteen thousand to twenty thousand years old—in the center a dart-head of typical shape

CHAPTER III

MOTHER MAIZE

I N SEARCHING through Central America for
the remains of ancient cities of white limestone,
one often has to clear a way for one's pack-animals
through the thick bush, with axes and machetes. Despite the frequency with which one stumbles on crumbling temples, monasteries, walls supporting agricultural terraces or marking off the land as parceled out
by the Government among various native families, it
is still often easy to forget that these tall trees and
these choking, suffocating vines that trip up the explorer to throw him headlong into thorny thickets
were not always there. The truth is that only a few
hundred years ago Central America was one great
garden. Land now held by the jungle once nourished
broad orchards, mile upon mile of white cotton, and
hundreds of miles of golden grain.

Of all the evidence indicating the great antiquity
of human culture in America and its complete independence of culture in Asia, Africa, and Europe,
the most significant is American agriculture, and the
most picturesque single bit is an ear of corn.

The men who excavate the dwellings and temples

of long ago, the men who dig up fossilized bones of remote man and the stone arrow-heads with which he slew mammoths, camels, and species of bison long since extinct have contributed an exceedingly convincing chapter to the story of the independent rise of human culture in America. But the botanist has done even more.

Botanists have pointed out that ancient Americans had an agriculture based on food-plants that did not grow outside of America before Columbus crossed the Atlantic. Moreover, these food-plants show a further development from their wild ancestors than is seen in the food-plants of Europe and Asia. This gives us some reason to suppose that Americans were the first primitive people to practise agriculture, and agriculture is the first stage of enlightenment among primitive peoples anywhere.

From the first farmers of America the world has gained a number of the most important food-plants in use to-day, including corn, potatoes, sweet potatoes, tomatoes, pumpkins, squashes, Lima beans, kidney-beans, peppers, peanuts, pineapples, and strawberries. But the basic plants of this prehistoric American horticulture were corn, beans, and squashes, because these three vegetables were grown almost everywhere that agriculture was practised in North and South America. And the most important of these three was corn, or maize, to give it its proper

34

native name. The word "corn" is of Anglo-Saxon origin and its use is misleading. It signifies a small, hard particle—that is, a grain—and in England it is applied to wheat, in Scotland and Ireland to oats. But American corn is maize, and is probably the oldest cereal in the world.

It is not yet certain whether primitive man was first of all a hunter of wild animals or primarily a food-gatherer, living on fruit, nuts, and seeds picked from wild trees. But when man invented agriculture —that is, when he began to gather seeds and plant them under conditions favorable for their growth— he took one of the longest of his early steps toward civilization.

We do not know where he took this step or how. A good many writers argue that cultivation was probably begun in arid regions where irrigation was practised, as Mexico and Peru in America, and Mesopotamia and Egypt in the eastern hemisphere. These writers seem to belong to a puritanical school of philosophy. They contend, like Dr. Spinden, that "theoretically, agriculture would be more likely to originate under conditions that were hard than under those that were easy. 'Necessity,' they say, 'is the mother of Invention.'" Therefore, declare these writers of the puritanical school, agriculture started in the desert. But Spinden seems to contradict himself in pointing out immediately afterward that "in the desert the clearing of the field is less laborious than in the jungle"!

It appears to be rather a fine question whether it would have been more difficult for primitive man to dig an irrigation ditch or to cut down wild, non-fruit-bearing trees in order to make way for trees and bushes that bore edible fruits and seeds. (Primitive man knew how to clear forests by bruising a ring of bark around the base of each tree and applying fire to the bruised area.) And it is an open question whether agriculture "would be more likely to originate under conditions that were hard than under those that were easy."

Agriculture may have been discovered accidentally when man dropped some of the wild seeds he was carrying to his cave for storage before eating them, and subsequently noticed the sprouting of plants from the seeds dropped. And perhaps irrigation was invented when plants sprang up beside water-holes where men had taken seeds for washing and screening. At any rate, the invention of agriculture, even more than the discovery of permanent fish and game supplies, made it possible for man to take up a stationary existence. And this gave him time to invent many of his most fundamental arts. For example, pottery, of little use to a nomadic people, is of great value to settled populations, and the boundaries of the territory in which pottery was made and of the

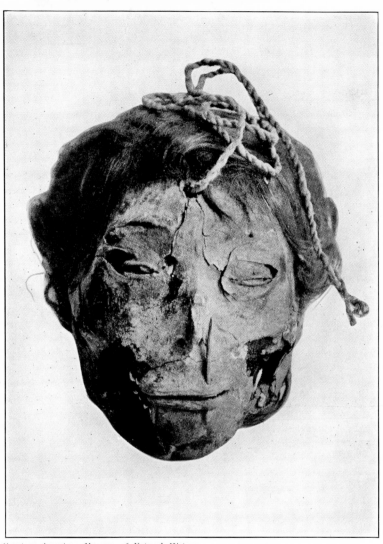

Courtesy American Museum of Natural History

Preserved human head discovered in Peru

area in which agriculture was practised are usually about the same.

In 1492, Columbus was looking for the famous Spice Islands of the East, described by Marco Polo. And when the *Santa Maria* dropped her anchor on American bottom, she had in her hold such samples of the products of the Spice Islands as cloves, cinnamon, peppers, nutmeg, ginger, and aloes wood— the last much used as incense in the East. The Genoese navigator was constantly showing his samples to the American natives and asking if anything of the sort grew in their country. There are American plants that produce somewhat similar things, and when the people of the Bahamas seemed to recognize some of his herbs Columbus jumped to the mistaken conclusion that these were native to the land he had just found. On November 4 he mistook a certain bark for cinnamon, and he proudly reported to the King of Spain that he had reached the long-sought islands.

After Columbus, Europeans continued to misunderstand and misname the plants of America, as they continued to misunderstand and misname various characteristic American products and institutions. The plants of America, like most other things distinctively American, were given European names and attributed to European or Asiatic origins. Not until 1884, when Alphonse de Candolle published his "Origin of Cultivated Plants," did the American source of many important food-plants receive proper recognition. But even De Candolle was not entirely fair to America and made some conspicuous omissions. These errors, however, have been corrected since his day, chiefly by experts of the United States Department of Agriculture. Such men as O. F. Cook and Lyman Carrier have devoted their lives—as the late W. E. Safford devoted his—to demonstrating conclusively the great variety and antiquity of the food-plants of the early Americans and the complete independence of these plants from those of Asia, Africa, and Europe.

*That American agriculture before Columbus owed nothing to contacts with other continents is now accepted as a definite fact by all the leading experts.* But Dr. Cook, just mentioned, has gone even farther, and has suggested that *the rest of the world got its agriculture from America.* Although his theory has not yet been accepted by many other savants, it has much to recommend it and is indisputably sufficiently interesting to deserve our attention. Dr. Cook predicates it on the assumption that there never existed in America that "primitive pastoral stage which so many writers have taken to be man's first step from savagery towards civilization. . . ." He goes on to say:

The comparative deficiency of the Western Continents in fruit and animals suitable for food is com-

38

pensated by numerous starchy root crops. The primitive culture people of the tropical regions of ancient America were accustomed to the cooking, grinding, and storing of vegetable food, and were thus prepared to appreciate and utilize the cereals by agriculture experience lacking among the fruit-eating aborigines of the Old World, who developed instead the arts of the chase, the domestication of animals, and the use of milk.

The Americans made a much larger use of root crops, points out Dr. Cook, than any other people. Moreover,

the more important and the more ancient of the distinctively Old World root crops, onions, leeks, garlic, carrots, radishes and turnips, are eaten, or are at least edible, in the raw state, while in America there seems to be no indication that the natives used any of their root crops in this way. Some of them, such as the sweet potato, the artichoke, and "sweet cassava," can be eaten raw, but throughout the tropics of America, the Indians, like the Chinese, preferred everything cooked. This habit must have been adopted very far back to have made possible the obviously ancient domestication of Manioc (cassava), Colocasia (taro) and Xanthosoma (yautia), since the fleshy underground parts of these plants contain substances distinctly deleterious until disintegrated and rendered harmless by heat. The same may have been true of the sweet potato, since the fleshy roots of its uncultivated relatives are

39

strongly purgative. Several of the yams, both wild and cultivated, are also poisonous in the raw state. Moreover, everywhere in tropical America maize is still prepared by methods adapted to root crops instead of as a cereal. The rough stone slab against which they had rubbed their cassava or other starch-producing roots was well suited to making paste from maize, softened by soaking in water with lime or ashes, and throughout tropical America has remained in use until the present day.

Dr. Cook then proceeds to construct a rather imposing argument, from these facts, that American root crops seem to have been more numerous than the root crops of Asia, seem to have been developed much earlier, and that they were treated with heat to make them palatable long before the Europeans or Asiatics took up cooking. In suggesting that agriculture reached Asia from America by way of the islands of the Pacific, he points out that the ancient Americans had *six of the seven chief food-plants of the Polynesians* (the Eastern, lighter-colored, and more advanced Pacific islanders), that the Americans had *all the root crops which attained any wide distribution in Asia and Africa, and that they had many other root crops besides.* Hence, says he,

since it is reasonable to suppose that the food plants which the Polynesians shared with the tropical peoples of both continents were carried by them across

40

the Pacific, it is also reasonable to seek the origin
of these widely distributed species on the continent
which gives evidence of the oldest and most extensive agricultural activity, and to the question in this
form there can be but one answer.

Dr. Cook's answer is America. And he goes on to
say:

The apparent superfluity of American root crops is
explainable by the fact that different plants were
independently domesticated in different localities,
which means also that conditions favorable to the development of agriculture were very general among
the natives of America. . . . The American origin
of agriculture is thus not doubtful, since not merely
one, but several, agricultures originated in America.
The same cannot be claimed for Asia and Africa,
where only root crops shared with America attained
a wide distribution, an indication that they reached
those continents before the uses of the similar indigenous plants had been discovered. . . . If we may
not know where man first began to encourage the
growth of the plants which furnished his food, we
are not without numerous indications that agriculture
proper, together with the agricultural organization
of human society which lay behind modern civilization, originated in America and has now completed
the circuit of the globe.

As already noted, Dr. Cook's theory that America
gave agriculture to the world is not generally ac-

41

cepted. But as the reasons usually given against acceptance of this theory are based largely on negative rather than positive evidence, Cook's courageous suggestion is worth bearing in mind as a stimulus to unprejudiced research. It cannot be denied that the western hemisphere had more root crops than the eastern, and it cannot be denied that America's food-plants show a further process of domestication than the root-plants of Asia and Africa. But it may be and often is said that this high degree of domestication of plants indicates an intensity rather than a long duration of the application of agricultural methods in America. *However, there can be no doubt at all that America has had her agriculture for a very long time and that she developed it without help from Asia, Africa, or Europe.*

Important as were the root crops to the first farmers of America, their use was diverse, according to locality. Maize, on the other hand, was used nearly everywhere, and if we could know the history of maize we should know the history of the human culture of North and South America. It is believed that maize was developed thousands of years ago on the uplands of Mexico or Peru, from a wild grass called *teocintli*. This grass grows in Mexico to-day, but the intermediate forms or missing links between *teocintli* and maize have never been identified. This fact alone would indicate the great age of maize, even had not archæologists discovered a fossilized ear of corn perhaps ten thousand years old, as well as numerous representations of the grain, in ancient American pottery.

The wide diffusion of maize in America indicates that there probably was exchange of other products of human culture. This fact has important implications which we shall consider later. Maize does not do very well in the hot lowlands of the tropics, but it will grow there on a pinch. It thrives in higher forest lands, on plains, and in mountain country in both our western continents. It was the food of the primitive "Basket-maker" who lived in caves and cliff-dwellings in New Mexico and Arizona, and it was the basis of the diet of the man of the "Archaic" culture who from Mexico into South America has left crude pottery remains of a unified type. It was the food of the laborers who built the roads and the stone walls of South America, and of the workmen who constructed the lovely limestone palaces and temples of Central America.

A surplus of maize gave the necessary leisure for artists to create the beautiful tapestries and pottery of Peru, and for scientists to build up the astonishing knowledge of mathematics which was current in Guatemala and Yucatan when the Romans were trying to civilize the barbarians of western Continental Europe and Great Britain. Far more than any other

43

food, maize supported the great population America had before the coming of the white man.

Of course we can only guess what that early American population was, basing our estimate on reports of the first Europeans, and on the extent and size of archæological remains found to-day, and on other deducible factors. The lavishness with which the remains of stone roads, temples, palaces, monasteries, and other structures are scattered through Yucatan indicates that at one time this locality was the most thickly settled part of the globe. That was perhaps about 1200 A.D. Dr. Spinden estimates that at that time there were on the American continents fifty million to seventy million red men. This seems a conservative figure.

Maize saved the first white men who settled in America. The Pilgrims in New England had the common sense to put their settlements in the cleared fields left by red-skinned agriculturists. But the colonists of Jamestown lacked this foresight, and, as they did not have time to clear land before seeding season, many of them starved. The proximity or remoteness of white settlements to native clearings proved a matter of vital importance in many other cases.

Three things are essential to agriculture—earth, sun, and water. Everywhere with maize went the worship of rain-gods, just the other side of which is the worship of sun-gods. The British colonists in Massa-

Maya pillars with damaged human figures, found by Mason on Cozumel Island

chusetts and Virginia may have sneered at the native deities, but they prayed to their own God to give them rain. And we Christians to-day need not laugh at the ancient rain-gods. In time of drought ministers and priests in our agricultural communities beg Jehovah for rain as the aborigines begged the Great Spirit. What was the Great Spirit, after all, but Jehovah? We must not forget that if the early Americans had lesser deities especially concerned with fire, water, and other elements, nearly all, like the Mayas, believed in a Supreme God who was invisible.

In the four centuries the white man has held our two continents he has not succeeded in domesticating a single important food-plant. American agriculture, which differentiated America from the rest of the world and united the American peoples with each other, deserves our increasing respect. That agriculture—original, diverse, and intricate—was unified by the wide use of the cereal to which for the last time in this book I shall apply the European misnomer "corn."

# CHAPTER IV

## AMERICANS WERE ONE PEOPLE

ONE reason why the growth of knowledge about America has been retarded is that learned but misguided men have attempted to apply in the western hemisphere the method of measuring the early history of man which is applied in Europe and Asia. This has done America a great injustice. Anthropologists have divided the early history of European man into a number of periods such as the paleolithic (early stone age), neolithic (late stone age), bronze age, iron age, etc. Because the exact parallels of these periods are not found in American pre-history, some anthropologists have concluded that American man is very young.

Now, tools which European man is supposed to have made in the early stone age were merely chipped. In the later European stone age his tools were polished as well as chipped. Whereas in America in very remote times stone tools were both polished and chipped. However, this fact is not sufficient to justify the conclusion that the early stone-age man in America was a better workman than the early stone-age man in Europe, although he may well have been,

46

for the later stoneworkers of America indisputably surpassed their European rivals.

As for bronze, the use of this metal was known in early America, but the western hemisphere had no sharply defined bronze age and iron age to parallel those periods in Europe. Copper implements were being used to a considerable extent in Peru and Mexico when the first white man arrived, yet for the most part the Western world was still in the stone age. This fact has been interpreted by partizans of the superiority of Europe as an indication of the inferiority of American culture. Yet no such conclusion is justified, for the truth is that Americans did much finer work with stone tools than Europeans or Asiatics ever accomplished, and the façade-decoration of Maya architecture which was produced with stone implements has never been surpassed by anything we know was done by a European of the same period equipped with chisels of bronze or iron! Again we see the folly of assuming that we can take the measure of a civilization in terms of mechanics. The European was a better mechanic than the American, but he was no better artist; and often he was an inferior artist.

Not only must a student of the history of man in America avoid the confusion of attempting to apply the chronology of prehistoric man in Europe to prehistoric man in America, but he must not be discouraged when he finds that there is no good tape-measure at hand for computing periods and epochs even in the later history of our aborigines. Only in Central America, where the Mayas carved many dates on stone monuments, do we find a continuous measuring of time. The tragedy is that although we are now able to read the Maya dates quite readily, we cannot yet read the inscriptions that accompany them and that may be historical. We are in a predicament like that of an explorer from Mars who might arrive here after the population of this earth had been wiped out by some catastrophe and who was able to decipher the dates in our histories without being able to understand the accompanying text.

But there can be no question that the Maya commonwealth was a great and powerful one, with trade routes flung far to the northward and southward. The cultural influence of the Mayas undoubtedly affected many other American peoples and probably affected most of them. It is quite possible, therefore, that in the books the Mayas made of wood fiber covered with stucco were set down comments on the state of civilization in many parts of America hundreds and perhaps thousands of years before the arrival of Columbus. To-day the world possesses only three of these books, or codices, as the experts call them. A great many others were collected by the second Spanish bishop of Yucatan, Diego de Landa,

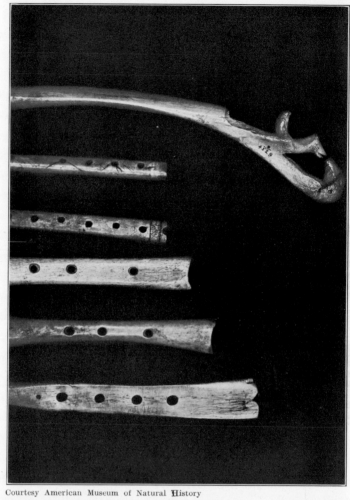

Courtesy American Museum of Natural History

Lutes of bone—coast of Peru

and destroyed by that zealous bigot, who considered them writings of the devil.

Landa's cruel and stupid act of destruction—a very pretty indication of the high standard of culture among Europeans of his time!—is just one more item in the long list of damages wrought upon America by ignorant and bullying Europeans, damages for which the civilization of the modern world continues to pay. Early Europeans wantonly destroy the history of culture in America. Then later Europeans blandly assume that America had no native culture worth writing about!

The first Europeans to come to our western hemisphere were adventurers greedy for gold, and religious fanatics convinced that a dead native was better than an unconverted one. Few of them had either aptitude or inclination for dispassionate study of local life. It is no wonder that some of the prejudices concerning Americans which they entertained have persisted even to this day, such as the ridiculous fancy that America was settled from the mythical "lost Atlantis." It is no wonder that, floundering amidst a mass of lies, myths, and illusions concerning America, handed down to us by our forefathers, few of us have been able to get any clear idea of the general scheme of human life in our continents before the white men came.

And yet there was a general scheme, and one easily

comprehended. The climate and topography of North and Central and South America is varied. But, *generally speaking,* the people were one people. And the way of living was marked by common features whether in North, Central, or South America; marked by many common features besides the use of a common agriculture, already noted.

In the first place, whether he lived on the frozen tundra of northern Canada, on the high plateaus of Mexico and Peru—where the air is like dry wine and where mere living is an intoxication—or in the humid lowlands of Florida, Yucatan, or the Amazon basin, the American was a fellow whose skin was reddish or reddish yellow in color, and whose hair was black and straight. His face was markedly broad from cheek-bone to cheek-bone. A less noticeable but no less characteristic feature was that his incisor teeth were usually shovel-shaped. Here we have a well-defined physical picture to remember.

The primary purpose of this chapter is to show the reader that there is a fundamental unity about all the American peoples. In this connection the fact that many different tribes have similar legends is significant, even though the legends themselves must by no means be given credence as history. The belief that a great flood once destroyed the world, which was afterward recreated in its present form, is found almost everywhere in America. Furthermore, many tribes in both of our continents have been discovered to entertain the belief that they were founded by a god with a beard, who arrived from the east arrayed in white cloth or white paint.

This legend was of great practical use to the European conquerors, who were hailed by the natives in many cases as representing reincarnations of the god. But it will not do to give it the importance of history, or to assume that it indicates that America actually was settled long ago by bearded individuals arriving from Europe. There is too much evidence to the contrary, especially in the entire independence of American languages and agriculture from those of the other hemisphere. Some scientists have contended that this god from the east was a personification of the sun. However that may be, to us the important thing about the legend of the white-clad bearded god is that it shows a widespread similarity in early American psychology and folklore.

What language did our American speak? This is an important question. One of the commonest ways of tracing relationships and historical contacts between different groups of people is through finding similarities in their languages. Consider the importance, then, of the fact that although the American languages are very numerous, and very diverse (there being as many as twenty-one language stocks in California alone), there has not yet been found a bit of

51

evidence indicating the intrusion of European, Asiatic, or African languages into the speech system of the ancient American.

It is true that a few Eskimo villages on the eastern coast of Siberia use the speech of the American Eskimo. But this may be ignored, for it is known that the Eskimo has gone back and forth across Bering Strait since fairly remote times—a fact which neither gives us much light on the origin of the Eskimo nor in any way vitiates the truth of the statement that the languages of the true Americans show no evidence of contact with the languages of the eastern hemisphere. Hence we may remember that whereas there were a great many independent languages in America, all of them showed a common "American" character, and a complete independence of the other hemisphere.

The tourist, who takes no pains scientifically to check up what he hears, often receives reports that there are parts of speech in use among the aboriginal races of America to-day bearing resemblance to parts of speech in some Asiatic or European tongue. An example of this is the frequent allegation that there are words in the tongue of the modern Maya of Yucatan which closely resemble words in one of the dialects of China. Such resemblances are superficial, coincidental, and entirely without significance. The unique character of American languages has

52

been established by scientists beyond any question.

The primitive American lived in dwellings of various types, as might be expected, considering the diversity of climate and the multiplicity of materials for house-construction in our two continents. The wooden totem-pole houses of the North Pacific coast, the conical skin tepee of many of the early residents of what we now know as Canada and the United States, the bark-covered community dwellings known as "long houses" of the Iroquois of New York, the conical earth-covered houses of the Missouri River region, various dwellings with thatched roofs and walls of upright sticks in Central America and South America, and different kinds of crude stone structures such as are found in Arizona, New Mexico, and parts of South America, present much variety.

But before man built these dwellings he lived in caves wherever caves were available. And, despite that diversity just seen, there are evidences of unity in later architecture than caves. For one thing, the true chimney was unknown in America. For another, the use of pyramidal mounds for burial-places and as foundations for habitations had a continuous distribution, from the Great Lakes in the north to the coast of Peru in the south. In the matter of fortifications also there was some unity. The employment of walls of wood or stone for purposes of protection is fairly widespread. Some villages in New York State were

53

protected with rings of earth, while others there and in New England were surrounded with wooden palisades which find their stone counterparts in the stone walls surrounding a few of the Maya villages in Central America, such as the ancient town of Xkaret, which Dr. Spinden and I discovered on the coast of Yucatan in 1926. However, it is in the absence of chimneys in residences, and in the frequent presence of supporting mounds of earth or stone, that early American architecture has its most conspicuous common trait.

A great variety of clothing was worn by our aboriginal American. In the tropics the earliest natives went naked or nearly naked, and in some colder climes, such as British Columbia, for the relationship of clothing to climate is by no means so simple as might be supposed. But in general, where clothing was worn at all the material was similar although the cut and hang were diverse. *Garments made from the skin of animals were the primitive and most widespread type.*

Later, cloth was used. The invention of weaving by early man is almost as significant as the development of agriculture, and certainly equals in importance the invention of pottery. When Americans began to weave they used three materials, wool, bast, and cotton. In South America the llama, the vicuña, and the

54

alpaca provided the wool. In North America the material was taken from the back of the Rocky Mountain goat or the buffalo. In parts of Canada a dog was specially bred for his hair, and there were local uses of the hair of other animals. Among the bast fibers which provided clothing were maize husks, cedar bark, willow bark, sage-brush, Indian hemp, pemmenaw grass, and the fiber of the maguey, a sort of cactus akin to our familiar century-plant. The sinews or tendons of animals also were employed to make garments.

Cotton probably was grown in most of those parts of what is now the United States where it is grown at present. But the great cotton area of the early American was from what is to-day New Mexico, all the way to Peru. Asia also had cotton, but the superiority of the Western product is shown by the fact that the commercial cotton of the modern world is the cotton of the early American.

There are many ways to twist fiber into thread—that is, to accomplish the process we call spinning. The European used the spindle whorl and the distaff. The American gave the necessary tension to the thread with his hand and rested the spindle in a bowl on the ground, or merely held it. *The uniformity of this primitive method throughout America shows us that the art of spinning and the use of cotton must*

55

*have been diffused from one center, as was the art of growing maize.*

The feathers of birds also played a large part in the costume of the Americans, especially in the way of head-dresses. As for footwear, in the tropics our American generally wore none at all. In colder regions he provided himself with straw sandals, or moccasins of animal skin.

No wheel in any form seems to have been used in America, and we have already noticed that in general our foster-ancestor was very un-mechanical. But we have also begun to appreciate that this was no reason why we should think less of him, a conclusion which will be emphasized if we bear in mind that Greece at the height of her glory had very little proficiency in mechanics. The first American was generally a rural soul, a hunter, a fisherman, a farmer, or sometimes all three. But, unlike the European, he made little use of domesticated animals. The dog in North America and the llama in South America seem to have been the only four-legged animals trained by man for his own service, but, among birds, the turkey, the curassow, and the muscovy duck were domesticated. The turkey was prized, not for its meat, as among us, but for its feathers.

The dart hurled by throwing-stick and the spear were much used as weapons and implements of the chase among the early Americans. The bow was a later development in some of the more nomadic tribes. Swords and clubs also were used for defense, and in New Mexico man acquired great proficiency in throwing a club at small game, the implement being somewhat similar to the famous Australian boomerang. The common American method of catching fish was with a net, and the notched stone sinkers with which the net was sunk to the proper depth have been widely found by archæologists. The blow-gun, which we think of to-day as essentially an arm of tropical man, was found not only among the natives of South America but among the Iroquois of northern New York State as well.

We have already noticed that bark was sometimes used for clothing. It was used for paper also. And one of the interesting indications of widespread communication among the early Americans is in the use of a type of ridged bark-beater on the west coast of North America similar to a tool much employed for the same purpose in Mexico and South America.

It is difficult to understand how any intelligent person ever could have doubted that there was a wide exchange of ideas and goods among the ancient nations of America. The goods were passed along from tribe to tribe, and the ideas went with them. An example of this sort of diffusion, as the scientists call it, is found in the presence of stone monkey heads among aboriginal remains discovered on the Columbia

River, a sub-Arctic area far from the tropics. Either those stone monkey heads reached the Columbia River valley in trade, from a people living in the tropics, or they were carved by Northern sculptors who had never seen monkeys but who had heard of them through the tales of far-traveled traders.

All over our twin western continents stone celts or axes were set into a mortise or hole in a wooden handle. In stone-age Europe, axes were perforated, with the handle inserted in the hole, but that method was used little, if at all, in America until it was brought here by white men. *The wide dissemination of the hafted stone ax is one more important indication of the cultural unity of America.*

Another general American custom was monogamy. Chiefs and shamans and priests often had several wives, but the layman was usually restricted to one. And life in America in those remote times also presented a resemblance to life in America to-day, in that divorce was comparatively easy. In Peru and Mexico dissolution of marriage was under the control of the Government. In most other localities husband and wife could separate at their own pleasure, although in some instances their families had a say in the matter.

So many of the early white explorers have testified to the universal kindness of aborigines to their children that there can be little doubt about this point.

The American was devoted to his child. As a rule he never punished the offspring, and when punishment was necessary the duty of administering it was often delegated to some relative. The fact indicates that the "This hurts me more than it hurts you," of the modern parent spanking his small son, could have been uttered very truthfully by our foster-ancestors!

In the main it may be said that the religion of early America was marked by two common traits, viz.: (1) a belief in dualism or the existence of contrasted and contesting sets of good and evil spirits; (2) relatively slight concern about the question of immortality. The second point often surprises Christians who study aboriginal religions, accustomed as they are to accepting religion as a device for removing or palliating the fear of death which afflicts western Europe and modern America.

Of course the all-important matter of agriculture was surrounded with religious observances, and some form of rain-god worship prevailed wherever maize or beans or cassava was grown. It has been well said that in America the great civilizations grew up around water-holes, which later came to be sacrificial shrines.

The shaman or medicine-man, to give him his more familiar name, held wide power in our two continents. It is a mistake to consider shamanism as identical with religion. Dr. Wissler points out:

We must not overlook the fact that the medicine man of the New World is not the priest. A large number of tribes have distinct names for each and their cultures give them distinct and sometimes antagonistic functions. It is a shaman rather than a priest who is called upon to treat the sick, foretell the future, etc. The priest is essentially the keeper and demonstrator of ritual, his right to do so arising chiefly from his near knowledge of the subject, but the native conception of the shaman is one who works directly by virtue of some extra-human power. Consequently, it is the shaman who goes into trances and mystifies by jugglery, not the priest.

When it came to the question of government, or the social grouping of people for mutual protection, in earliest America the fundamental unit was the family. Larger units were the clan and the gens. In cases where children of a number of people took the mother's name we have the clan; in those where they took the father's name we have the gens. Sometimes the woman ruled, but usually the best hunter or the wisest farmer was selected chief. As society progressed, leagues were formed, then nations and even empires. Examples of these were the League of the Five Nations of the Iroquois of New York State, the league of Maya trading cities of Yucatan, and the famous empires of the Incas in South America and of the Aztecs in Mexico.

Early American Governments were weakly developed with respect to the judicial function. In the heyday of their power the Peruvian and Mexican empires did indeed have provision for trying the cases of public criminals, but in general the American tribes had little machinery for dealing with the lawbreaker. Perhaps this means there was little lawbreaking!

We may conclude this survey of common social traits, which gave a large part of ancient America a conspicuous unity, by glancing at what is one of the most notable conceptions of them all. This concerns ownership of the land, a matter of utmost importance to agricultural communities. At the beginning of the second quarter of the twentieth century, when a great many of those who call themselves Americans profess to be deeply shocked at the spectacle of the communal ownership of land and other resources in Russia, it is amusing to reflect that in ancient America, from Point Barrow to Cape Horn, there was no such thing as private ownership of land. Private ownership of personal property, houses, furniture, etc., there was, but not of land.

It was the tendency to regard the house, the furniture, and the food as the property of the woman; the boat, the bow, the other implements of the chase as the property of the man. But land belonged always to the whole social group, and was used for the benefit of all alike. All ages, all sexes, all social ranks united to venerate the gods of the field, the gods of the maize, of the potato, of the bean, the special divinities of the rain. Good or bad crops meant success or failure to whole peoples, entire nations; and the suggestion that one individual should be permitted to acquire more land than a thousand of his neighbors, in the modern way, would have been regarded as tantamount to a direct threat at Society.

There is something very poetic as well as something extremely practical in the early American attitude toward the ownership of land. Whether we agree with it or not, we must observe that on the communal ownership of land as a broad basis was built up the agriculture which in turn was the foundation of all culture in the western hemisphere. To-day it is amusing to hear theorists arguing that socialism will never work. For throughout the Western world, for century after notable century, socialism worked like a perfectly oiled machine, producing enough surplus wealth so that the labor of men with special mental endowments could be released to create the art and the science that were the glory of America.

Thus, we may visualize a panorama of the earlier stages of human life in America: Men, women, and children living in caves, hunting and fishing close by, or planting the first domesticated grasses near the mouths of their caverns as agriculture was invented. Drawing pictographs on cave walls black with smoke, as art was invented. Then a few venturesome souls leaving the cave and going a little distance to pry up stones or stick saplings into the ground as walls of a primitive hut for which overlaid palmettos made the roof. Later, more pretentious wooden houses and the beginning of crude stone buildings, put up near water-holes. Following this, the beginnings of trade between tribes and the diffusion of culture traits, one group learning to imitate the better-shaped wooden canoe of another group, and in return teaching the latter how to improve its stone axes. The arts growing up—basketry, weaving, pottery. And all of this paving the way for the high sculpture and painting and the medicinal and astronomical lore of the men who thousands of years later were to build the great stone cities whose crumbling vestiges are the envy of our own age.

CHAPTER V

SPRUNG FROM ONE SOIL

W E HAVE just seen that, generally speaking, the ancient Americans were racially and—to a lesser extent—culturally one people.

We shall now see that our problem of understanding ancient America may be somewhat simplified geographically as well as racially. For the high spots in early American civilization were all within one rather large but definitely limited region. This extended from the northern border of Mexico—as it was before the war of 1846-47 with the United States —down through Central America into the northern part of Chile and including all of the northwest portion of South America.

The highest cultures America has given the world all bloomed within this compact area, consisting of southern North America, Central America, and northwestern South America.

Mexico, as defined above, of course included the highly developed social orders of the Pueblos of what is now Arizona and New Mexico. Farther south, in Old Mexico, were a number of fairly high cultures— Zapotecs, Mixtecs, Totonacs, and others—but the

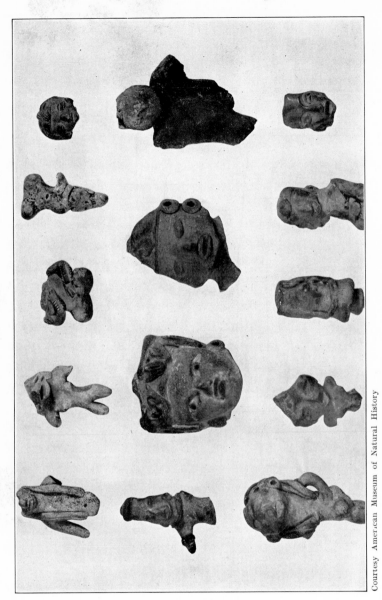

Courtesy American Museum of Natural History

Human figures done in clay—archaic type from Mexico

peak of Mexican development was represented by peoples speaking the Mexican or Nahuan (pronounced Nah-whahn) tongue. This means especially the Toltecs, and their more famous successors the Aztecs.

There was some fairly high culture in eastern South America, but man's highest achievements in the southern continent were in its western and northwestern parts. Colombia was the home of the Chibchas, famous for their skill as goldworkers. The Chibchas had so much gold that their life was almost a realization of the extravagant dreams of the avaricious Spaniards.

In Ecuador the Manabis left remarkable stone sculpture on the north coast, and the Cara people provided in their little empire of Quito a small rude model of what the great Inca Empire was to be. At the height of their power the Incas, of course, dominated Ecuador, Peru, western Bolivia, and the northern half of Chile. However, as the Chibcha and Cara nations preceded the Inca power in the north, so there were several mysterious early civilizations farther south than what became the Inca Empire, concerning which even the Incas themselves seem to have known little. Particularly there was the culture dominated by the city of Chanchan on the north coast (on which site Pizarro was to found Trujillo in 1535), and called "the kingdom of the Grand

65

Chimu," and the culture along the southern part of the Peruvian coast about the center called Nasca, and, finally, the upland culture about Lake Titicaca in Bolivia, called the culture of Tiahuanaco.

The art of Chimu is conspicuous for grace of line in pottery and painting, while that of Nasca is noteworthy for a wealth of coloration in textiles and pottery fairly dazzling to the eye. Tiahuanaco pottery is more elaborate and varied than either of the other two, but the remains of Tiahuanaco which have attracted the most attention are the examples of truly magnificent megalithic (big-stone) masonry. This early masonry is easily superior to the later stonework of the Incas, and other arts than stonework give us reason to think that in various respects the famous Inca culture was inferior to the mysterious ones which preceded it. These cultures of Chimu, Nasca, and Tiahuanaco are sometimes lumped together with others under the general term "Pre-Inca."

Finally, it was in Central America that the very peak of all American civilization was reached, of which we have indisputable proof in the accomplishments of Maya scientists and artists that have endured to our day.

Now then, to recapitulate: we see that southern North America, Central America, and northwestern South America are the three most important areas in the history of American culture, and that they form one compact region where the flower of American civilization attained its longest and loveliest bloom. Moreover, not only was it here that the American reached the peak of his self-development, but it was probably in this same region that American culture had its origin.

In trying to gain light on this origin, some research workers have given entirely too much credence to the myths and legends of the early Americans. The myths of any people are of great importance in reflecting its soul, its psychology, but it is dangerous to take them seriously as an accurate reflection of the course history has followed. And, indeed, data gathered by botanists, archæologists, and students of American linguistics indicate that we must be especially careful not to misinterpret the legend concerning its own origin which nearly every ancient American nation possessed.

For example, we saw in the last chapter how mistaken we should be to conclude that America had been given its first culture by Europeans, merely because many American tribes have a legend that their first learning was brought to them by a god with a beard, clad in white cloth or white paint (not necessarily *white-skinned*, mind you!) who had come from the east. For the evidence of the independent nature of American agriculture and American language, as well as of the American calendrical system,

67

indicate forcefully that whether the American man as a zoölogical specimen originated in America or not, he undoubtedly developed his own culture here.

As aids in reconstructing the pre-history of a vanished people old bones and old pots are much more valuable than myths. However, when a legend checks up with the findings of archæology it may be given an unusual amount of credence. This seems to be the case with a number of similar legends formerly current among peoples of the west coast of South America, describing how that region came to have its high degree of enlightenment. The substance of these legends is to the effect that learning was brought to western South America in remote time by immigrants who arrived on the coast in balsas, or rafts. These arrivals conquered the surrounding country, and amalgamated their own superior culture with the inferior one of the natives.

The most persuasive of these stories is called the Lambayeque legend, and states that the foreigners landed in Lambayeque Province, in Peru. It says that there were women as well as men in the party, and gives many circumstantial details about the arriving expedition, including the names of its leaders and the fact that they brought with them an idol made of a green stone. Now, jadeite, or nephrite, was a green stone considered sacred and much used by the Mayas of Central America and by the Nahua-

speaking peoples of upland Mexico, including the
Toltecs and Aztecs. Furthermore, the names of the
leaders of this Lambayeque party were much more
akin to the names of other American tribes than to
those of any people in Oceania, Europe, or Asia.

All in all, an analysis of these legends of the bringing of culture to South America by immigrants who
arrived from the sea on balsas suggests that they had
come no very great distance on their cumbersome
rafts; in short, that they had come from another part
of America. The most likely region for their origin is
Central America.

The findings of archæologists lend strength to this
supposition. These findings have frequently revealed
a resemblance between the ancient arts, crafts, and
customs of western South America, on the one hand,
and those of Central America and Mexico on the
other. It has long been known that there were cultural affinities between Central America and Mexico,
the indication being that an early migration from the
former locality to the latter gave the Mexican peoples
many features of Maya life, and that centuries afterward the Toltecs of Mexico returned the compliment,
and overrunning the Yucatan peninsula deposited
their own architecture upon what had been the parent
art of the Mayas. So if intercommunication between
South America and either Central America or Mexico can be proved, the rough but essential unity of

69

the three regions of high American culture—(1) Mexico, (2) Central America, (3) northwestern South America—will be established.

It is too early yet to say that this has been proved. But the tendency toward proving it is unmistakable as archæologists ply their spades in more and more burial-mounds of ancient rulers, and as artists copy the blurred outlines of painting and sculpture on the walls of this and that crumbling temple. The following are a few examples of the sort of evidence which has come in:

Superstitions entertained both by Peruvians and by some of the Mexicans induced them to mistreat dogs during eclipses of the moon, and to provide a dead man with a dog to lead his master's soul to the underworld. Geometric decoration in the stone of ruined cities in southern Mexico bears a striking resemblance to work in stucco on abandoned structures on the coast of Peru. And a certain arresting design found on pottery from the Mexican State of Oaxaca is entirely unlike anything else ever found in Mexico and is exactly matched by one of the patterns most frequently used in many colored textiles made by weavers who lived long ago near the busy manufacturing town of Truxillo, where on northern Peruvian beaches green Pacific combers break into quivering foam.

Further, a sculptured figure seated in a niche in

stone found in Manabi, Ecuador, looks like an imitation of figures found in the long abandoned Maya city of Piedras Negras. Then a very old monolith from Chavin de Huantar, in the Andes, shows a number of grotesque faces and other features characteristic of the stone carving the Mayas left in Central America before their somewhat mysterious decline just prior to the Spanish conquest. And the art of Nasca, on the southern Peruvian coast, has characteristics which inevitably suggest the Maya handiwork.

Such similarities as those cited in the last paragraph must not be given too much importance; as Thomas Joyce says, it is possible that they "may arise from no more than a common psychology, and may bear witness only to the 'American' basis shared by both cultures." But on the other hand they "might be taken as a vague indication of early coasting voyages down the west coast of South America," particularly in view of the many legends on that west coast concerning the remote arrival in rafts of a very learned and powerful people. It is quite possible that there was a maritime migration to South America from both Central America and Mexico, and quite possible that there was not one migration only from each of the latter two areas but several.

I said a little way back that "it has long been known that there were cultural affinities between Central America and Mexico." Not only did the comparatively late Toltec Empire, which seems to have been at its height a little before the Normans conquered England—not only did this Toltec Empire apparently get much of its astronomical knowledge from the Mayas and in turn implant its picturesque but inferior and rococo architecture upon their chaster and more poetic stone carving, but beneath remains of both the Toltec and Maya civilizations and all others of Mexico and Central America, archæologists have found traces of a culture which for lack of a better term has been called "Archaic." Primitive pottery objects apparently of this "Archaic" type have been found even in northern South America, and there are indications that the early manufacturers of these things had spread across Colombia and Ecuador into Peru.

I hope you are beginning to realize that archæology is not dry dust, but is frozen history. A bit of a pot means a great deal more in reconstituting history than a legend or a fairy-story. If the Greeks and Romans had not left written records behind them, the essential form and course of their civilization could have been traced by our archæologists. In that fascinating volume which is the story of the pre-history of America—and which is still being written—pottery is the most frequent page.

The artists of the "Archaic" era have left us a good picture of their age. They worked sometimes in stone,

Courtesy American Museum of Natural History

Pottery representing men playing musical instruments—Peru

being fond of carving boulders into a semblance of the human form. But more often they worked in ceramics. They made some globular bowls with narrow necks, as well as wide-mouthed bowls which sometimes had tripod legs and sometimes did not. And many of these vessels, of both kinds, were embellished with little clay faces affixed to the exterior. The faces, moreover, show a common resemblance to the most characteristic of all the surviving art forms of this "Archaic" people—namely, figurines of men and women, especially women. The ladies are perfectly nude and hold their hands upon their knees, hips, or breasts. There is some reason to believe that these female figures, five inches in height, represented the principle of fertility, and were used as charms by the early farmers of America to secure good crops.

Some of the figurines were painted, but most of them were decorated by incising or gouging with some chisel-like tool; or little balls of clay were affixed to them. A good deal of what we can learn from the life of the people who made these figurines is summarized by Dr. Spinden as follows:

We may gather much of an ethnological nature from the study of these quaint figures. Articles of dress and adornment are shown as well as musical instruments, weapons, etc. Head-dresses may consist of fillets, turbans, and objects perched on one side of the head. Nose-rings and earrings are abundantly

represented and in considerable variety. We may be
sure that weaving was rather highly developed, because many garments such as shirts, skirts and aprons
are painted, or incised with geometric designs. Body
painting, or tattooing, appears to have been a common usage. Among weapons, the *atlatl,* or spear-
thrower, was already known and knobby clubs seem
to have been popular. Men are shown beating on
drums and turtle shells, while women nurse children
and carry water. Since the large figures of clay are
often found in tombs it is not impossible that they
were intended to be portraits of the dead. Many have
a startling quality of caricature.

Archaic art is a pretty certain index of the religion then in vogue. There is a notable absence of
purposely grotesque or compounded figures representing divinities such as will be found in the later
horizons. Dogs are frequently modeled in clay and
were apparently developed into a rather special domestic breed. Snakes are sometimes found as a plastic
decoration on pottery but there are few signs of serpent worship. We can find no evidence that human
sacrifice was practised.

We saw in the last chapter that Americans were
one race. In that chapter and in this we have seen
that in addition to racial unity there was a smaller
but yet conspicuous cultural unity in America; that
all the more noteworthy instances of the flowering of
civilization in our two continents occurred within a
fairly compact area; and that, finally, there is reason

to believe American culture originated within the same area.

On the northern edge of this area the oldest relics of American man have been found; that is, at Folsom and Bishop's Cap, New Mexico; Frederick, Oklahoma; Vero, Florida, and other points within or very near the northern edge of Old Mexico. We do not know enough about these people to construct much of a picture of their life, but assuredly the Folsom people were far above the most primitive stage of stone-cutting.

Throughout this whole compact region except its southernmost part have been found the characteristic remains of the people called "Archaic," a nation apparently later in time than the makers of the Folsom arrow-heads. We know, however, that these "Archaic" gentlemen and ladies lived before the Toltecs and Aztecs of Mexico, because the remains of the former have been found underlying the remains of the latter. Apparently the "Archaic" people preceded the Mayas in Central America, too. And, accompanying traces of a very early and crude form of maize, the work of "Archaic" potters has been found in the Southwest of the United States, in sites belonging to the culture of the mysterious predecessors of the Pueblos called "Basket-makers," a people that buried their dead in dry caverns and that made baskets but no pottery. Moreover, although no such

75

clear "stratification" of remains has been found in South America as in Mexico, there is reason to believe that the "Archaic" potters worked in more ancient times than the potters of Nasca and Chimu, the stoneworkers of Tiahuanaco and Manabi, the expert Chibcha goldsmiths of Colombia, and other predecessors of the Incas.

In short, we are pretty sure that in early times Central America and Mexico had much the same sort of culture; indeed, it is quite likely that this was shared by part of South America as well. And if there *was* such far-flung unity about ancient American civilization as is indicated by the widespread discovery of the creations of these "Archaic" potters, that is additional reason for believing that there was some contact among the higher civilizations following the "Archaic." Not additional *proof* of this contact, mind you, but additional *reason* for believing in it; the reason being one which some scientists hate to hear mentioned—namely, the dictates of common sense.

But we must remember that there seems to have been a great gap between the sort of life these later nations led and the existence of the "Archaic" people. The relics of the two eras which have come down to us show scarcely any similarities and many divergences. (An interesting example of the latter lies in the fact that the commonest sculpture of the "Ar-

76

chaic" artists was the nude female figurine, already
mentioned, whereas the great sculptors of the Mayas
usually scrupulously avoided any suggestion of nude
femininity in their modeling.) It is quite possible that
the Mayas, Aztecs, and Peruvians were just about as
ignorant of these "Archaic" people as we are. It is
quite possible, too, that the former were studying the
latter as we are to-day, and it is quite probable that
nations so advanced as the Mayas, Aztecs, and Peruvians had their own schools of archæology.

At any rate, modern archæologists have found
among Maya objects samples of "Archaic" art which
the Maya scientists had apparently collected for their
own classification. This was as if—human beings having been wiped off the earth two thousand years from
now—strange creatures from Mars should come
probing through the ruins of New York and find
among the characteristic products of our own civilization, driveshafts of automobiles and twisted skeletons of Woolworth Buildings, the litter of our museums: a jasper arrow-head from Folsom, a gold
coin of the Chibchas, a lovely vase from the Chimu
country, and a little naked clay goddess of agriculture from "Archaic" Mexico. Yet even with such
diversity might the Martian savants conclude that
the makers of all these things were of one species.
And if a certain book had been preserved from rain
in a dry pocket under the fallen wall of a library, the

Martians might decipher from the following hieroglyphs this truest comment of that species on itself:

> Vain is man
> Who glories in his joys and knows no fears,
> While to and fro the chances of the years
> Dance, like an idiot in the wind.

Three great problems confront our scientists who
are trying to fill out conspicuous gaps in the pre-
history of America. The first is to trace back the connection between the high civilizations of Mexico, Central America, South America, and that "Archaic"
people. The second problem is to trace back the connection between the "Archaic" nation and the earlier
cultures whose evidences Dr. Vaillant has recently
unearthed near Mexico City. The most interesting
thing about Spinden's "Archaic" is the widespread
unity it seems to have had, whereas Vaillant's earlier
cultures present marked differences from the "Archaic," and from one another. The third problem is
to trace the connection between the peoples who made
these queer little figurines Dr. Vaillant has been finding, and the really primitive Americans. For certainly, although "archaic" means old, it does not mean
primitive. The people who made these "Archaic"
figurines were not extremely primitive. They evidently had the loom for weaving, and they had agriculture. And the people who made Vaillant's earlier

figurines may have been some distance from the primitive horizon.

Yet they were perhaps not out of sight of it. It is quite possible that maize grew up with this "Archaic" or with these "pre-Archaic" pottery-making cultures. If we knew where these little grotesque goddesses of agriculture and the curious naked but turbaned figurines that preceded them were first manufactured, we might know where maize was developed from the wild grass, *teocintli*.

More of these products of primitive potters have been found in Mexico than in any other part of the warm, central culture area of America. The testimony of archæology indicates that American culture probably started in Mexico or Central America. This conclusion is strengthened by the myths current in ancient South America. On the other hand, the testimony of botany seems to indicate that agriculture perhaps originated in Peru. At least, a larger number of anciently domesticated plants seem to have been possessed in Peru than in any other part of America.

Perhaps agriculture *was* originated in Peru, then carried northward to be the basis of a sharp development of human culture which was later borne back to Peru by adventurers and colonists on navigable rafts.

At any rate, we can be fairly sure that American culture originated within the same area to which its highest development was confined. We can pretty safely say that the American took his first important step toward civilization in a region somewhere between southern North America and north-central South America. This area is mostly warm country, much of it very hot. It includes some cool plateaus, but nothing below the snowy peaks of mountains which could be called cold country.

In modern times there is a theory that man develops a higher civilization in a cold climate than in a warm one. The history of America, like the history of the eastern hemisphere, is a refutation of that puritanical assumption. The flower of American culture was nurtured by the soft warm rains and ardent sun of the tropics or semi-tropics.

Gregory Mason and laborers of Mason-Blodgett expedition, with pottery from Rio Frio caves

# CHAPTER VI

## VEGETABLE-FED

"TELL me what you eat and I will tell you what you are," is the advertising slogan of a modern predigested food. There is a great deal of truth in it. As a man eateth, so is he.

As already seen, American agriculture was founded on maize, beans, and squashes. But one thing which made America great was the willingness of the early Americans to eat almost anything.

You may laugh at a man who lives in a hut and eats jack-in-the-pulpit and garter-snake, but reflect that he may be saving his leisure for philosophy! He may be ridiculed, but Diogenes, who lived in a tub, Christ, who turned the other cheek, and Einstein, who shuns the society of his neighborhood, have been ridiculed. Generally the ridicule comes from the broker, editor, college professor, carpenter, farmer, lawyer, and business man who lives in a rut, sleeps in a rut, dresses in a rut, and thinks in a rut. If we eat eels why should we not eat snakes? If we eat lobsters and crabs why should we not eat land-crabs?

Leisure is necessary for culture, and Americans secured this leisure by using whatever nature gave them.

81

There was nothing edible that the aborigine would not eat. All animal products of land and sea and lake, all fleshy roots, and all seeds went into his maw. But the bulk of the food of the first Americans was vegetable.

Among such products wild fruits perhaps came first in point of quantity. America abounded in berries—gooseberries, huckleberries, black raspberries, blackberries, cranberries, strawberries, and others. Among the wild fruits of America the strawberries and the pineapples were perhaps particularly appreciated by the Europeans, who had not the latter fruit at all and whose strawberries were of a miserable tiny, tasteless variety.

The fig, sugar-cane, coconut, and banana are doubtfully attributed to America; that is, the origin of these fruits is still a matter of controversy. Such an eminent authority as O. F. Cook, formerly director of the Bureau of Plant Industry of the United States Department of Agriculture, has insisted that the sugar-cane, banana, and coconut "existed, in pre-Spanish America," as well as in the eastern hemisphere, and as more intensive investigation is made of the rich flora of ancient America it is quite possible that the truth of his assertion will be established, to the discomfiture of American botanists with hemispheric inferiority complexes. But there is no doubt at all that the pineapple, and the better strawberry of modern horticulture, are gifts of the fertile West.

However, the white-skinned "discoverers" of America were hardly more pleased with the pineapples and strawberries than with the wild grapes and plums and persimmons. Colonial literature is filled with the praises of these native products, so rich and juicy and plentiful in the wild state that the aborigines had made no attempt to cultivate them. In 1621, Edward Winslow wrote from Plymouth to a friend in England: "Here are grapes, white and red, and very sweet and strong also; strawberries, gooseberries, raspas, etc.; plums of three sorts, white, black and red, being almost as good as damson."

Father Allouez, a Jesuit pathfinder toward the end of the seventeenth century, reported the natives of the Illinois country using "from trees and plants 42 different kinds of fruit all of which are excellent." Of course they ate every edible nut that grew wild, and of course they had known from time immemorial how to get sugar from maple trees. (This, obviously, has no bearing on the argument whether America shared the sugar-cane with Asia before the time of Columbus, for cane sugar is a Southern product and maple sugar is a Northern one.) It does the heart of a New Englander good to read some of the early accounts of native sugar-boiling.

Now, although it is true that the Americans ate

83

virtually everything the human stomach would digest, the fact remains that they were primarily a race of flour-eaters.

Early European explorers were much impressed by the amount of grain they found growing in America. The white observers were often ignorant of the fact, but some of these cereals were wild cereals. Wild rye was common on the Atlantic coast northward from Virginia. It was this that the Norse explorers, who "discovered" America to the glory of Scandinavians before Columbus "discovered" it to the glory of Latins, spoke of as growing in the form of "self-sown wheat-fields." It was this that Cartier in 1534 found filling the clearings in the Nova Scotian woods ("wild corn, that hath an ear like unto rye"), and it was this grain with "seede not much unlike rie, though much smaller" that gallant Captain John Smith found the Virginia red men using "for a dainty bread buttered with deare suet." Who can read such phrases as this last, frequent in the literature of the early European exploration of America, and not believe that the early Americans lived well!

Bread and gruel was made from the common wild cane of the Mississippi Valley, and another cereal much used by the aborigines was wild rice, the same plant that hunters now disseminate to attract ducks. This is probably the grain which the first French and Spanish writers on America frequently referred to as

84

"mill" or "millet." In our time we are apt to forget that when Columbus crossed the Atlantic more human beings in Africa, Asia, and Europe were living on millet than on wheat and all other cereals combined. It seems likely, however, that millet was not native to America. And it did not later ever become very popular in the western continents because of a widespread preference for the native maize and the imported wheat.

In their constant search for vegetable products which could be converted into flour, the ancient Americans used a great variety of wild nuts to make bread. Among these were the chestnut—now, alas, almost extinct!—the hazelnut, the walnut, the pecan, the chinkapin, and the acorn. The sunflower (*planta solis,* as the early explorers called it), also gave its seeds to the making of a kind of bread, and these seeds provided an oil much relished by the aborigines as a dressing. The Jerusalem artichoke—which is neither from Jerusalem nor an artichoke, the name probably being a corruption of the Italian *girasole articiocco,* or sunflower artichoke—was employed for the concoction of both bread and broth. This plant and the sunflower, however, became the object of deliberate cultivation. Whereas the nuts were so common in the wild state that cultivation was not necessary.

It is a natural assumption that man did not use

85

flour until he had begun to take that care of food-plants which could fairly be called the practice of agriculture. In short, it is quite likely that the American made flour from at least one of his cultivated plants, such as maize or the potato, before he made flour from such wild plants as cane or acorns. This is a very interesting point, but one that will probably never be determined.

A study of the history of maize reminds us that the conquest of America by Europeans meant that a civilization of artists flourishing in the western continents was forced to give way to a civilization of traders, of business men. The trader had an honorable position in ancient America, as he did in medieval Europe, but neither in ancient America nor in medieval Europe was the trader the dominant factor in society. In the modern United States, however, society at large is dominated by the business man. There remains virtually no aristocracy of blood; it has succumbed to the aristocracy of dollars. Almost any social gate may be "crashed" by the man with money. The professions have become commercialized.

It is true that the best type of modern business man in the United States is a man of generous cultivation, and is probably a more cultivated being than the traders of other civilizations and other ages. But interest in doing a good job for the sake of the work itself, interest in creating a product for the sheer joy

86

of creating, has in the United States of America been to a lamentable extent brushed aside by an interest in mere profit. It is characteristic that the work of white men toward improving maize, the basic crop of America, has been directed mostly toward increasing the quantity of the yield rather than toward improving the quality of the crop. Yet it would be difficult to prove that much success has been achieved even toward increasing the yield, so efficient were the early agriculturists of our continent. Speaking on this point, no less an authority than Mr. Lyman Carrier of the United States Department of Agriculture says:

A study of all available accounts of yields of early days fails to show that there has been any great improvement. The descriptions of plants, the numbers of ears to the stalk, the number of rows of grain on an ear and the number of grains in a row as given in the earliest accounts of Indian corn, while not equal to the extreme cases sometimes found, correspond very closely with average farm crops at the present time. The commercial varieties have been quite generally purified in regard to color, yet Indian corn still has strains distinctly pure as far as color is concerned, which they use in their religious ceremonies. On one point there seems to be a distinct difference in methods of breeding between white men and the Indians. The white men have been working towards the isolation of pure strains, the Indians with the exception of special purpose strains, allowed wide mixing of varieties. It is still a debatable question whether a heterozygous condition is not the better for this crop.

For Canada the early Americans developed a maize that would ripen in less than three months. But some of the varieties of maize they used in Texas required five months to reach maturity. There were special varieties of maize for popping, for parching, for making meal, for eating whole, and for roasting. The aborigines originated the dent maize of the middle West, the flint maize of New England, and the prolific varieties of the South. With maize, as with many other vegetables in the list of American food-plants, the white man has improved very little on his redskinned predecessor, and there is no doubt that he has forgotten a good many special technical points well understood by the original American.

The natives often mixed strawberries, raspberries, huckleberries, and other berries with their maize meal to make berry bread. An entire book could be written on the varieties of native ways of cooking maize flour, but the common method was to soften the grain with lime till the husks were removed and make it into the characteristic round, flat cake, shaped somewhat like our pancakes but thinner, which are known as tortillas in most of Latin America to-day. The *grrrck-grrrck* of maize being ground on a flat stone is the most *American* sound in America. It seems likely that "johnny-cake" is derived from "journey-cake," a name given small cakes of maize meal which were made for consumption on journeys.

To-day, where maize is found, beans and squash are usually not far away. We still plant maize in hills in the ancient American manner, and the yellow pumpkin is often seen mellowing in the sun between hills of maize. These are agricultural customs which the white man learned from the red. Botanists have established the fact that the common pumpkin as well as all the common squashes, such as the crookneck, Hubbard, simlin, and cushaw, were common foods of the prehistoric American.

It is hard to say what the early Europeans meant when they spoke of "pease" growing in America. Apparently the true pea was not native to the western continents. When they were speaking of Canada, these Europeans probably meant Lathyrus, a plant commonly found along the coast of Labrador; and when the Europeans were speaking of the southern part of North America "pease" may have been applied to a small bean.

But as to beans, every edible variety except horse-beans and soy-beans was given to the world by the aboriginal American. Of course this includes all the varieties of kidney-beans, Lima beans, scarlet-runner beans, and tepary beans. It seems likely that

89

the American beans were taken back to Spain by Columbus, to be a staple Spanish food from that time forth. How the white man learned to sow beans between rows of maize is indicated by the following quotation from a writer named Beverly, who was speaking of conditions in Virginia in 1705. It must be remembered that by "peas," he meant beans:

The Indians sow'd Peas sometimes in the Intervals of the rows of Corn, but more generally in a Patch of ground by themselves. They have an unknown Variety of them (but all of a Kidney-Shape) some of which I have met with wild.

There is no doubt that those indefatigable travelers the Spaniards did a great deal to mingle the indigenous products of one continent with those of another. Much confusion existed for a while because several products that had been considered particularly Asiatic were found in Mexico. Then it was remembered that for several years Spain brought her Asiatic goods from Manila to Acapulco, on the west coast of Mexico, and carried them overland to Vera Cruz for transatlantic shipment, owing to the fact that the pope had forbidden the Spaniards to round the Cape of Good Hope.

Leaving maize aside, the root crops gave the American much more bread than the grains. Americans developed for the world such roots as the potato, sweet potato, yam, yam-bean, taro, arrowroot, lleren, oca, Jerusalem artichoke, manioc, and many others.

Tapioca pudding is still a fairly common dessert in the United States, although the name "tapioca" is perhaps more familiar to our older generations than to our younger. But to few of us who are not specialists in botany do the names yuca, mandepore, manihot, mandioza, cassaba, cassava, manyoc, and manioc, mean anything. Yet these are all names for the plant which gives tapioca.

Manioc had a wide distribution in early America. Where the climate was too hot for maize, manioc was often the staple food-plant. Thus it was much used throughout eastern South America, including all the great Amazon drainage system. And in the West Indies and Central America, where maize also was eaten, manioc was a common food.

Manioc is a root, and the most interesting thing about it is that its juice is poisonous. Throughout the region in which it was eaten the manioc was treated in an identical manner in order to get rid of this poisonous juice, containing prussic acid. The root was grated and the pulp squeezed in a basketry press. When the juice had been pressed out the pulp was made into cakes and heated until the volatile poison remaining had been driven out. The result was cassava bread. The cassava which Europeans reported was being used by the natives in Virginia was not

91

true cassava at all, but a wild plant known as "wampee." As was the case with true cassava, this "wampee" required a careful preliminary process to rid it of poisonous juice before it could be eaten. Recently there have been some experiments made with cassava as food for hogs. But with the exception of these experiments and the use of old-fashioned tapioca pudding the modern American has ignored what was one of the most important foods of his foster-ancestors. A consideration of the elaborate process necessary to make it ought to disabuse any one of the erroneous idea that the Americans were a savage people when Columbus blundered into the Bahamas.

We do not think of the potato as a cereal, but the ancient Americans treated it as such. Perhaps no vegetable is more used in those parts of the modern world where civilization is highest than this tuber. Yet no food-plant has been so much lied about, not even the tomato. This common white root is usually known as "Irish potato," but as the late W. E. Safford of the United States Department of Agriculture pointed out, "It is only a potato by analogy and Irish by adoption."

The true potato is the sweet potato, which belongs to the convolvulus or morning-glory family. The misnamed "Irish potato" (*Solanum tuberosum*) is of the nightshade family, to which the tomato is related. Many plants of this family are poisonous, and that is

92

why the tomato was very little eaten by Europeans or their descendants in America until the nineteenth century, although this red "poison apple" was well liked in ancient Central America where it developed.

Mr. Safford, above mentioned, was largely instrumental in convincing the botanical world that before the Spanish conquest the "Irish potato" was never used north of Colombia. Europeans first found it in Peru, but, like maize, the potato has been domesticated for so many thousands of years that its wild ancestor has never been discovered. The Peruvians called the white potato *papa,* by which name Spanish-speaking peoples know it to our day.

The word "potato" comes from the native American *batata,* the name by which the sweet potato was known to the natives of the West Indies, where Europeans first encountered it. Of the first voyage of Columbus to this region it is written: "They [the natives] gave them [the Spaniards] some boiled roots to eat not unlike chestnuts in taste. . . . There was a great deal of tilled land, some sowed with those roots." Sweet potatoes rapidly reached great popularity with the early Europeans in America. Spaniards and Portuguese took them to Europe, Asia, and Africa, and the English colonists introduced them to what is now the United States, or at least widely extended their use there, for it is possible that the natives in the southern part of the country were

93

cultivating the sweet potato before the white men came.

Curiously the "Irish potato" did not reach the British colonies in North America until 1719. In that year it was carried to Londonderry, New Hampshire, by Irish emigrants. Englishmen were transporting it to the West Indies about the same time. Many early European writers, who made the mistake of thinking that the potato was in Virginia or the Carolinas long before this date, were confused by certain superficial resemblances between the "Irish potato" and a wild native tuber-bearing leguminous plant the Indians called "openawk" (*Glycine apios*). This was also known to the natives of the Virginia-Carolina regions as "tuckahoe" and as "wampee." Frenchmen called the tubers *chapelets,* or rosary roots, because of the fact that they were arranged on strings like beads. Englishmen sometimes called them ground-nuts, marsh potatoes, or Indian potatoes.

Neither Columbus nor Cortez ever saw the white potato. The first European account of it was written by Pedro de Cieza de León, in 1538. In a part of the Cauca Valley of Colombia, too high for maize to grow, he found the natives living on quinoa and white potatoes. In the diary that Cieza de León filled out at night after his companions had fallen asleep, he describes the potato as "a kind of ground nut, which

94

when boiled becomes as soft as a cooked chestnut, but which has no thicker skin than a truffle."

Many men after Cieza de León were to confuse the potato with truffles, including all the Germans, whose word for potato, *"kartoffel,"* is a modification of *"tartuffel,"* or truffle.

In the high regions of Colombia and Ecuador which Cieza de León traversed, quinoa—an American cereal similar to grits or rice—and the white potato are still the most important foods of the natives. Meanwhile, in the rest of the world, what an astonishing history has had the "laughing potato," as the sons of Erin have dubbed it!

Although the Irish have shown perhaps a greater appreciation of the potato than any other nation, making a drink from it as well as using it for food, they were not the first European people to cultivate the lowly "spud." The tuber seems to have reached Europe first in Spanish ships coming from South America soon after the year 1580. In 1588 it was cultivated by Charles l'Ecluse, in charge of the Botanical Garden at Vienna. Apparently it was not much used in Ireland before 1663. But when the Irish peasant at last did discover the potato, he began to employ it to the exclusion of oatmeal and his other previous foods, so that in rare years when the potato crop failed there was often much misery in the Emerald Isle.

The Irish were not slow in finding out that the potato made rather good whisky. And yeast added to the fermented juice of the tuber gave the isle without snakes another alcoholic liquor, the poteen. Baked or boiled potatoes dipped in a saucer of salted milk became the common food of the Irish peasantry. For the Irish the potato acquired an almost sacred significance, as the daily bread received by them in answer to their prayers. In certain localities it was customary at the time of planting for the parish priest to march solemnly to the field and bless it, praying for a bountiful harvest.

In this practice of blessing the potato crop by Catholic priests in Ireland, we see an analogy to the "maize masses," an invocation to rain-gods and sun-gods to be generous to crops, which native Americans have used in one form or another from time immemorial, and are using in Central America to-day.

In the middle of the eighteenth century, perhaps some thirty years after the potato had been carried from Ireland to New Hampshire, the Irishmen sent their beloved "flowery potato" into Jamaica. From Jamaica it spread southward through the West Indies until it was only a few hundred miles from Colombia, the northern border of its native land. Thus it had virtually completed a circuit of the world. Thanks to the dry climate of western South America, there can be little doubt that Peru was the original

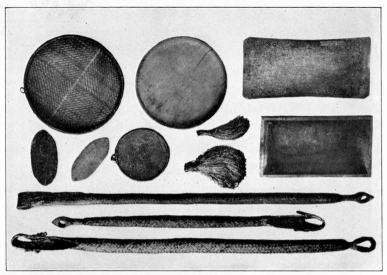

Courtesy American Museum of Natural History

Baskets, sifters, grinders, etc., used in preparing cassava

Vases representing vegetables cultivated in ancient South America

home of the potato: in a land of little rain vegetables buried with mummies hundreds of years ago have been preserved in graves to tell archæologists where originated the tuber that was to be a source of more wealth to the world than all the treasure of the Indies.

(Another valuable member of the vegetable kingdom given to the world by South America is the peanut. The original home of the "earth nut," as some of the early white explorers called it, was Brazil. Very soon after the discovery of America, the Spaniards took the peanut to Africa, and slave ships bringing negroes to North America a few years later brought the peanut with them. Thus the peanut, like the potato, had to cross the Atlantic from South America in order to get into North America.)

Although the Irishman makes whisky from the potato and the Russian makes vodka, there seems to be no record of the American having used this "goodly root" for beverage purposes. Maize was the universal drink as it was the universal food. Posole, which the Central American native uses to-day, was probably common in some form throughout the area in which maize was grown. This drink, which is non-intoxicating, looks like very thin gruel. It is made of boiled and ground-up maize mixed with water. Sometimes honey is added; indeed, there are several varieties of the beverage. With a tortilla or two it forms the breakfast of many a modern red man.

Yerba-mate, or Paraguay tea, recently sponsored in New York coffee-houses by the sons of the late President Roosevelt, was drunk throughout the Amazon basin. Like posole, it is non-intoxicating. So, of course, was the chocolate the ancients made from the native cacao—a word which the European "discoverers," with their customary inaccuracy, twisted into our word "cocoa."

But in no sense were the ancient Americans puritans. The thing that citizens of the United States today call "Prohibition" would have seemed to our geographical ancestors an insult to the sun-god who ferments the fruit when it drops from the vine. Possibilities of making many pleasant varieties of liquors to rest mind and nerves and bring new energy to the body—possibilities overlooked by later Americans —were utilized by the earlier natives of these continents. The Caribs of South America and the West Indies made a beer from cassava. Chicha, or maize beer (a much milder beverage than the "corn licker" of the Kentucky mountains) had many ceremonial uses among the Peruvians and allied peoples in addition to the happy common use of providing a little internal warmth and cheerfulness. Tizwin was a drink made from malted grain by the Mexicans, whose modern descendants make a malt beer as good as the best products of Germany and Austria. But the Aztec *octli* was far from being a concoction to trifle with

98

inasmuch as it was the ancestor of the Mexican pulque of our times. This opaque, sour, beer-like brew is made from the pseudo cactus called maguey, of the agave family. The word "agave" means "noble" in Greek, and is a fitting name for the plant that gave the Americans cloth, rope, dental floss, writing-paper, and the wherewithal to fill the cup that cheers.

The drink made from cacao, called by the Nahua-speaking peoples of Mexico *chocolatl* (from which we get the word "chocolate"), should not be confused with the drug coca, from which modern druggists have derived cocaine. Coca leaves played a most important part in the lives of the Peruvians and other South Americans. Offerings of coca leaves and of the maize drink chicha were made at roadside shrines, and maize and bags of coca leaves were buried with many a priest. The practice of the living was to chew the leaves, mixed with lime or bone ash, and it was believed that a bag of coca leaves would help the soul of the dead man on to his pleasant reward. To this day native carriers in western South America have a bag of coca leaves hung at their side, and there seems to be no doubt that the chewing of these leaves enables a laborer to exert himself prodigiously even if food is scarce or entirely wanting.

Cocaine is by no means the only valuable drug America has given to the world. Cascara sagrada is another, and a third is quinine—the bark of a tree, and the specific for malaria. This disease was brought to America by Europeans, who then found the cure for it in the land they had cursed with the malady.

The Americans have always been keen "herb doctors," and have been especially quick to recognize the value of narcotics and to venerate the plants endowed with narcotic properties. The "mescal-bean," which in the days of the early white settlements in Texas the aborigines considered worth the price of a horse, is probably a scarlet bean known to botanists as *Sophora secundiflora*. The consumption of this produces a delirious exhilaration followed by long sleep. Nowadays, however, the term "mescal-bean" is misapplied to the plant *Lophophora Williamsii*, a small, fleshy, spineless cactus, also commonly called "peyote," a word derived from the Aztec *peyotl*. This plant looks much like a carrot, but the severed top of it resembles a mushroom. It is the top which is chewed by the initiates who would see visions, and the Aztecs themselves seem to have been misled by its resemblance to a mushroom, naming it *teonanancatl*, "flesh of God." In the chewing of the "sacred mushroom," as the first Europeans called it, there is perhaps a rough analogy to the taking of communion in the Christian churches.

The ancients saw visions and experienced ecstasies through the use of other plants than this, including the fruit of the Cahoba tree, a sort of mimosa, which provides a ceremonial snuff to modern South Americans. Likewise the use of peyote has carried over into our own times, despite the strenuous efforts of the United States Government to stamp it out. Peyote seems to be not entirely evil, however. Those who use it say that it vastly increases their endurance, enabling them to walk great distances without fatigue. Witnesses summoned by the United States Government from the Menominee Indian Reservation, Wisconsin, testified that with them peyote had taken the place of alcohol, and they seemed to think that the former had far less ill effect on them than the latter.

During the Government's investigation it came out that among several tribes of red men to-day there exists a religious organization known as the Sacred Peyote Society, whose members use the misnamed "mushroom" to induce religious visions. Dr. Francis P. Morgan of the Government's Bureau of Chemistry experimented on volunteers with peyote, who reported that it gave them visions of various kinds, especially marked by moving objects, changing designs and figures of landscapes, friezes, balls of beautiful colors in constant motion. But an after effect was insomnia, whereas the Oriental practices of hashish-eating and opium-smoking induce sleep. "In this respect," says W. E. Safford, summarizing Dr. Morgan's testimony, "it somewhat resembles the active

101

principles of coffee and coca. Dr. Morgan further testified that as far as he knew no therapeutic or remedial value of the drug had been established."

But if physicians cannot approve this modern continuance of the immemorial use of native drugs, the ethnologist will travel many miles for the opportunity to see such ceremonies as these of peyote-eating, for often they contain vestiges of ancient ritual which throw a valuable light on the religions of America's youth. (By the way, *marihuana,* a drug considerably used in Mexico and the southwestern part of the United States at the present time, is not a native product, being, indeed, nothing else than *Cannabis indica,* or the "Indian hemp" of the Asiatic vision-seeker.)

Peruvian balsam, or Balsam of Peru, and copal gum are other gifts that have come down to us from the ritualists of ancient America. Copal incense was particularly valued by the Mayas, and many a ruined temple has been discovered by archæologists in the twentieth century with stone ceiling still black from the viscous smoke of copal burned to maize-gods and rain-gods centuries ago. Last but not least among the native gums in economic value is the chicle, from which we get chewing-gum. The early Americans were gum-chewers.

It is not on record that our foster-ancestors who ate maize and drank maize ever smoked maize—as farmer boys in the United States smoke corn-tassel cigarettes to-day. Tobacco was the smoke of ancient America, and the culture of tobacco was even more widespread than that of maize. It would be difficult for us to overemphasize the ceremonial uses of this antediluvian weed. Smoking of the famous "pipe of peace" was merely the particular ritualistic use of tobacco which the European conquerors happened to encounter most frequently, inasmuch as their chief contact with the natives was as victors making terms with the vanquished.

Tobacco was not only considered an incense to the gods, however; it was also considered an aid to everyday health as well as a minister to normal human comfort, and, as such, it was widely used by women and even by children, as well as by adult males. Long before Sir Walter Raleigh was undeservedly given credit for taking tobacco to England (a feat really performed by the sailors of John Hawkins) the Spanish adventurers returning from America introduced it into their own country. From Spain it was borne to Portugal, and Nicot, the French Ambassador to Portugal, took the fragrant herb to France about 1560 and also gave it the botanical name of Nicotiana, from which comes our word "nicotine."

Tobacco is a difficult crop to grow, and as a rule the aborigines of the West did not follow their prevailing custom with other plants of "mixing" crops, but raised it on a separate piece of ground. The European method of raising cabbages somewhat resembled the American mode of managing tobacco-culture. Naturally the European tobacco-planters imitated the native ways, but Lyman Carrier, who has made a historical study of tobacco-culture, thinks that the topping of tobacco, the removal of

the terminal bud after a certain number of leaves have set, appears not to have been practised by the Indians. It was used as an expedient to limit the production of tobacco to the very best grades inaugurated by the Virginia planters in 1621 and the tobacco growers in all parts of the country have followed this practice ever since.

Tobacco-growing became such a rage with the colonists that in some localities it was necessary to pass laws requiring the planters to sow enough maize or other food-crop to ensure the safety of the ardent tobacco-grower and his hands from starvation. John Smith reported that in the tobacco-plantation country of Virginia tobacco "passes . . . as current Silver."

Tobacco is not a food, but to-day as when the red man ruled our land, there are those who would go without food to get it. Thus there is perhaps a certain fitness in closing this discussion of American food-plants with the foregoing remarks on tobacco. Every American banquet ends with "cigars and cigarettes."

The late **Dr.** Safford did not forget this when, as a graphic illustration of the large contribution in food-plants which American agriculture has made to the world, he suggested the following "All-American Banquet" to be given to a visiting European botanist:

Cocktail of Virginia oysters with sauce of tomato and red pepper

Chowder of Little Neck clams, with tomatoes and green corn, with opossum fat substituted for butter; or terrapin stew made with turtle eggs

Barbecued shad à la Indienne, with white potatoes, and tamales à la Mexicaine

Black peppers or tomatoes stuffed with wild rice

Turkey stuffed with native chestnuts or oysters; cranberry sauce

Sweet potatoes, string-beans, succotash of Lima beans and green corn, stewed tomatoes, Jerusalem artichoke

Corn-pone or hoe-cake, guava jelly, salted peanuts

Sherbet, passion-flower à la Martinique, or Sour Sop à la Peruvienne

*For the game course*

Quail, rice-birds or canvasback duck, blackberry or grape jelly

Salad of avocado (alligator pear) with dressing of sun-flower or hickory-nut oil and maple vinegar and cayenne pepper and salt

*Dessert*

Pineapple ice, pumpkin pudding, stewed blackberries,
strawberries, grapes, wild plums, pecans, Brazil-
nuts, water chinquapins (or lotus-fruit), hickory-
nuts, pine-nuts, hazelnuts, popcorn, chocolate,
yerba-mate, cassine tea
Cigars and cigarettes
And—if you care to indulge—chewing-gum!

# CHAPTER VII

## AGRICULTURAL CITIES

THE reports of the first European discoverer~ are filled with allusions to the wide ~~ ton by the native Americans. Early in the ~ before Cortez had conquered Mexico, Hernandez de Córdoba touched at a small island off the northeast extremity of the Yucatan peninsula which he named Las Mugeres (The Women) because of certain statues in the form of women which he found there. Telling of Córdoba's visit to the island, the Spanish historian Gomara says:

The Spaniards were astonished, for the first time to see strong edifices, which had not as yet been discovered, and also to perceive that the inhabitants were so richly and tastefully clothed. They wore shirts and cloaks of white and colored cotton, their head-dress consisted of feathers, their ears were enriched with ear-drops and jewels of gold and silver.

Ferdinand Colon, the son of Columbus, reported that on the first voyage the Genoese navigator saw "above twelve thousand five hundred pounds of spun cotton in one house." Colon continues:

107

The cotton grows naturally about the fields like roses, and open of themselves when they are ripe, but not all at the same time; for upon one and the same plant they have seen a little, young bud, another open, and the third coming ripe.

Of course cotton was much used in the eastern hemisphere before the discovery of America. As early as the thirteenth century the famous traveler Marco Polo reported cotton trees "of very great size, growing full six paces high, and attaining to an age of twenty years," in India. But botanists are pretty generally agreed that the best commercial cotton of to-day comes mainly from American ancestors. The famous Sea-Island or Egyptian cotton, and the upland cotton are among the varieties attributed to America.

Cotton was the material used for the garments of the civilized people of ancient America. The *slap-slap* of clothing on flat washing stones was a familiar sound along the rivers from Peru to Arizona, as truly an American sound as the *grrrck-grrrck* of maize on the metate.

To-day farmers of the United States bind up their grain crops chiefly with sisal fiber. This comes from the leaves of the henequen plant, a member of the agave family and a relative of our common century-plant. Most of the henequen thus required by our farmers is raised on huge plantations in the State of

Yucatan, the easternmost State of the Mexican Republic. There have been periods when the henequen of Yucatan, as a revenue-producer for Mexico, ranked second only to the oil of the Tampico district. These henequen plants that give our modern farmers the twine with which to bind up their crops are the lineal descendants of the henequen plants that furnished twine for the binding of bundles of maize to feed the workmen of the Maya city-states, and rope for the hauling of the great stone blocks used in the ancient Maya temples—some of which still stand in the midst of fields gray-green with henequen.

Early in the twentieth century, Mérida, the modern capital of Yucatan built by the Spaniards in the sixteenth century on the site of the Maya city of Tihoo, had more millionaires per capita than any other city in the world. And all these millionaires of clean and beautiful Mérida had made their fortunes in henequen, the "Green Gold of Yucatan." Then, from 1915 onward, the Mexicans began experimenting in Yucatan with a kind of communism more radical at its extreme than anything seen elsewhere in Mexico or even in Russia, and also more radical than the communistic ownership of land practised in Yucatan and throughout America before the advent of white men. This disrupted the fortunes of the great *henequeros* and seriously affected the prosperity of the whole State, which did not begin to come back until,

109

toward the end of the third decade of the twentieth century, socialists with more moderate ideas gained control of the government of Yucatan. Under proper administration this State founded on fiber is capable of producing both fortunes for the few and prosperity for the many.

Members of the agave family were used in the making of textiles in America, all the way from Mexico to Peru. The cultivation of plants that provide fiber for clothing doubtless came after the cultivation of food-plants, but the agave, which produces both drink and raiment, was pretty surely one of the first fiber plants to be used in ancient America, where, after he began to become civilized, man was vegetarian in attire as well as in diet.

One variety of agave, the *Furcræa,* was converted by the Peruvians into the cloth with which their mummies were clad. They also made of it nets, laces, and twine of lovely design. Beyond the northern border of the agave plant's habitat the natives used wild hemp and various grasses to make their textiles.

The hammock is probably one of America's gifts to the world. The best hammocks are made of agave fiber or of cotton. The cotton area and the agave area both are virtually coterminous with the region of highest artistic and scientific achievement. That is, they extend from northern Mexico to southern Peru. From graves in Peru archæologists have dug up three

110

kinds of cotton, a white, a tawny, and a red-brown. The white is considered the best.

Rubber is of course an American contribution to civilization. The oldest pieces of rubber yet found were dredged out of the sacred cenote at Chichen Itza, Yucatan, a pool into which virgins were thrown as sacrifices to the gods of rain. These same ruins of Chichen Itza contain the remains of a characteristic ball-court where the ancients played a game somewhat similar to our basket-ball, the object of the contest being to push the ball of solid rubber through goals which were stone rings set in the parallel stone walls of the ball-court. (More of these two uses of rubber later.)

Rubber was also used for incense, to tip drumsticks, and for waterproofing as we use it to-day. In the Nahua language of Mexico rubber was called *olli,* and a tribe inhabiting the damp country in what is now the Mexican States of Vera Cruz and Tabasco was known as the Olmeca, or Rubber People. Most of the rubber came from this region, which has produced a great deal of it in modern times.

Rotation of crops was very unusual in America. The Americans preferred a rotation of fields. When one field had been exhausted the native farmer would clear another one. The first European colonists imitated the natives in this respect, as they did in many others. Much of our picture of what early American

111

agriculture was like we get from reports of the European colonists, who were far more interested in it than they were in other native arts. And there is no doubt that agriculture at the time of the European conquests was very little different from what it had been when American civilization reached its peak about 1200 A.D.

The native practice of "resting the land" has been much condemned by European writers. Yet where land is plentiful this practice is cheaper and easier than fertilizing worn-out fields. As white immigrants from Europe poured into America there came to be insufficient land for the "resting" method, and more and more resort had to be made to fertilization. Yet even before the white man came, there was little land to spare in the more populous districts of America. In the thirteenth century, Central America, the site of the highest native civilization, was probably the most thickly settled part of the globe; to-day botanists declare that there is not an acre of truly virgin forest to be found there. At one time or another all of it has been burned over to make native maize-fields. Or else it has been cut down to supply native homes with fuel. To this day the native method of clearing land for maize-fields in Central America is to burn down the trees.

Because the Americans in a land of plenty preferred rotation of fields to the rotation of crops it should never be assumed that they made no use of artificial means of fertilization. The great deposits of guano, or bird dung, on the islands off the west coast of South America were much used by the natives of the southern continent to increase the yield of their gardens. And it was a general practice in both continents to bury in each hill of maize a small fish, which, rotting, fertilized the ground. Naturally, such fish were used as could be netted in large numbers. In North America it was often the herring; in South America the sardine.

The origin and development of the scarecrow would provide a subject for some writer with a flair for the curiosities of agriculture. At any rate it is known that the natives of the northern part of North America had tame hawks, trained to drive away from the maize-fields small birds seeking to rob the grain. Crows and blackbirds did a great deal of damage of this kind.

In the days when mammoths and camels roamed the land, there may have been members of the horse family in America. But from the time these Pleistocene animals became extinct until the white "discoverers" brought their cavalry mounts to the Western world the American had no horses. Attempts to domesticate the buffalo never succeeded, and although the llama of South America was successfully tamed, he seems not to have been used in plowing.

113

The only thing resembling a plowshare which was used in America was a stout stick. To this stick was attached a rope by means of which a number of men dragged it through the earth to break up the ground into clods, and these in turn were smashed to bits by the women who followed their husbands. In South America a stick of this kind was sometimes equipped with a crosspiece, by which the foot could force it into the ground. On the northern coast of South America the digging-stick was shod with copper and looked much like a large chisel. Ancient American stone hoes and clod-breakers may be seen in many of our museums to-day. But as often as not these instruments were made of a very hard wood. Writing of native farming methods on Roanoke Island in 1585, Hariot said:

A few days before they sow or set, the men with wooden instruments made almost in form of mattocks or hoes with long handles; the women with short peckers or parers, because they use them sitting, of a foot long, and about five inches in breadth, do only break the upper part of the ground to raise up the weeds, grass, and old stubs of corn stalks with their roots. The which, after a day or two days' drying in the sun, being scraped up into small heaps, to save them labor for carrying, they burn into ashes.

These methods were in operation for many centuries before the whites came.

114

The natives often accomplished prodigious feats with their hoes, feats which were the admiration of the European colonists. Writing of the cleanliness of the native cultivation of maize, in his "New England Prospect," in 1629, Wood says:

They exceede our English husbandmen, keeping it so cleare with their Clamme shell-hooes as if it were a garden rather than a corne-field, not suffering a choaking weede to advance his audacious head above their infant corne, or an undermining worme to spoile his spurnes.

The first farmers of America were scrupulous to keep weeds out of the hills of maize, and as these hills were used season after season they eventually became so sizable that some of them have remained to our time. The European settlers were not so careful about weeding and it is on record that the squaws of the aborigines often ridiculed them for this shortcoming. On the other hand, the Europeans, especially after they began to make use of animals in cultivation, broke the ground between the hills of maize, which the natives did not do. But Mr. Carrier reports that recent investigations by experts do not indicate that the white man's method of cultivating maize is superior to the red man's.

Hariot said that no fertilizer was used on Roanoke Island, but speaking of conditions in New England in 1632, Morton said:

115

There is a Fish (by some called shadds by some allizes) that at the spring of the year passe up the rivers to spaune in the ponds: And are taken in such multitudes in every river that hath a pond at the end that the inhabitants dung their ground with them. You may see in one township a hundred acres together set with these Fish, every acre taking 1000 of them and an acre thus dressed will produce and yield so much corne as 3 acres without fish and (least any Virginia man would inferre hereupon that the ground of New England is barren, because they use no fish in setting their corne, I desire them to be remembered, the cause is plainne in Virginia) they have it not to sett. But this practice is onely for Indian Maise (which must be set by hands) not for English corne.

The native American had decidedly fixed ideas regarding the division of labor between men and women. Modern Americans and Europeans who see Japanese women working in the rice-fields of Japan or in the potato-fields of California assume that the Japanese is unkind to his women. The same mistake was made by the colonials who saw the women of the aborigines working in the maize-fields and laboring homeward with heavy burdens of farm produce. The preservation of the whole community in ancient times depended largely on the agility of the male as a warrior, which would have been lost by much labor in the fields, so that work was largely left to the women.

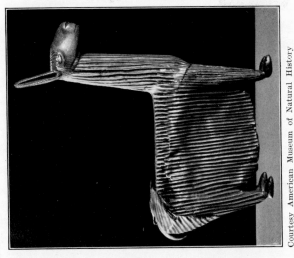

Courtesy American Museum of Natural History

Silver alpaca

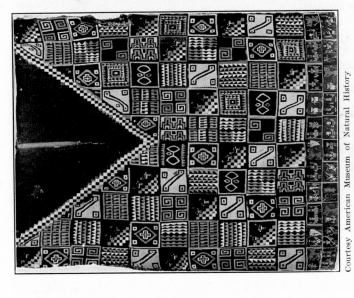

Courtesy American Museum of Natural History

Tapestry poncho with silver tinsel yarn

Along the eastern side of the Yucatan peninsula, almost within earshot of the Caribbean Sea smashing from green to white on the barrier reef, and in the depths of great mahogany forests in upland British Honduras, I have found the broad, low agricultural terraces inclosed with walls no higher than the land itself which have been reported by other explorers in many other parts of Central America, and which have puzzled many agricultural experts. Dr. Cook has suggested that the presence of these low terraces indicates that the ancient people practised dry farming. He says, in a report to the United States Department of Agriculture:

The motive of the prehistoric people in building these broad terraces is not easy to understand unless they are considered as a method of dry farming. The walls are only a few feet high, though the area enclosed may be several acres in extent. Even without the terraces the land would often appear quite level, the slopes being extremely gentle. This makes it quite improbable that the terraces had the object of avoiding erosion, like the system of terracing followed in our Southeastern States. There is also no indication that they were intended to impound running water or that artificial irrigation was applied. The walls do not rise above the level of the land inclosed. The probability is that the complete leveling of the land was found useful to prevent the running off of any of the rather slight rainfall which comes to

117

these semi-arid districts. While the terraces are not high, the walls are often half a mile or more in length. The leveling of the land must have required vastly more labor than the building of the walls, but the work may have been done gradually, if a regular practice of hoeing the earth toward the wall were followed.

The fact that land was always owned by the Government and never by the individual made the construction of great works of irrigation much easier than it would have been otherwise. With a vast reserve of specialized labor at its disposal the city-state could undertake enterprises of this sort that would seem considerable even to so powerful a modern Government as that of the United States. On the Salt River, in the southwestern part of what is now the United States, an ancient people called the Pima built an extensive system of huge irrigation canals. Moderns have heard more of the extraordinary public works of the Aztec city Tenochtitlan. The historian Prescott has made famous the network of causeways connecting the island capital with the mainland. Think of the labor that went into the construction of these, and into the building of the great dike, ten miles long, from Iztapalata to Atzacualco, punctured by many sluices which were used to protect the city against floods. Then there was the remarkable beveled stone aqueduct that brought to this

118

city in a lake the purer drinking water of Chapultepec.

Most of the Mayas lived in a land of superfluous rain, and were more in need of drains than of aqueducts. An example is the stone-lined subterranean drain that carried off excess water from the city of Palenque. But the Peruvians were afflicted—or blessed, according to your point of view—with a climate as dry as that which taught the natives of Arizona and New Mexico the need of irrigation. The Peruvians thought little of bringing water miles out into the desert from snow-moistened mountains far away. Such main aqueducts of irrigation were of course split up into scores of smaller streams, to fertilize as much land as possible. In the Valley of Nepena still stands a tremendous stone dam, eighty feet thick, at the end of an ancient reservoir which was three fourths of a mile long and half a mile broad. The traces of most of the sixteen-mile-long aqueduct from the Santa River to Chimbote may still be seen. Modern engineers attribute to this work of their remote predecessors a capacity of sixty million cubic feet of water *per diem!*

In hacking my way through the thick bush that grows now in Yucatan where a thousand years ago were thick fields of waving grain I have often stumbled on the remains of the well-made stone walls which marked the limits of the parcels of land the

119

governments of Maya agricultural cities doled out to
their inhabitants. Each married man was given a
piece of land four hundred feet square (3.67 acres),
called *Hun Uinic* (one man). This was measured by
a stick twenty feet long, called *Kaan*. That is, the
stick was one twentieth of the length of each side of
the square piece of land allotted to the individual
farmer. In eastern Guatemala to-day *canquib* or
*kankib* is a term applied to a small palm that makes
an excellent measuring-rod. *Quib* means "small
palm" and *can* means "yellow."

Bishop Diego de Landa, the same man who began
his career in Yucatan by ruthlessly destroying many
of the native books, in his later years partially atoned
for this grievous sin by writing his "Relacion de las
Cosas de Yucatan." This volume, describing native
customs at the time of the Spanish conquest, tells us
the Mayas estimated that each plot of ground above
mentioned would yield forty man-loads of maize.
This would amount roughly to eighty bushels, and
would not be a large yield for such an area of land.
But maize does not yield as highly on the low plain
of Yucatan as it does in higher parts of America.
Dr. Cook has made very interesting investigations
resulting in the conclusion that under the Inca Empire in the Cuzco district of Peru at a height of from
nine thousand to eleven thousand feet above sea-level
the land yielded from sixty to seventy-five bushels of

maize per acre. In Peru each individual householder was granted one *topo* of land. A modern *topo* is equal to about seven tenths of an acre, but in those days it may have been somewhat larger. However, taking the yield per acre just given and considering the *topo* as seven tenths of an acre, this computation gives us only from forty-two to fifty-two bushels of maize annually for each householder. Dr. Cook concludes that the fact that "the family requirement of maize under the Inca system should have been smaller than among the Mayas could be explained by more extensive use of other foods, as potatoes, ocas, ullucus and quinoa, in the Peruvial table-land."

To-day the Pima tribe of Arizona allots about ten acres of agricultural land to each household. In ancient days the Pima allotment was four acres. Which may mean that agriculture was more intensively practised then than it is at present.

In 1931 there were perhaps twenty-five million members of the red-skinned race living in the western hemisphere. About two and a half million of these live in Central America, and a large proportion of that number belong to the Maya race. In point of cultural level they are among the best aborigines still left with us. Yet they have sunk a long way from the height of the builders of the great temples, from whom they are undoubtedly descended. However, they are a fruitful source of study for the ethnologist,

121

because they still maintain many of the ancient customs and traditions. The difficulty is that many modern customs, derived from the white man, have been grafted upon ancient ones. Thus the religion of the modern native is a mixture of Roman Catholicism and the pagan beliefs of his forefathers. This is illustrated no better than in the solemnization of "maize masses" and other rites performed by the present native in the hope of gaining a fertile crop of his favorite cereal.

Yet so far as the actual performance of agriculture is concerned, it is much the same to-day as it has always been. The milpa, or maize-field, is cleared in December or January, all the bush being cut down but the very largest trees. The possession of modern steel axes makes it unnecessary to destroy trees in the ancient manner by bruising a ring of bark around the base and applying fire. The old-time spirit of co-operation still exists and neighbors help one another in clearing the land, sowing, and harvesting. A score or more of neighbors move from farm to farm until all fields are sown or harvested.

All winter the dead bush dries on the ground and in the spring it is burned. March and April are the hottest months of the year in Yucatan—or at least the most trying months to the foreigner, because to the natural heat of the sun is added the heat, as well as the smoke, of burning maize-fields. After the burning, men go over the ground with sharp-pointed sticks, making little holes at regular intervals into which are dropped a few kernels of the grain. Just before the cereal is ripe in October, each stalk is bent about a foot below the ear and permitted to hang, so that rain may not enter the ear and spoil the grain. At this time the farmer is never long absent from his milpa. He sleeps in a little hut of palm leaves at the edge of the maize-field, in order that he may scare away wild birds and animals, and the tame pigs of his neighbors, which are even more dangerous robbers. When the maize is ripe the ears are gathered and stored either in a hut at the edge of the garden or on a platform erected to protect it from marauders. It is shelled on the spot as it is needed, although the surplus nowadays is often sold in the near-by village of the white man in exchange for steel machetes, axes, and, alas, too often, rum.

When man became certain that he had mastered the secrets of the fertile soil and need no longer follow the migrations of salmon or buffalo, or move along when he had exhausted the supply of wild fruit and nuts, he put his mind to the construction of houses that were more comfortable than most caves. Then it was that the human village was invented.

Old indeed are the mysterious cities of pink porphyry recently uncovered by the drifting sands of a desert on the southern coast of Peru. Old is Pachacamac, a holy city centuries before the mailed fist of the first Inca began to build a socialistic empire which was to rule most of the western coast of South America. Older are the pre-Inca fortresses of Sacsahuaman and Ollantaytambo, with their astonishing walls of huge stones sometimes as much as eighteen feet high and eight feet wide, yet fitted together as closely and as delicately as the machine-carved wooden blocks of a modern child. And certainly there is great antiquity about the cone-shaped, three-storied structure at Cuicuilco, near modern Mexico City, whose stone foundations are twenty-five feet deeper than the lava flow about them which geologists are certain occurred at least three thousand years ago. Old, too, are some of the scores of stone cities abandoned by the great Maya race in Central America to be overrun by the jungle, and by the bats and owls and lizards that are the only living things occupying them to-day.

But we know man built towns of wood before he built towns of stone. If we did not have other evidences of the fact the testimony of some of the stone cities would itself be conclusive. In Central America it is common to find a stone or stucco imitation of wooden latticework or of the upright log walls of the huts where lived the humble sculptors who carved the stone, and where even the Maya rulers lived before the art of carving stone was mastered.

124

"El Cartillo," Tuluum's chief temple, the most conspicuous landmark on the east coast of Yucatan

The growth of agricultural cities was an important phase in the development of America, as it was in the development of ancient Greece. Situated in the midst of a wide farming area, each of these cities gave some of its inhabitants leisure to develop basketry and pottery, weaving, painting, sculpture, astronomy, medicine, and other refinements of civilization.

Pottery-making, as we have seen, is an art which seems to have gone side by side with agriculture and to have spread wherever agriculture spread. Before pots were made, gourds were used as household receptacles, as they are still used among tribes too primitive to conceive of ceramics. It is interesting that the common gourd (*Lagenaria vulgaris*), from which ceremonial and toy rattles were made by many tribes, is the only plant known to have been in wide use in both hemispheres of the world, as well as in the Pacific islands, before the European conquest of America. The close connection between pottery and agriculture is symbolized by the many vessels in the form of squashes, melons, potatoes, and other vegetables made in ancient America, especially in Peru.

It is one of the ironies of history that culture is often spread by warfare, the conquerors giving the benefits of their civilization to the conquered and frequently learning more from the latter than they teach. Nevertheless, trade is the commonest method

125

by which culture is disseminated. And we may ima-
gine that as maize, manioc, potatoes, or beans were
traded for fish or game or minerals or baskets, the
pottery vessels in which the vegetables were carried
served as models for crude imitations by the nation
acquiring them. Thus the dissemination of agriculture was followed by the dissemination of other arts,
and the agricultural cities became trading cities. It is
as characteristic of America as of Greece that all the
civilization worth noting grew up around the city,
and the city-state was the common form of American
political organization.

The city-state was developed to its highest point
by those Americans who had, in general, the highest
culture. These were the Mayas of Central America.

Maize was the chief item in the diet of the Mayas.
Now, lime is required in the process of making the
cakes of maize which the Spaniards have called "tortillas," and which were the commonest form of food
among the Mayas. Limestone was the basis of the
whole peninsula of Yucatan, the home of the Mayas.
Yucatan is also the habitat of bromelia, a type of
water-hoarding plant used by thirsty hunters to the
present day. One of the West Indian names for
bromelia is Maya, and it is possible that the great
race which produced the most learned astronomers
of their time got its name from this plant. Finally, it
should not be forgotten that henequen, used by the

natives for making rope, cloth, and other textiles, thrives in Yucatan, where cotton does well, too. In short, the agricultural possibilities of the Yucatan peninsula, offering clothing of henequen and cotton, the water of bromelia, the food of maize, and the lime with which maize cakes are mixed, may be the reason why this narrow area became the site of the highest of all American civilizations.

Like the other civilizations of America, the Maya civilization was erected on a vast supply of socialized human labor. This made the possession of an abundant food supply a matter of prime importance. Hence, even in the lush tropics the danger of exhaustion of the soil was ever present, particularly as land must be rested after it has produced two or three crops of maize. As soon as the population begins to equal the capacity of the soil to produce food the entire existence of society is threatened. The Greek city-states seem to have reached the danger-point in the eighth or seventh century before Christ. Apparently some of the Maya city-states were reaching this point in the sixth or seventh century after Christ, and the abrupt abandonment of several cities in the southern part of the Maya area is believed to have been due to exhaustion of the arable land in their neighborhood.

We can readily understand now why the Mayas felt that the control of all good available agricultural land must rest in the Government. Our modern governmental regulation of food prices and of rates for gas, electricity, and water is in its way just as "socialistic" as the regulation of the use of land by the governments of the Maya agricultural cities.

The red man depended on agriculture even more than the white. He got drink and clothing as well as food from the products of the earth. Agricultural statistics of the United States show that to-day crops for which the world is indebted to the aborigines are valued at more than three thousands of millions of dollars! The bounty of the soil meant life itself to the American, and it was impossible for him to do too much to appease the gods of fertility. The great fear of the American—a fear now near and now far but never entirely out of his consciousness—was exhaustion of the soil. As men herded together more and more with the growth of civilization, this fear grew upon man, until when cities were built an elaborate ritual was developed in order that the gods might know man never forgot his crowded existence in towns depended on the fertility of the broad fields outside the city walls.

## SOME AGRICULTURAL PRODUCTS AND BY-PRODUCTS GIVEN THE WORLD BY AMERICA

### FOOD-PLANTS

Maize
Potato
Sweet potato
Tomato
Pumpkin
Squashes
Lima bean
Kidney-bean
Scarlet-runner bean
Tepary bean
Jerusalem artichoke
Peppers
Cassava (tapioca)
Cacao (cocoa)
Taro
Yam
Yam-bean
Arrowroot
Lleren
Oca
Pineapple
Strawberry
Guava
Peanut
Alligator pear
Watermelon?
Coconut?
Sugar Maple?

### FIBERS

Cotton (best varieties)
Henequen (sisal)

### GUMS

Rubber
Balsam of Peru
Copal
Chicle

### DOMESTIC ANIMALS

Turkey
Curassow
Muscovy duck
Llama
Alpaca
Guinea-pig

### DRUGS

Quinine
Cascara sagrada
Cocaine
Tobacco
Peyote
Ipecac

129

# CHAPTER VIII

## THE RULE OF RELIGION AND SCIENCE

WHEN did a poet more clearly foretell the fate of his people than the Maya bard who wrote the following lines?

> Eat, eat, while there is bread,
> Drink, drink, while there is water.
> A day comes when dust shall darken the air,
> When a blight shall wither the land,
> When a cloud shall arise,
> When a mountain shall be lifted up,
> When a strong man shall seize the city,
> When ruin shall fall upon all things,
> When the tender leaf shall be destroyed,
> When eyes shall be closed in death,
> When there shall be three signs on a tree,
> Father, son, and grandson hanging dead on the
>    same tree;
> When the battle flag shall be raised,
> And the people scattered abroad in the forest.

*When ruin shall fall upon all things and the people be scattered abroad in the forest.*

There is a warning for you, proud and powerful nations of to-day—arrogant, self-satisfied British

Empire, priggish, boastful United States, Narcissistic Italy, strutting in puny pride with your ridiculous Mussolini! "A day comes when there shall be three signs on a tree, father, son, and grandson hanging dead on the same tree!"

For look at the Mayas, look at the Mayas, who like the Greeks surpassed you in most of the points that justify man in thinking himself more than an animal by as much as you surpass the *jivaro* headhunters. Never did the Mayas invite the vengeance of the gods with such conspicuous arrogance, boastfulness, and peacock strutting as you exhibit. The Mayas fell out among themselves, and that was their doom; but as nations go they were unmaterialistic, shunning conquest, appreciating the tinsel folly of imperialism, and adoring the gods as not even the Greeks adored them.

And now their descendants, pitiful and degenerate, though still the best natives in America, are scattered abroad in the forest whose leaves hide the fallen stones of palace walls which tearing roots have tumbled. No temple bell for sacrifice rings, but only the lonely moan-bird wings; under the jungle of Yucatan lies the mystery of Mayapan.

Yet the beauty the Mayas created is not wholly gone. Some of it has been recovered by the few white men with wit enough to realize that the history of America is more than the story of the successful

131

effort of European adventurers, fanatics, and convicts to wrest a material paradise for themselves from the Western wilderness. Whatever remains to be found will be recovered more quickly, now that more and more Americans, vaguely dissatisfied with the dull materialism of their own lives, are turning back to the mystery and beauty which was Maya.

The Mayas, the Mayas! Expect no neutrality in words of them from one who has seen the towers of Tikal and Tuluum; Tikal's turrets swimming in mist at dawn above the dim green of the "big bush," Tuluum's crenellated profile majestic and serene above the heaving limpid green of the Caribbean Sea. How can one be dispassionate to whom the Mayas have been wife and child, alcohol and morphine and cocaine, who knows what one knows who knows the connotation of the lovely, ridiculous place-names: Balantun, Saban, Okop; Kimil, Hobonpich, Bolonchenticul; who can never forget the smell of Yucatan at dawn—the dewy petal smell of other tropic mornings plus the spice of the oxide of iron that makes every littlest trail a ribbon of red?

Much as one regrets seeing the Mayas being made the object of such fancies as the thin theory which would connect them with that most mystical "lost Atlantis," one must admit that our maddening lack of knowledge about their origin partially excuses even the most fantastic theorist. Here is a nation which

132

suddenly appeared on the fore-line of history with all its civilization highly developed and functioning like the smoothest machinery. Of the crude beginnings, of the trial-and-error period of youth that all nations must have, we know nothing. Between the men who built the observatories of Tikal and Chichen Itza and that crude "Archaic" people on this land before them there is a gap of oceanic width.

The territory of the Mayas constitutes to-day the Mexican States of Tabasco, Chiapas, Campeche, Yucatan, and Quintana Roo, and British Honduras, Guatemala, and the northern part of Spanish Honduras. The Maya language was used in a wider area than this, having prevailed among the Totonac people of what is now the Mexican State of Vera Cruz, and among the Huaxtecs of the Panuco Valley, in the region of the famous modern oil town of Tampico. There is a good deal of topographical variety in the Maya country. On the Pacific side an extension of the Sierra Madres, which runs down the whole western rim of North America, provides a cold climate in the Tierra Fria, as the modern natives call it. Below this is the Tierra Templada, or temperate zone, sloping down to the plains of northern Guatemala, Campeche, and Yucatan, which last is a limestone formation young in geological time, being nothing more than the remains of a tremendous coral reef.

The Maya race was divided up into a number of

tribes, of which the Tutul Xiu (pronounced *shoo*) of Yucatan, the Quiché and Kakchiquel in Guatemala were the most prominent. The world has an interesting account of the origin of the Mayas according to the belief of the Quiché, in the Popol Vuh, a collection of Quiché traditions and legends written down soon after the Spanish conquest by a native who had embraced Christianity. According to this book, man was created by three gods, Hunahpu, Gukumatz, and Hurakan. These are simply the Guatemalan names for the three important deities whom the Mayas of Yucatan knew as Hunapku, the omnipotent and invisible Creator, Kukulcan, the feathered serpent rain-god, and a wind-god (compare our modern term *hurricane*) whom archæologists dealing with Yucatan have given the unimaginative name of "God K."

These three gods cried, "Earth," and the world was created. Animals were made to fill it, but the animals were dumb and could not thank the gods, so the latter made men out of clay. Finding these clay men had no intelligence, the gods became angry and killed them. Next they made men of wood, but a flood came over the world, the water rotted the men of wood, and birds pecked their eyes out. All these wooden men were destroyed except a few who escaped into the mountains of Guatemala, to become the ancestors of the monkeys that swing in the trees to-day.

Then the gods made up their minds to create men out of maize. The coöperation of various animals was engaged to grind the grain into flour to make this possible.

Four men were formed this way. One of these had no children, but the other three became the ancestors of three branches of the Maya race. Supposedly based on the hieroglyphs that baffle modern attempts at interpretation, two books were written by Christianized natives who understood the ancient writing. Both the books of Chilam Balam and the annals of the Kakchiquel branch of the Mayas speak of a place called Nonoual which seems to have been somewhere between the mouth of the Usumacinta River in Tabasco, and the mouth of the Rio Papaloapam (River of Butterflies) in Vera Cruz State. That is, in the central pocket of the shore line of the Gulf of Mexico. This coincides with a site called by the early Mexican peoples Nonoualco.

Some of the Maya traditions point to a place called Tulan, a place of seven caves, as the starting-point of the early tribal migrations. It seems quite likely that this Tulan of the seven caves is the Chicomoztoc where legend says the Nahua tribes of Mexico gathered before descending upon the Mexican Valley. In other words, the legends or mythical history of the early nations both of Mexico and Central America seem to designate identical locations of historical im-

135

portance. And it is quite possible, indeed very likely, that the Maya and Mexican cultures—which interacted upon each other so considerably during historical times—had a common racial background.

It will not do to lean too heavily, in reconstructing Maya history, upon such accounts as the Popol Vuh and the books of Chilam Balam. The fact that apparently dates suddenly ceased to be carved on stone in the southern part of the Maya area—Honduras and Guatemala—after the close of Cycle Nine of Maya chronology, which would be toward the end of the sixth century A.D. by our count if we accept Spinden's correlation, for a long time led archæologists to put great credence in the statements of the books of Chilam Balam to the effect that southern Yucatan was not discovered and colonized by the Mayas until the middle or close of the fifth century A.D. But recently Maya dates corresponding to the early fourth century A.D. have been found in Yucatan.

Yet it seems still a fairly reasonable working hypothesis to assume that the Maya civilization developed first in Honduras and Guatemala, and later spread northward. By the end of the second century A.D. the great cities of the south were flourishing. This era has been called the golden age of the Mayas, and it is often compared to the classic period of Greek art, for at this time the Mayas produced their best sculpture. Their architecture, however, continued to

136

develop up to the time of their mysterious downfall shortly before the arrival of the Spaniards, and the architectural embellishment of the cities of northern Yucatan is not surpassed by anything in the southern area.

It is common to make a political as well as an artistic division of Maya history. A centrifugal tendency, or tendency of cohesive States to split up into smaller units, has been conspicuous in Central America from the earliest times to the latest Latin-American revolution. Now it is believed that the early Mayas who produced the great sculpture lived under a fairly centralized form of government, and this period in their history is often called the period of the First Empire. We are not certain just what bonds united the earlier cities, but it is fairly well established that the independence of each city-state increased throughout Maya history until we find the later city-states of northern Yucatan unable to cohere even in the loose federation of trading cities known as "the League of Mayapan," a confederation of the three great municipalities of Maya, Chichen Itza, and Uxmal.

It is a curious fact that throughout the higher cultural centers in America there seems to have been a great deal of political and social uneasiness about the year 1000 A.D. This was true of Peru, of Central America, of Mexico, and of what now comprises the Southwestern States of the United States. It was about this time that there began that civil war among the Maya cities of Yucatan which was to contribute much toward their downfall within the next two hundred years. It was about this time that the Toltec monarchy of highland Mexico fell into disruption, leaving restless bands of Toltec mercenaries to roam about the country, and eventually, it is believed, to hire out their arms to the Maya city of Mayapan, in the destruction of the Maya city of Chichen Itza.

However, there is almost as much mystery about the breakdown of Maya civilization as there is about its origin and as there is about the mysterious abandonment of the southern cities of Honduras and Guatemala toward the end of the fifth or beginning of the sixth century A.D.

There seems to be no doubt that some of the Maya cities in the interior and several on the eastern coast of Yucatan were occupied when the first Spanish discoverers arrived. Juan Diaz, sailing-master of the expedition of Juan de Grijalva, which explored the east coast of Yucatan for Spain in 1518, reported sighting a city on that coast "so large, that Seville would not have seemed more considerable nor better; one saw there a very large tower; on the shore was a great swarm of Indians, who bore two standards which they raised and lowered to signal us to approach them.

138

The commander did not wish it." This is generally believed to have been the city of Tuluum.

Of course it is possible that these natives were not actually occupying Tuluum, but that they lived in the bush around it and used its temples for religious ceremonies. But for that matter, it is generally thought that none of the stone buildings found in the Central American bush to-day were ever used as residences. It is believed by most experts that these were merely the public buildings of the ancient cities, and that the inhabitants lived in wooden houses not unlike the huts with thatched roofs and log walls that house the modern natives.

The relation of the modern Mayas to the ancient temple-builders is one of the outstanding facets of the entire riddle. There can be no doubt that the natives of the Yucatan peninsula to-day are descended from the great builders. Again and again one sees a native cutting leaves of henequen for the sisal fiber of commerce, or boiling chicle to provide masticatory exercise for the jaws of New York stenographers, who is a living replica of the intaglio figures on the walls of old temples darkened by centuries of smoking incense. The modern natives speak a language called Maya, but they do not write it, and it has been put into writing only by ethnologists, who of course use Latin characters.

The natives cannot read the ancient hieroglyphs

139

at all, and can tell the white explorer virtually nothing about *los Antiguos* (the ancients). But unwittingly they often reveal to the investigator irrefutable evidence of their connection with the race that built Copan and Chichen Itza. For example, the archæologist finds in one of the three codices or in a scene painted or carved on a temple wall the representation of certain ancient ceremonies in progress. Then, living among one of the few branches of the Mayas who still keep themselves fairly uncontaminated by the white man's civilization, he gains their confidence until he is permitted to see the performance of a religious rite that exhibits unmistakable analogies to the others.

Do you begin to see the fascination of this game of anthropology?

There is pathos in the way the natives jealously watch over the ancient temples, a fact with which every explorer is familiar. Again and again I have stumbled on some crumbling shrine, far from the nearest native village, and have begun to photograph it or draw a plan of it, only to have a silent red man saunter out of the bush and hang around suspiciously until I left the neighborhood.

Thus, you see, we learn about the ancient Mayas from a number of sources—from the books, from ceremonial objects and objects of everyday life the archæologist digs up, from accounts written by a few

140

Christianized natives or a few intelligent Spaniards soon after the conquest, and from a close study of the degenerate Mayas of to-day. But especially we learn by comparing the information to be had in one of these sources with the information to be had in the others. The task of solving the riddle of the Mayas is essentially a synthetic task, a work truly creative.

Men who have argued that the present natives of the Yucatan peninsula are of a race different from that which produced the great architects and sculptors have based their contention largely on the natives' undoubted ignorance of the hieroglyphs and alleged ignorance of the ancient ritual. The error here lies in the mistaken assumption that the religious life of the Mayas was organized like the religious life of our own time. Apparently the Maya commonwealth resembled a feudal European State of the Middle Ages in that there was a tremendous gulf between the upper and lower classes. It seems unlikely that any but an educated, aristocratic priesthood ever was able to write the hieroglyphs or to read them. Likewise it seems probable that the religion of the Maya masses was a crude conglomeration of automatic ritualism, lacking the spiritual range and artistic richness of the religion of the Maya priests.

The history of other races shows that a peasantry is apt to develop greater physical and moral strength than an aristocracy. Hence it is reasonable to suppose that the civil wars, epidemics of terrible sickness, and other disasters which destroyed the Maya civilization, or at least brought it to its knees before the arrival of the Spaniards, wiped out the effete aristocracy while permitting a large part of the peasantry to survive. But that peasantry never understood the high artistic and scientific achievements of the race. And it is quite credible that the Mayas of twentieth-century Yucatan are descended from that ignorant working class which piled the stone blocks of the great public buildings that have remained to astonish us moderns, but which was incapable of planning those buildings and decorating them, much less of entertaining the intricate religious concepts lying behind their plan and decoration.

In my "Silver Cities of Yucatan," I said, "It is difficult to name another race in which the religious emotion so dominated the artistic expression of a whole people, or worked to produce so ardent a search for the secrets of the universe."

That is stating the matter too mildly. I should like to amend that statement now to say *it is impossible* to name such another race. There has never been a nation to which religion meant so much as it did to the Mayas. And unless we wish to go far astray in our estimate of this greatest American people, we must remember not only the all-pervasive quality of Maya religion but the extreme intricacy and highly

142

esoteric quality of some forms of ritualism among the Mayas. The gods of the ceremonies our archæologists and ethnologists have succeeded in interpreting are mostly the gods and ceremonies of the common people. But we know that the Maya priests had their own very special secret ceremonies and their own very special secret gods, which the Maya laborer was forbidden to worship, was forbidden even to hear mentioned.

The Mason-Spinden expedition found at Muyil a certain unimportant temple raised upon the conventional type of masonry mound. But as we were about to leave Muyil we fortunately discovered under the broad stairway leading to the top of this mound a blocked-up passage leading to a temple directly beneath the other one. This secret, subterranean temple may very well have been one of those places of worship which the Maya priests kept for themselves, and to profane which probably meant death for the layman. If scientists are ever able to unravel the nature of the intricate ritual and religious beliefs the Maya priesthood reserved for itself, they will make an exceedingly important contribution to the history of the speculative thought of the human race.

But of the religion of the Maya people as a whole we know a good deal. The Mayas did not believe in the resurrection of the body, but they did believe in a definite heaven and a definite hell. Those persons who

143

had led a virtuous life on earth went to a heaven where there was no suffering, but much feasting and dancing, and much resting in the shade of an enormous tree. But when a man died who had led a bad life on earth his soul went to Mitnal. This was located underneath heaven. And in Mitnal, Hunaphau, prince of all devils, presided over the ingenious application of countless forms of torture.

It is interesting to note that one of these tortures was cold. We should expect a tropical people to look upon cold as a form of suffering and to look upon the enjoyment of shade as a concomitant of a heavenly existence. But as Dr. Morley says, "the materialism of the Maya heaven and hell need not surprise, nor lower our estimate of their civilization. Similar realistic conceptions of the hereafter have been entertained by peoples much higher in the cultural scale than the Maya."

Most native American religions are marked by the existence of dualism, or a belief in a group of beneficent gods constantly at war with a group of evil gods. The Maya pantheon showed this dualism to a high degree. There was a number of malevolent deities, but by far the most important was Ahpuch, or the Black Captain. He was the God of Death. The deities whose protection was most frequently sought by man against the Black Captain were Itzamna, the Creator God, and Kukulcan, the god who brought

144

The Maya maize-god

the fertile rain. Of course the chief concern of the highly organized Maya priesthood was to keep alive the affection of the good gods, in order that these might be ever alert to succor man against the gods of evil.

The sculptors of the old Mayas left behind few things more beautiful than the young God of Maize. He was one of the few gods to whom they gave a human form. He is often depicted in association with the sign *Kan,* the symbol of the harvest, and some authorities consider him as identical with Yum Kaax, the Lord of Agriculture. At any rate, he is always represented as having a young maize plant for a head-dress, waving in the wind above his handsome, youthful features. As Mr. J. Eric Thompson has well said, the maize-god "gives one the impression that spring is in the air and the whole spirit of joyfulness permeates the land—youth is in control."

The maize-god, of course, was under the domination of the gods of the rain and the gods of the sun. The Maya pantheon contains many deities, and a discussion of them is likely to become intricate and involved. But the fact that many of them are portrayed in semi-animal form should not prejudice us against them. The Mayas believed in a supreme god who was invisible, just as we do. They called him Hunabku, and they did not draw pictures of him or make sculptures of him, just because he *was* invisible. Their art

145

was concerned mainly with portraying the lesser gods, just as the art of Christianity has been concerned with painting Madonnas and saints, and has never attempted to delineate the Creator of the Universe.

Second only in importance to the Supreme Deity the Mayas held Kukulcan, the plumed serpent. Kukulcan was a sky god, apparently a sun-god, wind-god, and rain-god rolled into one. The city of Chichen Itza, whose magnificent ruins in modern Yucatan are only just beginning to be appreciated by tourists, seems to have been particularly the city of Kukulcan. The elongated snout with which this god is depicted when the side of him concerned with rain is being invoked protrudes from the façade of many a building in Chichen Itza, with an effect picturesque and bizarre.

Another Maya god who seems to have been a deity of the rain is Chac-Mool—half man, half jaguar. He was probably borrowed from the Toltecs of upland Mexico. Then there were four gods concerned with the four points of the compass who also were the custodians of the rain. They were sometimes called Pahahtunes, sometimes Bacabs, and sometimes Chacs. The ancient Mayas called them individually Kan, Muluc, Ix, and Cauac. The later Mayas, influenced by Christianity, called them Saint Dominic, Saint Gabriel, Saint James, and Mary Magdalene, respectively. Kan was yellow, Muluc was white, Ix was

146

black, and Cauac was red. These four names are among the twenty titles given by the Mayas to the twenty days which constituted their month.

All very well and very quaint, you may say, but much of this sort of thing would soon be a bore. Be assured, however, that there is no need of bothering ourselves now with the names of a great many different deities. *The significant thing to notice is that the Maya religion grew out of agriculture, and was dominated by gods of earth, sky, and water. With these ancient Americans agriculture was the parent both of mythology and of astronomy.* In his eagerness to understand the right period for planting corn, and in his superstitious reverence for forces which he felt were about him in the earth and the sea and the sky, the early Maya became a student of the rotations of the planets, of the periodic comings and goings of the heavenly bodies.

All over the world a knowledge of when it will rain is the most valuable piece of information a farmer can have. Now, there were certain times of the year when a farmer in the highest cultural centers of America could be almost sure that it would rain. The most advanced American civilizations were all situated between the tropic of Cancer and the tropic of Capricorn. Twice each year within this zone the sun passes through the zenith of the heavens, and at these times, all perpendicular objects are without a shadow.

147

These passings of the sun through the zenith are followed by heavy rains caused by the heat of the vertical solar rays. Hence it was of great importance to determine just when the sun reached this point in his course. Garcilasso de la Vega, a descendant of the Incas of Peru, informs us that in the neighborhood of Quito, which is virtually on the equator, the natives used columns of stone erected in open spaces before their temples of the sun to tell them when the season of rain was approaching as the sun's shadow grew less and less each day. The occasion on which there was no shadow was called "the descent of the sun." De la Vega says that the sun pillars on which the sun-god was supposed to have rested when he descended—that is, when his vertical rays cast no shadow—were of the greatest sanctity.

Mrs. Zelia Nuttall has devoted a great many years and a great deal of effort to gathering evidence relating to the observances of this "descent of the sun" among all ancient American peoples. Mrs. Nuttall believes that the phenomenon was waited for and greeted with profound ceremony in all the centers of high culture between Peru and Mexico, inclusive. She thinks that many ancient monuments of a vertical nature which have puzzled archæologists were used as gnomons, that is, measurers of the shadow of the sun. Pointing out that to this day the Pueblos celebrate their New Year's festival "by laying the

148

seeds and roots of all food-plants upon the altar so that the sun might descend into them and give them life and vigor," she contends that the mysterious *intihuatana* of Peru served a similar purpose. These *intihuatana* consist of large circular platforms in the center of which is a conical altar. The name *intihuatana* means, literally, "the point where the sun stays." Mrs. Nuttall thinks that the conical altar was used to measure the sun's shadow.

In 1926, behind the modern coastal village of **Paalmul**, Yucatan, **Dr.** Spinden and I found a temple with an ancient pineapple-shaped object of stucco erected on an altar before it. I have shown a photograph of this object to Mrs. Nuttall, who argues with a good deal of conviction that it is another gnomon, or measurer of the sun's shadow. She attributes the same use to many of the other stone cones, columns, and stelæ found in Central America and Mexico.

Mrs. Nuttall also believes that one of the most puzzling features of Maya architecture was used for the same purpose. This is the *chultun,* a jug-shaped underground chamber with a narrow neck or opening which is very common in Yucatan. Other archæologists have contended that these *chultunes* are the remains of the efforts of the Maya architect to get the softer limestone used in making plaster, or that they were used for storing food or for ceremonial chambers or for sepulchers. However that may be, Mrs.

149

Nuttall contends that the *chultun* was "obviously admirably adapted for the accurate registration of the passage of the sun through the zenith by persons occupying the wide chamber below." (Quite possibly the *chultun* was used for several purposes.)

Mrs. Nuttall adds, "A new light is also thrown on the purpose of the deep vertical shaft that has been discovered in ancient ruins." Noting that in several important archæological regions the interval of days between the two descents of the sun-god, or between the two occasions at which the sun cast no shadow at noon, is 282 days, or the average period of human gestation, Mrs. Nuttall suggests that this might furnish "a plausible explanation of the origin of the native local belief in 'sons of the sun' of divine descent, who formed a ruling, privileged class."

As will be seen later, the Mayas made much of a ceremonial time-count, the *Tzolkin*. To-day this is often called the *Tonalamatl,* a name given it by the Mexicans, who borrowed it. This device for counting time was a combination of the twenty named days of the Mayas, with thirteen numbers applied in unceasing rotation from 1 to 13. With each day both numbered and named it will be seen there can be no repetition, for 13 x 20 equals 260 days. This *Tzolkin* was of great importance as a divinatory calendar, and it ran in a continuously recurring circle throughout the many years that the Mayas counted time. Mrs. Nuttall puts forward the interesting contention that this 260-day period was determined for the ancient Mayas and Mexicans by the number of the days between the two passages of the sun through the zenith in the territory in which these nations lived.

Certainly there is a good deal of evidence to indicate that the ancient Americans attached much importance to the passage of the sun through the zenith, and that not a few of them regarded it as the beginning of the "natural" year. Diego de Landa is authority for the statement that the beginning of the "natural Maya year" in the region of Mérida, modern capital of Yucatan, fell in the month of July. And it is easily verifiable that in these latitudes the sun reaches the zenith on its way south on the nineteenth or twentieth of July. Partly owing to the efforts of Mrs. Nuttall, many municipalities in the modern Republic of Mexico have resumed the ancient custom of celebrating the sun's attainment of the zenith.

As the Mayas perfected their knowledge of astronomy and meteorology, their agriculture became more and more efficient. In turn the cities fed by the wide fields of maize grew larger, and an increasing number of hands were free for other pursuits than tilling the soil. Many arts were developed besides agriculture. But as has often been the case with other commonwealths, the arts in which the Mayas attained perhaps their greatest skill—painting, sculpture, and

151

architecture—were not those that brought in the largest contemporaneous returns. It was the potters and weavers of Yucatan and Guatemala who brought the largest revenue to the State.

The pottery and textiles of the Mayas came to be much sought after by neighboring nations, so international trade in early America was begun. In return for their exports of pottery and textiles, the Mayas imported emeralds and pearls from Colombia, turquoise from New Mexico, cacao from southern Central America (where the United Fruit Company is now experimenting with the revival of this ancient drink), and a variety of other things, some precious, some useful. Great stone roads were built across country on which the human beasts of burden carried their packs; but the bulk of the commerce was probably carried on by sea. As maritime trading grew the importance of a knowledge of the heavenly bodies was emphasized. Thus the impetus of trade as well as the impetus of agriculture contributed, among the people of Central America, toward a development of the knowledge of the heavens, until the Mayas became the best astronomers of their time in the whole world.

One of the first astronomical events they learned to recognize was the arrival of the vernal equinox. In 1928, in the little village of Succots, British Honduras, I saw a survival of an ancient Maya ceremony which was devised by the be-feathered priests of other times to solemnize the passage of the sun over the equator, on his way north. This ceremony in Succots was also a very good example of how parts of the ritual of the pagan Mayas remain to this day intertwined with the Roman Catholic religion among the modern natives. The sun crosses the equator northward-bound on March 21. Now, it happens that the Roman Catholic San José (Saint Joseph) is the patron saint of Succots, and his "day" is March 19. In ancient times the Mayas celebrated the vernal equinox by planting a small cottonwood tree, a bit of ritual that was to the Mayas what the festivities about the May-pole were to the Anglo-Saxons. But when Roman Catholic missionaries began to teach the later Mayas to celebrate the fiesta of Saint Joseph on March 19, the natives found it convenient to incorporate some of the ritual of the old fiesta of the equinox with the new fiesta. So it comes about that in British Honduras to-day the natives celebrate the fiesta of Saint Joseph by bringing in a small cottonwood tree from the forest and planting it before the pavilion in which they still dance the shuffling step of other times.

This sort of thing has happened again and again since the conquest of America by Europe. To this day, in many parts of our two continents, descendants of the original redskins who are presumably converted to Christianity are actually not nearly so much

153

converted as their religious mentors believe. Very early during the conquest the astute natives discovered that so long as they would stick up a cross during their ceremonies they could continue to pronounce the old charms and call upon the names of the old gods, without much interference. Since that day in 1502 when Columbus sighted a great Maya trading canoe off the Bay Islands of Honduras, the oppressed natives of America have been wont to adopt with more than usual enthusiasm any Catholic rite which somehow resembled one of their own ceremonies, or whose proper celebration synchronized with one of their own fiestas, as is the case with the day of Saint Joseph and the celebration of the vernal equinox.

The pathetic thing is to see how often to-day the natives—while continuing to use part of an ancient ritual—have forgotten its true significance. Thus at Succots, when I inquired why they were using a cottonwood tree, the majority of the merrymakers replied simply that they were using it because their fathers had used it in connection with this same festivity.

Even more pathetic, however, was an explanation given by a smaller number of celebrators, who told me it was said that wherever the great Spanish Captain Cortez had camped in America he had planted a cottonwood tree. (It is true that cottonwoods are found at the sites of most old Spanish towns in this

neighborhood.) Thus, in planting this small cottonwood, some of these poor descendants of the first
great Americans thought they were celebrating the
conquest of their ancestors by the hired cutthroats
and professional looters who brought the colors of
Spain to the western hemisphere in the early sixteenth
century! Only one or two of the older men of Succots would admit even suspecting that the true significance of the cottonwood tree was quite otherwise,
and it was obvious that they did not want the Catholic
priest of the village to know that such theories were
entertained even in the depths of their aboriginal
souls.

Any one who sees such a thing as I saw at Succots
will read only with irony the frequent accounts of
early Spanish writers regarding the ease with which
the Spanish priests were able to convert the natives
of America to Christianity. The mistake of these
priests was in thinking that, because the natives had
been willing to accept the form, they had really accepted the substance. The truth is that to this day,
in many parts of our two continents, Christianity and
the religion of America's noble pagans have been so
mixed that the people who use the fused product no
longer know where the one ends and the other
begins!

My interest in this phenomenon perhaps somewhat
put me out of the proper spirit to enjoy the fiesta at

Succots. The chief outward activities of the celebrators consisted in dancing and drinking. Both were done with intensity, but I cannot say with fury or abandon. The fact is that the modern Mayas always seem a phlegmatic and pathetic people, a race in whose minds resignation and sadness ever lurk. And they drink with the cold purpose of men determined to forget something. Would that they might begin by forgetting the outlandish theory that the cottonwood ceremony is a form of homage to the dead chief of their conquerors!

In short, although fragments of many such ancient ceremonies as that just described may still be found in observance, on the whole they are more decayed than the remains of canals and causeways and "lighthouse temples" used by the early American mariners, and more crumbled than the astronomical observatories in which the scientist-priests of other times studied the heavens.

Fortunately, there are remains of ancient astronomical observatories sufficiently well preserved in the Maya territory to give us a vivid idea of how much concerned were the ancients with the heavenly science. The most interesting observatories yet studied are those at Uaxactun, Guatemala, and Copan, Honduras, and Chichen Itza, Yucatan. (An interesting round building which Dr. Spinden and I discovered at Paalmul, on the east coast of Yucatan, in 1926,

156

probably had important astronomical significance, but this has not yet been worked out.)

At all three of these observatories the most notable feature is the permanent recording by the Mayas of astronomical bearings relating to solstices, equinoxes, and positions of the heavenly bodies at other phases of their travels which would be significant in a farmer's almanac. Following the suggestion of Mr. Frans Blom, Dr. Oliver Ricketson demonstrated that bearings between certain parts of temples and mounds in the so-called "solar observatory" at Uaxactun give the direction of true east, the direction of amplitudes of the sun on June 22 and on December 22, and marked the points of sunrise on certain dates which seem to have been significant to the Maya farmers, including April 6 and September 6.

About the time that Dr. Ricketson was establishing these interesting facts, Dr. Spinden was surveying two stone monuments four and a half miles apart, which lie at opposite sides of the ruined city of Copan, in Western Honduras. He reports:

As viewed from the eastern stone the sun sets behind the western stone twice during the course of a year, one occurrence being about the same interval after the Vernal Equinox that the other is before the Autumnal Equinox. It seems from the dates on these two markers that the base line was first arranged in 392 A.D. to reach April 5th and September 6th. The

157

dates are also those of new and full moons, so there was a co-relation between sun and moon in the farmer's almanac of the Mayas. Other monuments at Copan show that the base line was re-set, first to yield April 9th, and September 2nd, and secondly to yield April 12th and August 30th, which are the dates recovered by the last survey.

Probably this "re-setting" of these monuments was the result of an astronomical congress which evidence gathered by archæologists indicates the ancient Mayas held at Copan several hundred years before the Spanish conquest.

Three windows in the famous Round Tower, or Caracol, at Chichen Itza, were found by Dr. Ricketson to have most important significance. This lay not in the direction of the windows themselves, but in the directions indicated by lines drawn diagonally from the inner jambs of the windows to the outer jambs of the same openings. For example, a line of sight from the right inner jamb of Window 1 to the left outer jamb turned out to be due west. And a line of sight from the right inner jamb to the left outer jamb of Window 3 is due south. Two other directions given by these most interesting windows in America indicate where the moon sets at two important stages of its career through the skies.

Discoveries such as these increase our respect not only for the Maya astronomers but for the Maya architects, for these window-jambs at Chichen Itza must have been built into place after astronomers had determined by observation the significant bearing to be recorded by the jambs. But with regard to the astronomers, we can be pretty sure that they did their extraordinary work without the help of any telescope whatsoever. Infinite patience and the assistance of a remarkably effective science of mathematics were chiefly responsible for the successful results obtained by the star-gazers of ancient Central America.

It is pathetic to observe how far the degenerate modern Mayas have sunk from the one-time standard of intelligence. In 1928, when I was exploring Quintana Roo with Mr. Sheldon Yates of the American Chicle Company, who was looking for new stands of the *sapote* trees which give the valuable sap that is the fundamental ingredient of chewing-gum, we almost had serious difficulty with the chief of the Tuluum Indians because a surveyor, coöperating with Mr. Yates, was seen taking a star sight at night. The chief of the Tuluum branch of the Mayas threatened to have the man shot, because, "we don't want you white men moving our stars around!"

At about this stage in their description of the wonderful society of the Mayas, other writers have confused their lay readers by introducing a compressed description of the mathematics and astronomy of the men who built the observatories at Copan and Chi-

159

chen Itza. I do not wish by such an error to lose the attention of those of you who may still be reading. The names of several books containing descriptions of the Maya mathematical and calendarical systems are contained in the bibliography at the end of this volume for any one who may be interested. I shall merely mention a few of the most outstanding features of the high science developed by Maya mathematicians and astronomers.

Regarding their mathematics, suffice it to say that the Mayas used a vigesimal rather than a decimal system of counting. That is, they counted by twenties instead of by tens as we do. Our decimal system probably originated in primitive man's taking his ten fingers as a basis for counting. But the most common numeration systems among primitive peoples are the quinary, based on the five fingers of one hand, and the vigesimal, based on the ten fingers and ten toes found on the complete man.

As for the Maya calendar, the first thing we ought to notice is that it was founded originally on a lunar year rather than a solar year. This was also characteristic of the calendars developed by the empires of the Aztecs and the Incas. This is a point worth remembering when you hear the victims of American inferiority complexes arguing that American civilization must have been derived from Egypt because the Incas were sun-worshipers like the Egyptians. Sun-

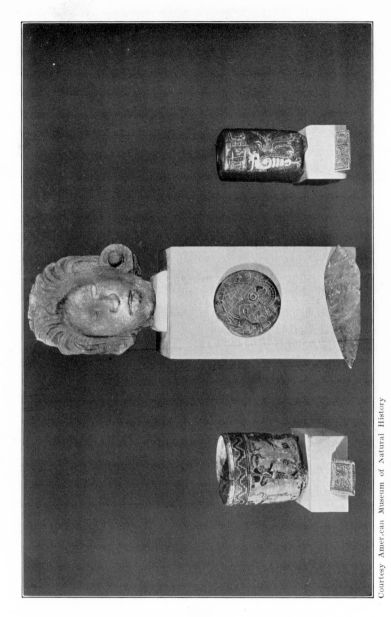

Courtesy American Museum of Natural History

Synoptic survey of middle American plastic art—from the region between northern Costa Rica and southern Mexico

worship in America as a whole was much less accentuated than rain-worship and, as we have just seen, the earliest American astronomers gave much more heed to the moon than they did to the sun.

A fact which helps us to appreciate the originality and scope of the Maya mind is that the Mayas had three other systems of counting time besides their lunar count. These others were a year of 365 days, (the "vague year," as the late Dr. Teeple called it), a year of 360 days (the *Tun*), and a ceremonial period of 260 days (the *Tzolkin,* already mentioned). The alternation of light and darkness on this terrestrial sphere of ours furnishes the most obvious method of counting the passage of time, and it is not surprising that many archæologists consider that the day was the fundamental unit by which the Mayas counted time. However, Mr. William E. Yates and Dr. J. E. Teeple have stoutly maintained that the *Tun* or 360-day year was the fundamental unit. The controversy is too complicated to develop here.

At any rate, it is a fact that the perfected calendar of the Mayas was in no sense astronomical, but was a mere counting-machine. We call this machine the Long Count. It was by means of this device that they could accurately distinguish any day from 136,655,-999 other days; that is, fix the position of any date in 374,400 years. The Long Count employed six units of measurement. First, the day was called *Kin;*

20 days made 1 *Uinal* (month); 360 days or 18 *Uinals* made 1 *Tun* (year); 7,200 days, or 20 *Tuns*, made 1 *Katun;* 144,000 days, or 400 *Tuns,* or 20 *Katuns,* made 1 *Baktun,* or cycle; and 2,880,000 days, or 8,000 *Tuns,* or 20 *Baktuns,* made 1 *Pictun,* or great cycle. But the Mayas counted only actually elapsed time. Thus they would consider our year 1931 to be the year 1930 until it had actually been completed at midnight on December 31. This is really a much more logical method of counting time than the one we use. As Dr. Teeple says, the Mayas "counted time just as the meter on a motor car counts miles. It does not register one mile until the whole mile has been run. While Christian chronology, like a taximeter, registers a unit the instant it starts."

Virtually all the dates the Mayas have left behind were reckoned from the date 4 Ahau 8 Cumhu (which fell in 3113 B.C. by Goodman's correlation, or in 3373 by Spinden's). This is believed to refer to an event not historical but mythical.

In one of the three Maya manuscripts which have been preserved for us, not only was the end of the world described by these extraordinary artists and scientists of Central America, but periods of 34,000 years (12,500,000 days) are referred to as casually as we might mention the "gay nineties," or "befo' de war."

In that ancient Maya book known to modern scientists as the Dresden Codex, calculations involving revolutions of the moon over a period of nearly 33 years are set down so accurately that out of 11,959 days recorded there is an error of only 89/100 of a day less than the true time computed by the best modern methods! Archæologists believe that revolutions of the planets Jupiter, Mars, Mercury, and Saturn are recorded in the same manuscript.

The Mayas regarded their twenty days as gods who had once lived on earth, tilling the maize-fields and weaving cotton like ordinary mortals. All the important planets also had the status of godhood. Among the planets, Venus in particular was much worshiped, and in addition to the four time-counts commonly in use among the Mayas their astronomers built up a theoretical Venus calendar, so accurate that if it had been in practical use up to the present, its error in computing time over a thousand years would not have amounted to more than one day! In all probability magic played a much greater part in Maya mathematics and astronomy than most modern archæologists have realized, and the search for evidence of this is a fascinating field of scientific effort.

We should never forget that the priests were the scientists of the Mayas, who found no such conflict between religion and science as some silly mortals of the present time profess to see. Indeed, these educated Central Americans whom the ignorant Spanish "discoverers" called "barbarians" would have considered barbarous a society in which a man could be persecuted as Galileo was persecuted for holding that the earth moved round the sun. Only in a country where the softness of too much prosperity has persuaded some people to forget the fundamental verities of human existence—such a country as the United States of America to-day—can any one be so absurd as to see a conflict between religion and science. This would not happen in our time if our business men, bankers, sculptors, and musicians remembered that all of them are supported by the efforts of the farmer.

The Mayas never forgot that religion and science are one, and that each is the child of agriculture. They could no more have forgotten it than the Maya astronomers in the observatories rising above the dwellings of the crowded cities could have forgotten that their next meal, that their every meal, was dependent on the bounty of the gods looking after the broad maize-fields whose miles of waving green made a pleasant rest for the eye dazzled by the glints on limestone walls and towers under the tropical sun.

Courtesy Museum of the American Indian, Heye Foundation

Maya turtle stone of Quirigua, Guatemala

# CHAPTER IX

## ASTRONOMER-PRIESTS

THE Spanish bishop Diego de Landa has told us that the high priest of the Mayas was called Ahkin Mai, or Ahaukan Mai. This functionary was supported by the public, and was very much respected. He took part in only the most important religious ceremonies, and it is believed that he spent most of his time working at astronomical problems and keeping the calendar in order. It was his duty, however, to manage the training of candidates for the priesthood, who were generally chosen from among the second sons of the nobility.

Below the high priest were the Chilans. They had many duties, and were much employed in managing feasts and sacrifices, but they were above all oracular priests. That is, it was believed that messages came to the people direct from the gods through the mouths of the Chilans. Inasmuch as the Mayas considered all science as part of religion, it is not surprising that they delegated the practice of medicine to these Chilans. The latter cultivated the good-will of the gods of medicine, who included Ixchel, the goddess of childbirth and the wife of Itzamna, and Zuhuykak,

165

a goddess who looked after little children. Evil spirits were often exorcised by the priests in their pursuance of the medical arts, but bleeding was the most frequent treatment employed, and this was often done by piercing the tongue and ears. Several monuments discovered in Central America show this painful operation in progress.

Below the Chilans were the third rank of the priesthood, whose members were called Nacons. The sole religious function of the Nacons was to cut open the breast of the victim of religious sacrifice and pass the bleeding heart on a plate to the Chilan in attendance. Like the priests of higher rank, the Nacons enjoyed office for life, but they also had a military duty for which they were elected for a period of only three years. That is to say, the commander of the Maya army was a Nacon chosen to hold his job for three years. It does not seem as if this method could have led to a very efficient military service, but, as we shall see later, the Mayas, although brave enough, were not at all militaristic either in practice or in spirit. The placing of an ecclesiastic at the head of the army is one more item of the many that indicate how religion permeated the life of the ancient Central Americans.

The lower priests were called Chacs. They always went in quartets, like the subsidiary rain-gods whose names they bore, and who were essentially gods of the

166

four points of the compass. (The Mayas, like all the American peoples, gave a great deal of attention in their ritual to the points of the compass, which is not surprising when we consider the importance of agriculture and maritime commerce in their lives. To-day many of us who live in apartments and go out only in the streets of great cities, where huge buildings hide us from the kindly sun, would be unable to tell offhand on a cloudy day which was north and which was east. But no Maya ever forgot this for an instant.)

The special duty of the Chacs was to hold the human victim as the knife was being plunged into his breast, in order that the streaming heart might be offered to the gods of rain. This seems barbarous to us, who, instead of dedicating a few lives to horticultural deities, sacrifice hundreds of thousands of young men in bloody warfare in order that nations may seize from one another territory rich in agricultural or mineral resources.

Although the Maya priests had many duties which brought them into contact with the masses, they lived apart in monasteries close to their temples. A similarly isolated habitation was set apart for the "nuns" or "vestal virgins," who were under the supervision of a "Mother Superior." One class of these vestal virgins was used as sacrifices to the God of Rain, as we shall see later. Unchastity on the part of a nun

167

was punishable by death, but one who made proper application was permitted to resign from her religious order and marry.

The Spanish historian Cogolludo has given us a vivid picture of the enactment of human sacrifice:

The high priest had in his hand a large, broad and sharp knife made of flint. Another priest carried a wooden collar wrought like a snake. The persons to be sacrificed were conducted one by one up the steps, stark naked, and as soon as laid on the stone, had the collar put upon their necks, and the four priests took hold of the hands and feet. Then the high priest with wonderful dexterity, ripped up the breast, tore out the heart, reeking, with his hands, and showed it to the Sun, offering him the heart and steam that came from it. Then he turned to the idol, and threw it in his face, which done, he kicked the body down the steps, and it never stopped till it came to the bottom, because they were very upright; and one who had been a priest, and had been converted, said that when they tore out the heart of the wretched person sacrificed, it did beat so strongly that he took it up from the ground three or four times till it cooled by degrees, and then he threw the body, still moving, down the steps.

The Spaniards of course never came into contact with the Mayas until long after the latter had exchanged cultural influences with the Toltecs and Aztecs. Human sacrifice was common among these two

168

peoples, but there is good reason to think that the Mayas indulged in the bloody rite very little before the peninsula of Yucatan was overrun by Toltec mercenaries and Toltec ideas. In the Maya cities of the old empire only one illustration of human sacrifice has been found depicted on the sculptured monuments. We are warranted in believing that the Mayas were much less bloody in religion than the Nahuatl-speaking people of Mexico, as they were undoubtedly much less militaristic and imperialistic in politics.

The sacrifice of animals, however, was a usual proceeding. The human beings offered up were generally slaves or prisoners of war. When in 1511 a Spanish ship was wrecked near Jamaica, and an open boat containing a number of survivors drifted to the coast of Yucatan at a point situated in the province called Maia, several of the unfortunate Dons were used as sacrifices to the American gods.

The Mayas seem to have had no such frequent and regularly recurring holiday as our Sunday, but they probably had even more miscellaneous religious holidays than Greek Catholic Russia and Shinto-Buddhist Japan, which is saying a great deal. Everything the Mayas did was governed by religious consideration, and nothing was undertaken without the consultation of augurs and portents. Life was just one religious festival after another.

An unusual amount of importance, however, was

169

attached to the New Year's ceremonies, which began during the five unlucky days of the expiring 365-day "vague" year, called the Uayeb days. According to Bishop Landa, the year in the calendar of that branch of the Mayas living in Yucatan at the time of the conquest began on July 16 by the Julian calendar, which the Spaniards were then using. This day was 1 Pop in the Maya calendar. Priests and members of the aristocracy fasted for thirteen days or more in preparation for the purification ceremonies of the month.

Other months were sacred to particular trades or industries; witness the private festivals of the hunters and fishermen in the month Zip, the festival of the bee-keepers in the month Tzec, the great festival to Kukulcan in the month Xul, when new fire was made and five nights were spent in singing and dancing, many offerings of food and drink being made to the genial god, who was considered the god of learning and culture as well as the deity of the wind and the rain. In the month of Muan, the Maya ranchers who had cacao plantations held special festivals to their particular deities.

Ceremonies to maize-gods, rain-gods, and other gods of fertility were always in order, and special days for the ritual considered pleasing to these deities are too numerous to mention.

In order to do the thing up properly, a fiesta in honor of all the gods indiscriminately was held in the month Mol. Domestic utensils and the tools of all workmen were painted with a secret blue ointment. Paint was also applied freely to children, who were given, into the bargain, nine raps on the wrist by an old woman dressed in a feather robe. "The object of this ceremony," says J. Eric Thompson, "was to ensure that the children grew up expert each one in his or her trade."

The ancient Mayas were as ardent religious pilgrims as the Japanese are now. They thought nothing of walking two or three hundred miles to visit a sacred shrine. Cozumel Island, off the east coast of Yucatan, was the most popular objective for these pilgrims. Cozumel, only about twenty-five miles long and nine miles wide, remains to this day one of the most extraordinary places in the world. Mr. Ludlow Griscom, then of the American Museum of Natural History, naturalist attached to the Mason-Spinden expedition in 1926, established the fact that on Cozumel there are some eighteen species of birds not found anywhere else in the world—not even on the mainland twelve miles away. The ruined sites of three towns have recently been discovered there by expeditions organized by me, and undoubtedly others remain to be found in the thick bush, for most of the island is still virtually a wilderness.

One of these sites, which I named Ucul Ha, (Drinking Water), contains what I believe to be the

171

best preserved building in the entire Maya area. It is, unfortunately, a tiny building, a little shrine to the god of water, erected by the Mayas within a cave in which there is a limpid spring. The fact that the natural roof of the cave is just above the roof of the building, protecting it entirely from the weather, explains why this shrine looks as if the limestone stucco had been applied to its walls only yesterday.

Ixchel ("the Lady of the Rainbow") Goddess of Medicine and wife of Itzamna, was one of the deities whose worship was particularly emphasized at Cozumel. Bishop Landa tells us that women who expected to become mothers placed images of Ixchel beneath their beds and counted confidently on her protection during their hours of pain.

Another special divinity of Cozumel was Teel Cuzam, the "swallow-legged." Although he gave the island its name, very little is known about him.

It is interesting to know that the Mayas had a number of religious ceremonies similar to those of other lands. But there is no reason to interpret the fact as indicating an interchange of culture between them and those countries, as many misguided enthusiasts have been over-eager to do. The physical attributes of culture—the clothing, the furniture, the utensils man makes—are determined by the physiography of the human body. In the same way the mental and

172

Round building believed to have been an astronomical observatory,
discovered by Mason-Spinden expedition—Paalmul

spiritual attributes of his culture are determined by the limits of his mind and spirit.

There is no reason to seek for any remote physical communication between Central America and Japan merely because Japanese priests of to-day walk through fire for purification as the Maya priests did long ago. Having marched through the red-hot embers of the Shinto ceremony myself in Tokio, I can appreciate that the fire-walking of the Mayas was a more intricate performance than that of the Shintoists of Japan. For one thing, the Japanese get their embers merely by burning a large pile of brush. But the Mayas went to the pains of constructing a hollow mound of wood with a doorway like a small temple, and before the mound was burned to produce the embers the priests were to walk through, a man sat on top of it singing and beating a drum, while the loyal congregation danced about him.

The Spanish priests who accompanied the first explorers were astonished to find the Mayas using both the confession and baptism. As the European superiority complex invariably urges the conclusion that where similarities exist between practices in America and practices in Europe, the American practices must have been derived from the European, these Spanish friars made up their minds that Christian missionaries must have reached America fifteen hundred years before them and spread the Gospel. Of course

173

there is not a scintilla of evidence to support the view that Christianity crossed the Atlantic till it came with the bloody swords of Columbus and Cortez.

The baptismal rite of the Mayas was called by a name meaning "to be reborn." The priest, who was assisted by the four minor priests, or Chacs, sat down beside a brazier and as each child entered the room in which the ceremony was performed he passed the little one a few grains of maize and some incense, both of which the child threw on the fire.

As for confession, children were often asked to confess their sins. When they had done this the priest blessed them and sprinkled them with water which he threw from a short carved stick.

The Mayas married young. Twenty was considered the proper age, but in practice they married earlier. Marriage was arranged very largely by the parents of the two persons concerned, but it was not supervised by the Government in the strict manner observed in Peru. It was customary for the young man's father to make a present to the bride's parents, and among some branches of the Mayas this was so developed that marriage was virtually by purchase. As is the case in the United States to-day, polygamy was not openly practised and in theory the Mayas were monogamous. But divorce was so easy and desertion so common that persons of fickle disposition found little difficulty in changing their mates. In

174

cases of adultery the guilty man was put entirely at the disposition of the aggrieved husband, who might kill him or pardon him as he pleased.

On the whole the Maya women were chaste and modest, as they are to this day. But drunkenness was common among them, as it is likewise in our time; the women, however, indulged in this vice much more secretly than their husbands. The Mayas believed in the occasional tremendous spree rather than in the steady tipple. I have often seen men stagger out of the *cantinas* of their little villages and fall face forward on the ground, lying there in a drunken stupor for half a day unless their friends came to carry them home.

The Mayas were very much afraid of death, yet in times of depression almost forced themselves to die by will, as they do now. Men bitten by snakes have been known to die from sheer fright, and it is common for a modern native depressed by some minor ailment to get into his hammock and refuse food or drink until he dies. The common people were buried in much the manner current among us now, but members of the nobility often were cremated.

We do not know enough about the details of the Maya social system to understand just how this nobility was constituted. Apparently the whole Maya Government was of a religious nature, and the rulers were the priests. It is natural to suppose that all the

175

members of the upper class got their superior position by virtue of some religious grading of society. The ceremonial insignia shown in the monuments and paintings are nearly all those concerned with religious symbolism.

Possibly toward the end of Maya history there was a tendency to develop non-religious rule—such as became noticeable among the Mexicans later. But if we think of the Mayas as a people living under a feudal form of government in which the Church was the State we probably have a pretty accurate general idea of the organization of their commonwealth. There was no more conflict between religion and government than there was between religion and science. Religion was regarded as the obvious means to get sustenance and health and comfort for the people, government and science were simply two of the tools by which this was accomplished.

It is fairly obvious that the Mayas, like most early Americans, were both gregarious and bashful. The spirit of individualism seems to have been strangely absent throughout early America. The stubborn passion with which an Englishman clings to what he considers his rights as a separate entity in society would have been incomprehensible to the ancient American. The Peruvians under the Inca emperors carried this abnegation of individuality to its highest point of

176

development, yet the same tendency was very marked in the social life of the Mayas.

They were a conventional people and eccentricity even in such a small matter as dress was frowned upon. Like their modern descendants, the ancient Mayas were a fairly short people, sturdily built but not fat. A first glimpse of some of the representations of human figures carved on monuments might give one the impression that they were a people of small brain content, so markedly do their foreheads recede. But this appearance was not natural; the skulls of many infants were artificially flattened in front to give their heads a sugar-loaf look.

Another abominable practice among the Mayas was deliberately to make children cross-eyed by hanging something attractive from the forelock. The practice of chipping the teeth and of "ornamenting" them—by inserting plugs of jadeite, hematite, iron pyrites, or other materials—also was popular among the Mayas, as it was among some of the Mexican peoples. Men of importance did not consider themselves properly dressed if they appeared in public without heavy plugs of jadeite or some other semiprecious stone dangling from nose and ears, and such plugs are among the commonest objects found by archæologists in Maya graves. Beads, necklaces, masks, and a host of other ornamental objects of

177

stone or of shell are found in great numbers in Maya tombs. No people in the world ever used more stone ornaments than the Mayas.

The ancient Central Americans were very fond of tattooing themselves; the men thought the more they were tattooed the more beautiful were they, and the women tattooed their entire bodies except the breasts. The New York belle of to-day could learn much about the application of paint from a study of Maya practice. Red was the usual color used by women and by married men. Bachelors, whether in chagrin at their lot or otherwise is not known, painted themselves black. Some branches of the Mayas considered hair on the face inappropriate and ugly, and the Spaniards found the natives of Yucatan applying scorching damp cloths to the faces of their children in the hope of obliterating all hair. But in the Maya books and on some of the pottery rediscovered by archæologists men of the Maya race are depicted as wearing mustaches and even beards.

There was no aversion to hair on the head, and it was usually worn very long. Men in Yucatan wound their hair around a clipped spot which they maintained on the top of the head, permitting one small plait to hang behind, while the women's hair was suspended in two long braids down the back. Males seem to have formed the brilliant half of the Maya family, and their methods of ornamenting their hair and

178

heads were legion. Feathers were much used and so were masks representing animals or gods.

As to clothing, the only garment necessary for a man was a sort of girdle, but a good many wore broad shoulder mantles. The common people often went barefoot, their superiors using sandals of skin or woven hemp. Some sort of buskin or else a sort of crisscross puttee seems to have been worn on the legs by men of rank, to judge by the testimony of sculpture and painting.

Women wore a skirt, and some of them covered the upper part of their body with a tunic, but many of them went naked above the waist.

Next to what they did in mathematics and astronomy, the art of the Mayas was the greatest achievement they accomplished, particularly their sculpture. But Maya art is a subject in which it is very difficult to interest the layman. This is because the Maya artist dealt with subjects incomprehensible to us without considerable study, and through the medium of a technique unlike any used by the artists of the modern world. The first thing to notice about Maya art, and the last thing, is that it was utterly inspired by and dominated by religion. In his excellent work "A study of Maya Art" Dr. Spinden says:

The influence of a national religion upon a national art was never more unmistakable than in the case of the Maya. But, indeed, it is universally important.

179

Religion is able to furnish the deepest and truest inspiration which the human mind is capable of receiving. Being ideal in itself, it develops the imagination so that this in turn finds secret meanings in common things. Moreover, religion, as a communal element in the life of the nation, turns the attention of all artists to a common purpose. Through this focusing of the attention religion leads inevitably to an intensive rather than a diffuse development of art. But once this intensive development has exhausted the possibilities of the established ideas, then religion throws its powerful influence against further disorganizing change. Thus religion enriches art and makes it permanent.

In the case of the Maya the art might almost be termed the concrete expression of the religion, since all the great monuments were apparently connected with religious practices and no minor object was too humble to receive decorations with religious significance. Clearly this wonderful art rose under the communal inspiration of a great religious awakening and was conserved by the persistence of ritual. Doubtless the art reacted strongly upon the religion which gave it birth, filling that religion with symbolism and imagery. The two worked hand in hand. The spreading of the religion meant a spreading of the art, and the graphic representations of the art rendered the religion intelligible. It was probably through the objective ritual on the one hand and the objective art on the other, that the religion of the Maya was enabled to leap the bounds of language and impress itself so strongly upon the Nahuan and Zapotecan peoples,

Have you never thought what a pity it is that the artists of medieval Europe spent all their time painting the heads and modeling the busts of saints and virgins and infant Jesuses? How much more might we not know about life in those times if painters had given even twenty per cent of their time to contemporary subjects! Likewise it is perhaps regrettable that the Maya artists gave so much attention to religious subjects. For it is as true of the Maya land as it is of medieval Italy that the art was far more advanced than the religion which so engrossed the attention of the artist.

So many of the Maya gods were in forms that appear grotesque to us—a number of them, indeed, being in semi-animal form—it is not surprising that we have been slow to appreciate the technique of the Maya painter and sculptor. But if you will give this technique a chance, weigh it by the same tests you apply to the technique of the Italian or the Frenchman, you will heartily agree with the statement of Dr. Spinden, that "upon technological grounds—such as the knowledge displayed of foreshortening, composition and design—Maya art may be placed in advance of the art of Assyria and Egypt and only below that of Greece in the list of great national achievements."

On the whole we have rather more vestiges of Maya art preserved for study than we have of Greek

181

art. Examples of sculpture are plentiful, though naturally the paintings surviving the ravages of Central American climate are not nearly so numerous. The methods and materials used by the Mayas differed but little from those employed on the other side of the Atlantic. There was a great deal of carving in wood and stone, and the technique of working metal was highly developed, but as metal was scarce this particular art was not widely practised. Painters worked on paper and on plaster, some of the best examples of their labor which have survived being the extensive murals of temples. Sculptors modeled in clay and stucco, and made terra-cotta figurines from molds.

So excellent is the stone carving of the Maya monuments and temple façades that many critics have refused to believe that these Americans did not have metal chisels. However, although several well-made chisels of hard copper have been dredged out of the pool at Chichen Itza in which virgins were drowned as sacrifices to the gods of rain, it remains the consensus of archæological opinion that most of the Maya stone-carving was done with stone knives.

The Maya sculptors who decorated the huge monuments and the expansive outer and inner surfaces of public buildings with millions of feet of modeling, used all three of the common methods of modeling employed by their contemporaries in Europe; that is, low relief, high relief, and full round. But the low relief was far more common than the other two types.

There has been a good deal of arguing among the experts as to whether any of the many sculptures the Mayas have left behind were portraits of individuals who actually lived on this earth. The probability is that this was not so, and that the figures carved by the Maya sculptors were always somewhat idealized. Proceeding on this assumption, we may be pretty sure that the Mayas found beauty in flattened foreheads, receding chins, and prominent noses. Individuals with these distinguishing facial characteristics may be found in Central America now, but it is by no means certain that this type of face ever prevailed among the Maya nation. Any one who has studied Japanese art remembers how partial the painters of Nippon were to a long narrow face with aquiline nose, especially in the case of women. Such faces may be seen in Japan to-day, but they are not the common type and probably never were. It seems, however, that the type they represent has been idealized by the Japanse artist; and, similarly, it is quite possible that the Maya artist selected a particular form of human visage and idealized it for his own purposes, and that the artificially flattened skulls taken out of burial-mounds are the skulls of an aristocracy or special class addicted to skull-deformation.

Any one who doubts that the Maya artists were superior to the painters and sculptors of Egypt, Assyria, and other ancient transatlantic lands, with the exception of Greece, has only to compare these arts in the matter of perspective and foreshortening to be quickly convinced of the clear superiority of the American. The Mayas knew well how to cope with profile delineation. They knew how to draw the hand or foot on the far side of the subject of a portrait so that its relation to the hand and foot on the near side appeared as it really does appear to the human eye. Whereas the more primitive artist remembers that an individual has two hands and two feet and draws them in equal conspicuousness; witness much of the work of Egyptian artists.

Modern critics have found fault with the Maya artists on the grounds that they did not appreciate the uses of blank space for obtaining contrast, and that they did not know how to subordinate. But we should remember that in all probability many shades of paint which have long since disappeared were used in the more intricate designs. Another thing to remember in attempting to understand Maya art is that the early Americans were much inclined to simplify.

Dr. Harrison Allen has written an illuminating paper on this matter of simplification. He finds that artists are inclined to do one of four things, as follows:

184

Back view of building, believed to have been an astronomical observatory, discovered by Mason-Spinden expedition at Paalmul

1 Repeat the normal lines of the model.
2 Diminish the normal lines of the model.
3 Modify according to a symbol.
4 Modify according to mythological or religious conceptions.

He uses the term "radical" for the somewhat ideographic figures that hold the elementary lines of a number of variants of the original form. In Maya and Mexican art he sees a very common radical in what he calls the "crotalian curve," which is a line maintaining the profile of the rattlesnake (*Crotalus durissus*). Once you learn to recognize this crotalian curve you will begin to appreciate Maya art. Then what appears to be a mass of meaningless whorls becomes a pattern of the beautifully twisted bodies of the serpent god, the deity of rain.

As Spinden well says, "the trail of the serpent is over all the civilizations of Central America and Southern Mexico," and there is much reason for the belief of this learned writer that the serpent came to mean even more to Maya art than he did to Maya religion, owing to the fact that his sinuous body lent itself so readily to decoration. The serpent was often drawn with the feathers or foot of a bird, in which case he was Kukulcan, God of Wind and Rain. He was also idealized with human features, and very often a human head was shown in the open jaws of the snake. Any animal depicted by the Mayas with

185

human features was a sacred animal or divine animal, and this snake holding a human head in his jaws is perhaps the *divinest* of the many forms the Mayas gave the snake, although unfortunately we do not know just what this half-human serpent stood for.

As the snake was used more and more in decorative art, the processes of simplification and conventionalization were carried so far that no one who had not made a specialty of Maya art would recognize the drawing as that of a snake at all. However, the Mayas always knew what their paintings represented. They were never in doubt, as we are concerning the works of some of our modern artists, as to whether a painting is meant to represent the wreck of a speakeasy or a nude descending the stairs!

In general it seems that the tendency toward conventionalization in art developed with the advance of Maya history, and that there was much more realism in the early Maya art than in the later. Yet stone pieces of realistic depiction dating from the last days of Maya rule have been found.

Of Maya music and Maya literature we know next to nothing, thanks to the ruthless efforts of the Spaniards who destroyed the old books. But if the poem at the opening of the preceding chapter is a fair sample, we may be certain that Maya literature was worthy of standing beside Maya painting and Maya sculpture. As for the plastic arts, it is hard to find adjectives in the English language with which to do justice to them. We may say that above all else Maya art was virile, bold, free, and original. Perhaps the art of no other nation has ever so throbbed with vitality as the art of the Mayas.

How the snake came to have such tremendous importance in the religion of early America no one has ever satisfactorily explained. Why rain has great importance to primitive peoples is self-evident, and it may be that in the following words J. Eric Thompson has given us the right explanation for the popularity of divine snakes with primitive worshipers:

The snake is throughout the New World closely connected with rain. Possibly its sinuosity recalled the lightning which so often preceded rain in these latitudes, or the fact that snakes show themselves in large numbers before and after a storm may have given rise to the connection.

The very peak and culmination of rain-god worship in America took place at Chichen Itza. Here is a big cenote, or natural pool, two hundred and fifty feet long by one hundred and seventy feet wide. Its sinister jade-green water lies some seventy feet below the top of the perpendicular side of the sacred well. An elevated stone road still runs several hundred feet from the foot of the great pyramid of Kukulcan to a platform built out over the south side

187

of this pool. After ceremonies in the pyramidal temple the vestal virgins, who had been living in the nunnery near by to await their turn at sacrifice, were led down this roadway by the Chac priests, the special attendants of the rain-god. From the platform these maidens of between fourteen and twenty years of age —to judge by their bones, which have been recovered in large quantities—were cast into the pool. This was done at sunrise. Any maid who might still be alive at noon was considered rejected by the rain-god and was fished out. But it is doubtful if this happened very often, for the girls of those days were not swimming the English Channel much.

Mr. Edward Herbert Thompson, to whose faith, persistence, and ingenuity the world owes its knowledge of the secrets of the Sacred Cenote, dredged out of this pool, with the bones of maidens just mentioned, innumerable sacred objects which had been cast into the water with the human sacrifices. Embossed gold disks, gold rings, basins and cups of gold, brooches, beads, pendants, ear-plugs, nose-plugs, and countless ornamental articles of jade and other semi-precious stones were found.

Such work as this—indeed, all archæological excavation—is more like roulette than anything else I know of. As you scan each spadeful of earth thrown out, wondering if it will prove to contain a jade bead or a fragment of pottery decorated with an ancient

188

hieroglyph, your sensations are almost identically those of the man who is watching the little rolling ball that may bring him temporary fortune by stopping on his number.

I shall never forget the thrill that came when I had the good fortune to find an unusually well-made stone "coffin" only six inches below the top of the first Maya burial-mound I ever opened. And inside the grave, with the crumbled bones, were two scalloped shell ear ornaments and a lovely little incised cylinder of jadeite which had once hung upon the breast of the priest who had been laid to his last rest here within earshot of the tumbling water of Monkey Falls, on the upper reaches of the Belize River. A few hours later, in another mound close by, I found the fragments of an ancient mirror of pyrites. What would I not have given to be able to put together that mirror and see all that it had reflected since it was made, centuries before!

Thoughts like these will come to the digger, particularly in late afternoon when the excitement of the hunt has given way to fatigue, when the bush is stilling for the night and when the big hole where your pick-and-shovel men still stir up old bones is filling with shadow. Strange to think that these bones which crumble when you touch them once walked about—yes, ran, fought, loved, hated, and suffered! Strange to reflect that here is a bit of the stuff that

189

made a noble nation, a nation which was on a high level of civilization when our own ancestors were savages in the bush of the British Isles. Strange to hold in your hand a bit of the skull of the high priest who once ruled the city here beside this river—brown and rapid then as now, but with banks corn-tasseled which to-day are tangles of thorny trees—a bit of the skull of the man who mayhap knew more of the planets and their courses than many an astronomer of the present age.

# CHAPTER X

## ANCIENT AMERICA WAS BUILT BY BUSINESS MEN

IN NO country since scribes began to record history has the business man had so much power or used it so wisely as in the United States to-day. The soldier, the farmer, the jurist, the teacher, and many others have contributed generously of their brains and energy to put our country in the enviable position among the nations which she occupies as 1931 goes out. But perhaps the largest single contribution has been made by the man of commerce. It is quite fitting that he should enjoy a prestige and influence among us greater even than that he enjoys in the two other most developed economic nations of the modern world, Great Britain and Germany. From the days of prairie-schooner and clipper-ship the trader and manufacturer have been in the very skirmish-line of the forces that have carried ever outward the particular brand of civilization developed from the conceptions of the men who met in Independence Hall in 1776. Ford, Eastman, Woolworth, Morgan, Rockefeller are logical successors of Hamilton, Jefferson, and Franklin.

191

But also in that America more ancient than the thirteen colonies, in that society of highly civilized peoples which flourished on our two western continents before Columbus saw his saving pin-point of light in the dark early hours of October 12, 1492, the business man held a position of much importance. At long last we are beginning to acquire something like a just measure of the high achievement of the pre-Inca, Inca, Maya, Toltec, and Aztec commonwealths in art, architecture, medicine, mathematics, and astronomy. Late is better than never.

We may congratulate ourselves on even our tardy appreciation of the fact that in the Middle Ages no Europeans or Asiatics surpassed in their respective fields the masons of the remote pre-Inca nations, the engineers of the Inca and Aztec empires, the surgeons and textile artists of Peru, the architects and astronomers and mathematicians of the great Mayas of Central America whose civilization on the whole was the highest in all ancient America. But we do not yet give due recognition to the first business men of our twin continents. And the fact is that all the high lights of culture just summarized were made possible by the industry, ingenuity, and social responsibility of the traders and manufacturers who were sending their goods up and down the interiors and coasts of both our continents centuries before Norman tapestries were first being hung on English walls.

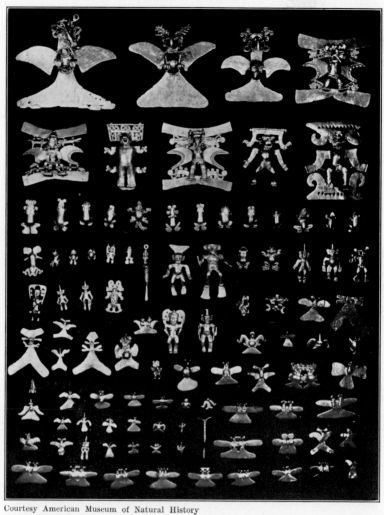

Courtesy American Museum of Natural History

Costa Rican gold specimens from the Minor Keith collection—
American Museum of Natural History

It is a question whether agriculture is older than trade. Scientists believe that before man learned to cultivate the soil he was either a hunter or a "food-gatherer," i.e., one who lived by collecting nuts, berries, and other wild edible products. It is quite possible that there was a primitive barter between the man who had killed a supply of meat and the man who had gathered more than he needed of this or that berry or nut. But in any case, agriculture was never long in practice before, *ipso facto,* it begot commerce. One of the first results of the invention of agriculture was the invention—or at least the development—of basketry and pottery. The reason is, of course, that such receptacles as baskets and pots are needed for the gathering and storing of the food products of the soil.

In America the use of pottery was practised over virtually the same area as that in which maize was grown. We know that maize spread northward from the south, and it is reasonable to suppose that pottery followed it in the hands of the first traders.

To-day plows made in Boston are found in South America. In 1200 A.D. the one type of plow was used in both continents, having been carried abroad by aboriginal traders, but we do not know in which continent it originated.

In the wide diffusion of copper objects lies one of our most striking evidences of the extent of ancient

193

American trade, albeit it cannot equal the record of the calabash rattle, which spread from the tropics throughout the area where agriculture was practised and was even imitated outside this area in the hollow wooden rattle of the Canadian Northwest and the rawhide rattle of the non-farming, buffalo-hunting tribes.

Mexico and Peru were two important centers of the copper industry, and for the production of gold, silver, and, in the case of Peru, tin and platinum, as they are to-day. These two regions were also noted for the stone produced by their quarries; this, like the other minerals, was often shipped long distances by the exporting houses of those times. The huge monoliths of Quirigua, Guatemala, from fourteen to twenty feet high and weighing several tons each, are believed to have been conveyed there by water, because of canal-like excavations which have been found. The copper knives recovered from the famous pool at Chichen Itza, Yucatan, with the bones of virgins who had been sacrificed to the rain-god, are believed to have been imported from the highlands of Mexico, six hundred miles distant.

So far as the less cultured groups of North Americans are concerned, their copper came mostly from the region of Lake Superior, where to-day we have extensive copper workings of our own. This was "free copper"; that is, all the natives had to do to make it

194

serviceable was to beat it into the desired shape. Traders hawked copper replicas of the fundamental stone tools of those times from Lake Superior over all of what anthropologists call "the eastern maize area," which embraces all our States east of the Mississippi and two or three immediately west of it.

"Lake Superior Copper" must have been quoted high on the stock-exchange of those times. There were other deposits of "free copper"—in the country west of Hudson Bay and in Alaska—but the Lake Superior region contains far more vestiges of ancient mining operations. Dr. Clark Wissler, whose researches have thrown much light on the activities of the first business men of America, reports of the Lake Superior workings:

Stone hammers to the weight of twenty-six pounds have been collected in the ancient pits; in one instance a wooden shovel, a bowl and a ladder were recovered. The aboriginal method of taking out the virgin copper seems to have been cracking by heat, breaking and wedging. In one pit twenty-six feet deep a six-ton piece of copper had been worked out and raised five feet on an incline of logs by wedging; most of the supporting timbers and wedges were still in place.

Wide as was the distribution of knives and axes and other tools fabricated from Lake Superior ore for the first American farmers and manufacturers, it is not yet certain that the copper implements un-

195

earthed in our Gulf States did not come from the Appalachians, for copper *has* been found in "them thar hills," too.

Northern exporters did not make any headway getting sales for their finished copper south of the Rio Grande, for the art of smelting, casting, and beating in dies was well comprehended in Old Mexico. Peru, however, was where these matters were best understood, Peru whence the United States imports thousands of tons of copper every year nowadays. For smelting, the medieval Peruvians used cylindrical pottery furnaces known as *guayras*. Having no bellows, the furnace men exerted their own lung-power through copper tubes. Some ores, and especially silver, needed more heat than could be blown up by human bellows, and for these ores hopper-shaped furnaces were built on windy hills. Dr. Wissler reports that "at the various intakes to these furnaces, fires were placed to heat the air, a mechanism employed by some Old World smelters."

There can be no doubt that the Peruvians knew how to make bronze by mixing copper and tin. As for the more precious metals, Professor Marshall H. Saville has amply demonstrated how cunning were both Peruvians and Mexicans in the arts of casting, soldering, hammering, and inlaying gold and silver. From one Peruvian pyramid a plundering Spaniard

196

took gold and silver objects valued at 4,450,784 Spanish dollars. The gold and jewels which the Peruvians raised as a ransom for their last Inca, Atahualpa, in the vain hope of saving him from the Spaniards, was estimated as having been worth $15,-000,000. As for the Chibchas of Colombia, they had so much gold that rumors of their wealth may have been the origin of the Spanish legend of El Dorado—a country so rich that its men were supposed to have worn golden armor.

In the United States at present, industry engages the attention of a somewhat larger number of our people than agriculture. It is probable that the proportions were about the same in ancient America. The chief commercial products involving some process of manufacturing or artificial treatment were rubber, cacao, feathers, paper, textiles, and pottery.

In 1502, on his fourth and last voyage, Columbus met off Bonacca Island in the Caribbean Sea a Maya trading canoe. Although hewn from a single log, it was so large that it required the manning of thirty paddlers. In the waist Columbus saw a merchant, richly clad, surrounded by bales of bright cotton goods and stacks of brilliantly painted pottery which he was taking southward to exchange for the cacao and feather-work of Honduras.

Let us keep the picture of that maritime merchant

197

in our minds, for it induces a more accurate conception of pre-Columbian America than we can get from any historical text-book in our schools.

America was the domain of nations whose high achievement in the arts and sciences was founded on and supported by a solid basis of trade and manufacturing, as well as on the highly developed agriculture already noted. Both coasts of both continents were washed by the bow waves of countless canoes of commerce—canoes even larger than the one Columbus hailed off Bonacca. The extensive grain- and cotton-fields of the interior were crisscrossed by fine roads linking industrial city with industrial city. And "fine roads" means not narrow, muddy trails, but *fine roads*—broad raised highways of stone that surpass the famous thoroughfares of the Romans, great causeways well-preserved remains of which may still be found running through the bush of Yucatan, Colombia, Venezuela; roads runnings over well-made suspension bridges such as those of Peru, whose central artery of commerce traveled the whole empire, a distance of about twenty-two hundred miles. There were pontoon-bridges, too, culverts, aqueducts, and splendid paving.

It cannot be too much emphasized that those foster-ancestors of ours were traders and manufacturers as well as farmers. They knew the uses of credit as a supporting fabric for the life of a commercial nation, and loans were made without excessive interest.

Finally, they even had their rotary clubs and their chambers of commerce! And trade guilds—in the medieval European manner—were very common, with patron saints for each craft and fasts and festivals for the special god of this or that trade, such as the special fiesta to their own beneficent deity which the members of the Maya cacao trade held in the month Muan.

It is no exaggeration to say that ancient America was built by business men. But there are fewer traces left of the Maya business men than of some others. The archæologist who is delving into the past of the people of Central America works under a much greater handicap than he who is trying to gain light on the nature of the ancient people of Peru or of Arizona. For the arid climate of the coastal regions of Peru and of our Southwestern States has permitted objects of wood and skin and even of cloth to survive until this day, whereas the dampness of Central America has wiped out nearly every vestige of the Mayas except such articles as are made of stone and metal. Only two or three small samples of Maya textiles have ever been found, but we may be sure that the Mayas were expert in the textile arts, because of the representations of elaborate dresses carved on the stone monuments.

The ancient Mayas evidently were masters of interweaving and embroidery, as the Mayas of even modern times have been. There are still some parts of Central America in which the women make their own *huipiles,* one-piece garments that hang from the shoulders to midcalf. But, alas, the advance of the white man's machine civilization is ending embroidery as it is ending most native crafts and industries, and nowadays the great majority of Maya women buy cheap cotton-print dresses from Mexican and other mixed-breed traders, or from the Syrian peddlers who dominate much of the small business of Central America.

The reports of the early Spanish explorers and discoverers are enthusiastic about the beautiful and intricate designs on the costumes of the natives of the Maya territory. Indeed, so highly did the Spaniards think of the Maya ability in the textile arts that much of the tribute demanded of the Mayas by the Spaniards was in cloth. When Lieutenant Cook—who afterward became the famous Captain Cook who explored the Pacific Ocean—traveled overland from Bacalar to Mérida in Yucatan in 1765, he wrote describing the beauty of the Maya women and the loveliness of their white-cotton smocks embroidered with flowers around the bottom, the identical garments worn by many Maya women to this day. It is too bad that the Spanish discoverers did not take a few artists

200

with them so that we might have actual drawings of the designs used in Maya handiwork. But we do gain a fairly good knowledge of the textiles from the reproductions of them in stone, just as we know that the Mayas were skilled in basketwork from the imitations of basket weaves that have been found painted on pottery.

Of course pottery will withstand dampness, if cloth will not. Enough Maya pottery has been found for us to know that the people who lived in Guatemala in the time of Charlemagne and in Yucatan in the time of William the Conqueror had reached a high point of development in mastering the art of ceramics. The best Maya pottery yet found, however, is not equal to the best product of Peru. A comparison of the types of pottery discovered in different areas is often of great use to the investigator who is trying to trace ancient trade routes. For instance, the distinguished German anthropologist Seler has pointed out that the discovery of pottery in Guatemala similar to vessels of the Tarascan region in Mexico indicates a trip of some seven hundred miles.

Some of the better-class ware of the Mayas is made of well-mixed clay skilfully fired, and covered with a lovely slip on which designs were often beautifully engraved or painted. Reds, yellows, greens, and terra-cotta are shades much used by the Mayas. White and brown are sometimes found, black is rare.

But the figures used in decorating vessels are often outlined in black. Much Maya pottery was shaped by hand, but a considerable percentage was made in molds. Where vessels are decorated in relief, this superimposed work was often done by hand.

The majority of experts are convinced that the Mayas did not have the potter's wheel—which is also supposed to have been unknown to other American nations. But Mercer, who made extensive investigations of this subject, maintained vigorously that they did have the potter's wheel, and described a similar device he found in use in Yucatan in modern times. At any rate, we know that in some localities a block turned by the heel and the toe was employed beneath the pot while it was being shaped, and this block is still being used in northern Yucatan. It was very usual to decorate pottery with incised designs as well as with paintings and applied decorations in relief. Pottery was sometimes stamped, but not many vessels with designs of this kind have been found yet.

Although the best Maya pottery, which is called the polychrome variety and is decorated in two, three or more colors—generally red, yellow, orange-and-black, or some of these colors—looks so glossy that one would at first believe it to be glazed, the truth is that it is polished. In fact, it is questionable whether any of the ceramic workers of America understood the process of glazing. Natives of the valley of the

Rio Grande, which now forms part of the boundary between the United States and Mexico, did make some use of a glazed paint, but a knowledge of this art seems to have died out soon after it was discovered, and it is not known to the modern natives of that region.

Inasmuch as a great deal of the peninsula of Yucatan consists of a coral reef, throughout much of it no metallic ores may be found. Despite this handicap the Mayas attained a high degree of proficiency in the art of metalworking, using ores they brought in from outside. They worked gold and silver skilfully, as well as various precious or semi-precious stones.

Such pearls and emeralds as the Mayas may have had were probably imported in their large sailing-canoes from Colombia—about twelve hundred miles away. It is even possible that some of the pearls and emeralds possessed by the peoples of upland Mexico reached them through the services of the Maya traders who had been to Colombia. The Maya turquoise is supposed to have come from what is our State of New Mexico, a distance of fourteen hundred miles by sea and land, or eighteen hundred by land alone, from the heart of the country where Kukulcan was worshiped. Even if the trade range of the Mayas was limited to Colombia on the south and New Mexico on the north, these are very respectable distances indeed to have been covered by people who were forced to travel either on foot or by canoe and sail-boat.

Copper bells and copper anklets were among the forms of currency used by the Mayas, with coco-seed, stone disks, red shells, and feathers.

Such things as we have been discussing—textiles, pottery, metalwork—and any other vestiges that have come down to us from the nation which once made the Yucatan peninsula a bee-hive of industry, help us a good deal in reconstructing ancient trade routes, but much painstaking classification must be done before we shall know as much as we should like to know. For example, the finding of similar types of pottery in areas wide apart assuredly indicates the existence of trade between those areas, but we might know a good deal more if we would take the pains to analyze the materials of which the pottery was made, and thus locate not only the places where it was used but the places where it was manufactured.

Maya pottery, wood-carving, and textiles of cotton and the "nequen" cloth (probably made of the plant we call henequen) were carried north and south in the great sailing-canoes that sought pearls in Colombia and copper in New Spain (Cuba); and, as we have seen, the interior of Central America was a net-work of commercial roads and trails. A great high-way of commerce linked the cities of northern Yucatan with the towns of the Toltecs and other peoples

204

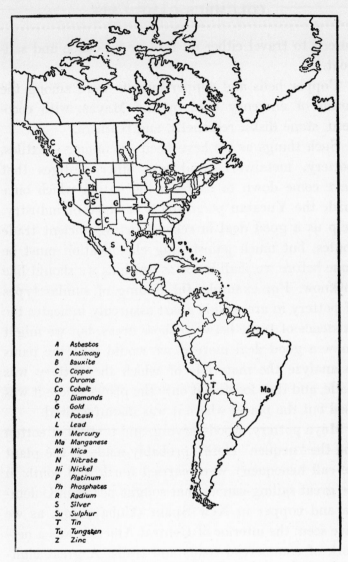

A   Asbestos
An  Antimony
B   Bauxite
C   Copper
Ch  Chrome
Co  Cobalt
D   Diamonds
G   Gold
K   Potash
L   Lead
M   Mercury
Ma  Manganese
Mi  Mica
N   Nitrate
Ni  Nickel
P   Platinum
Ph  Phosphates
R   Radium
S   Silver
Su  Sulphur
T   Tin
Tu  Tungsten
Z   Zinc

Map showing disposition of minerals and rare stones in
North and South America

in upland Mexico. An offshoot of this runs backward through the modern State of Campeche to connect with the Gulf of Honduras near the Guatemala-Honduras boundary. Cortez reported that after crossing the Usamacinta River, which starts in the highlands of Guatemala and flows into the Gulf of Mexico near the border of the States of Campeche and Tabasco, he came to a district called Acalan, whose inhabitants had trading-posts on the Honduras border and in the region of the Golfo Dulce, in the southeastern part of the modern Guatemala. There is not much doubt that such people were in touch with an ancient trading city the ruins of which I discovered in 1928 and named Ollitas, as it is called by the modern natives on account of the many little jars (*ollitas*) found there among the ruins of the buildings that once stood upon the great acropolis. Ollitas is in an ideal location, having been built mainly on two slight elevations of dry ground with good drainage and with a brook passing between them that supplied the ancient inhabitants with their water for drinking. This brook flows a quarter of a mile to a creek, navigable for large canoes, which flows into the Sarstoon River two miles away, just above its mouth on the Gulf of Honduras.

Sarstoon Hill, which throws its afternoon shadow from its twelve hundred feet of steep height almost over the ruins of the old town, probably supplied the necessary stone for the temples the inhabitants of Ollitas erected to various gods, among whom very likely was Ekchuah, the Maya god of trade and travel, worshiped by merchants. It is known that the inhabitants of the interior of the peninsula of Yucatan had a considerable trade with Uloa—part of modern Honduras—in salt, textiles, and slaves exchanged for cacao and stone money. Ollitas is so situated as to have been very probably concerned with this trade. But I believe it was even more important as a post on a route crossing the entire peninsula of Yucatan.

Ancient traders who had brought pearls and perhaps emeralds in canoes from Colombia, destined for Mexico, could have avoided a rough voyage of approximately six hundred miles around the peninsula of Yucatan by going up the Sarstoon River to the head of navigation, and carrying the freight overland from there a short distance to the head-waters of the Pasion River, which flows into the Usumacinta River, which in turn eventually flows into the Gulf of Mexico near the border between Campeche and Tabasco. The head-waters of the Pasion River have been very little explored, and I should wish to make a first-hand inspection of that region before proposing a detailed reconstruction of the ancient overland connection I believe existed between the Sarstoon and rivers flowing into the Gulf of Mexico.

But any tourist to Guatemala City who will look

at the large and excellent outdoor relief map maintained by the Guatemalan Government, in one of the parks of its capital, will see that the Sarstoon-Pasion route I am suggesting seems to offer both a shorter and a more level overland trek than a carry from any other river in the eastern part of Central America to any other river connecting with the west coast of that isthmus.

It is not, then, using more than a legitimate amount of reconstructive imagination to visualize Ollitas as a once busy seaport, where canoes were repaired, crews rested, and goods brought up from the south in the heavy sea-going Maya canoes, with thirty or more paddlers, were transhipped to lighter, smaller river canoes capable of following the northern upper branch of the Sarstoon to where its dimensions are hardly greater than those of a brook.

In 1926 the Mason-Spinden expedition found a number of ruined trading towns with vestiges of ancient harbors, canals, lighthouse temples, and other adjuncts of trade suggesting that there had once been a rather important maritime trade route down the eastern side of the Yucatan peninsula. It is likely, however, that the trade was purely Maya, and that this route served to connect the great cities of northern Yucatan with southern Central America. Goods from Chichen Itza, Coba, and other cities in the interior doubtless reached the east coast by such roads

Building at Chichen Itza showing masks of Kukulcan—about tenth
century A.D.

as one fifty feet wide and from four to ten feet high found by the Mason-Blodgett expedition in 1928, linking the city of Ixil with the city of Coba.

There is much more evidence of trade between northern Yucatan and southern Central America over such a route than there is by inland trails southward from Yucatan. On the other hand, there is good reason to believe that goods destined for Mexico and North America from southern Central America or South America passed over the Yucatan peninsula by taking advantage of such river routes with short carries as the Sarstoon-Pasion route suggested above. In modern times vicious hurricanes assail the eastern shore of Yucatan during the rainy season, from May to December. The waters of the Yucatan Channel, between the northeast tip of Yucatan and Cuba, are notoriously treacherous. Ancient mariners in their big sailing-canoes, even the double ones described by the Spaniards as unusually seaworthy, would have had every reason to avoid the dangerous voyage around Cape Catoche—the northeast tip of the Yucatan peninsula—if they could possibly do so.

Up until nearly the end of their history, before the arrival of the Spaniards, the story of the Mayas was the story of the growth of manufacturing and commerce. It is difficult to give too much significance to the fact, already mentioned, that the Spaniards considered *cloth* to be the typical Maya product for the

209

levy of tribute, rather than some kind of precious stone. That is, a manufactured product rather than a natural raw material represented the wealth of the Mayas. The Mayas dealt drastically with thieves, which is not apt to be the case with a purely agricultural people. If the Maya thief were unable to return the property he had stolen, he was made a slave.

We have already seen that the tendency in the history of Maya government was centrifugal, that is to say that, as time went on, whatever central power there may have been originally, rapidly declined, while the power of individual trading cities rose and rose. By the twelfth century A.D., the network of Maya trading cities presented a very good analogy to the famous Hanseatic League of trading cities in Europe. Communications among these cities were extraordinarily close, despite the fact that the Mayas had no draft animals. But they had human couriers capable of covering many miles in a day's run, and there was a certain advantage in this very absence of beasts of burden. Whereas in the United States to-day four fifths of the cereal foods we raise is consumed by domestic animals of one kind or another, the Mayas had their entire food supply for the sustenance of human kind, including that large percentage of the population concerned with building public works such as the great roads constructed for the

210

combined use of the pilgrims of religion and the caravans of commerce.

To have a true picture of Maya life, however, not only must we visualize these ancient Americans as manufacturers and traders; we must keep in mind the fact that *they were essentially a peaceful people.* Of course, as the world goes, nomads and pirates are probably the most warlike of all human groupings. Yet there have been many nations conspicuous for their success in manufacturing and commerce which have not been loath to push the boundaries of that commerce at the point of the sword. Rome and Carthage are ancient examples, and for modern ones we have only to look at France, Germany, Italy, the British Empire, and the United States.

But the more we learn about the Mayas the more are we impressed with the essentially peaceful nature of their civilization. On the whole the scenes depicted on the walls of temples or on the surfaces of monuments are very little concerned with soldiers and war. At some of the older sites, such as Copan, Quirigua, and Palenque, "armed figures are not seen at all," as Joyce points out, "for the axe which appears at the two latter sites is obviously a purely ceremonial object." However, as the same distinguished authority has shown, one weapon in the hands of a figure shown on a monument at Menche (also called Yaxchilan) seems to be similar to the "swords seen by

211

Columbus in one of the Bay islands of Honduras, consisting of sharp flakings of stone set in a groove in a wooden haft, held there by a lashing of fish gut."

To judge by the testimony of Maya art, neither bows, slings, nor the dart-throwers which were widely spread over America were used by the main body of the Maya nation until very late in their history. An exception is the Kakchiquel branch of the Mayas, which was always warlike, and which had the bow as a weapon, in addition to the sling, the blowgun, the ax, and the club. The other divisions of the Maya people probably did not possess the bow until it was brought down to Yucatan by the Toltec mercenaries from the highlands of Mexico in the twelfth century after Christ. After the bow was introduced, it was used mainly by the lower classes, the spear continuing to be the weapon of the nobility.

The Mayas employed a variety of armor and devices for protection. In Chiapas the Spaniards found them using long shields which covered most of their body and could be rolled up and carried under an arm when not in use. A commoner shield was a good deal smaller than this and was either square or round. In the well-known scene depicted in relief on the wall of the Temple of the Tigers at Chichen Itza, one warrior is seen wearing a turtle-shell as a corselet. And Bernal Diaz speaks of the use of turtle-shells as shields by natives in the country west of the Tabasco

River. Cotton armor, heavily quilted, was in wide use in Yucatan at the time of the beginning of the conquest. Probably it had reached Yucatan from Mexico, for heavily quilted cotton armor was much employed by the Aztecs in their wars with the men-at-arms under Cortez.

Sometimes the cotton corselets were filled with salt to make them more resistant, and a wooden helmet was worn by some of the officers. The skins of jaguars and pumas seem to have been used as badges of rank. The Popol Vuh says that the Quiché, in defense of a fortress, used an ingenious bomb consisting of a gourd filled with hornets! The Yucatecans, as the Mayas living in Yucatan were called by the Spaniards, had a custom of appropriating the jaw-bones of their dead enemies, not to be used as weapons in the Biblical manner but to be worn as armlets.

Drums and trumpets of conch-shell were much employed to move men into battle, and we have an ancient account of how frightened the Kakchiquel were by the terrific noise made by these drums and trumpets of the Quiché in descending on them from a mountain. However, in this battle the warlike Kakchiquel were victorious as they generally were, and succeeded in capturing two of the kings of the Quiché, who gave over to the victors one of the Quiché gods. It was always considered very desirable to capture a god of the enemy. The gods were

213

probably idols, and it is believed that most of them were made of wood, so few have archæologists succeeded in finding.

The very manner in which their armies were organized, with a priest at the head as already noted, indicates that the Mayas were not a warlike people. No large standing army was maintained, the real strength of the military force lying in the reserves called Holcanes, who engaged in ordinary commercial, industrial, and agricultural activities except when war was actually in progress. These militiamen were paid by the generals rather than by the State, which seems a most unfair as well as inefficient procedure. However, the food of the militiamen was provided by the public, although the soldiers' wives were expected to cook it.

In times of great national danger every man capable of bearing arms was called to the colors. Bishop Landa tells us that old men of the Maya nation who were still alive in his time could remember what a nuisance the demobilized soldiers were after peace had been declared, inasmuch as they seemed to expect the whole nation to provide a long-lasting picnic for their benefit.

Maya history contains one lesson clearly written for all who care to read. This lesson is pointed out by the unmistakable evidence that as the Mayas became more warlike, toward the latter part of their domination in Central America, they became less and less efficient in the arts and sciences, with the exception of one art—architecture.

Indeed, one who studies the history of the early American peoples can find much reason to conclude that an important factor in bringing the earlier Mayas to a higher degree of civilization than any other American people was that they wasted less effort on war than any other nation except perhaps the Pueblos. The people of the Incas and the Aztecs, to take two examples, were far more warlike than the Mayas and far more successful in imperialistic schemes, but were demonstrably inferior in civilization. And there can be no doubt that the Mayas of the Late Empire, as the period of the League of Mayapan is sometimes called, were more belligerent than the Mayas of the First Empire, and were inferior to the latter in all arts but architecture, an art which often receives impetus from release of the warlike spirit.

However, I strongly disagree with the statement of J. Eric Thompson that "the Mayas of the Late Empire were a highly warlike nation." Mr. Thompson thinks this is proved because the Central Americans bitterly resisted the Spanish invasion and were not entirely subdued until the end of the seventeenth century. But the fact that a man fights stubbornly in defense of his home does not mean that he is a belligerent person. And the same thing is true of entire peoples.

Taking the Mayas as a whole, they were assuredly not given to extending their own territory by raiding weaker nations on their borders in the manner of the Incas and Aztecs in America, and of the Romans, Goths, and Normans on the other side of the Atlantic. Even when the Spaniards came, the Mayas received them peacefully at first, and did not fight until it was evident that the white strangers were ruthless robbers. When they did begin to fight they put up a desperate struggle, but although they greatly outnumbered the invaders, the latter, with their steel armor, guns, and cavalry, had a tremendous advantage in weapons. Many of the natives considered the Europeans gods or half-gods, and some of them thought that the cavalryman and his horse were one animal of supernatural power. How pathetic is the account of that battle in which the natives attempted to seize the legs of the horses!

By this time, of course, the Mayas had bows and reed arrows tipped with obsidian, or volcanic glass, yet such missiles could make little impression on steel armor. The Spaniards never underrated their own valor in their accounts of their combats with the natives, and usually greatly overestimated the size of the latter's forces. We must bear this in mind in reading about the Battle of Tihoo, where two hundred

216

Spaniards routed an American army variously estimated at from forty thousand to seventy thousand
fighting men. This was the most sanguinary battle in
the history of the conquest of Yucatan, and ended in
the complete rout of the Mayas. They never rallied
again for a general battle, but they kept up guerrilla
warfare for nearly two centuries, or until their last
stronghold was snuffed out on Flores Island in Lake
Peten. And after the Mexicans had thrown off the
Spanish yoke, the red men rebelled against the Mexicans and some of them have succeeded in keeping
their virtual independence to this day.

Traces of defensive works are rare throughout the
Maya territory, and with the exception of a few remnants of fortifications on the summits of mountains
in western Guatemala, most of such vestiges are in
northern and eastern Yucatan—that is, the site of
the last stronghold of Maya culture. There are walls
around the three cities of Tuluum, Xelha, and
Xkaret—all on the east coast of Yucatan. But even
these are defensive in nature and are not very for-
midable from the point of view of military engineering. Xelha and Xkaret each has a small harbor capable of holding a few Maya canoes. There is no reason to think, however, that these were ever anything
but trading vessels, and there is no record of the
Mayas indulging in naval warfare at all.

If you have ever visited Bermuda you will understand what an easy time most of the Mayas had making their public buildings of stone. In Bermuda when you wish to build a house you simply buy a piece of ground, and then excavate the limestone which is the basis of the whole island, sawing it up into blocks of suitable size for your dwelling. This is what the Mayas did throughout most of their territory. However, their walls were often very thick, with a heavy rubble inside faced by cut stone, which itself was sometimes covered with stucco. Façades were decorated lavishly, especially the upper part. The Mayas were fond of cornices, or projecting tiers of stone. These are even more in evidence in the northern area, where architecture reached its height, than in the southern area. In many cases hardly a square foot of wall space was left unembellished and door-jambs and lintels also were a favorite place to apply decoration, irrespective of whether the lintels were of stone or of wood. Most of the Maya woodwork which has survived in architecture consists of heavy lintels of the *sapote* tree. The Mayas were much given to painting their sculptures, as the Greeks did. In some cases so many successive coats of paint were applied that the effect of the original stone carving has been somewhat injured.

The outstanding form of façade decoration was what archæologists call the mask panel. This mask panel was used to embellish the fronts of buildings

218

and was adorned with faces carved in stone, but so highly conventionalized that the lay observer might not recognize them as faces at all. A good example is shown in the frontispiece of this book, a photograph of the faces of rain-gods from the chapel and nunnery at Chichen Itza. The adjoining parts of these two buildings are literally covered with such representations of the great god Kukulcan with the grotesque long snout which he was supposed to assume when he was concerning himself with rain.

Sometimes instead of the conventionalized god faces, buildings were decorated with realistic human faces affixed to the walls, as in temples which the Mason-Spinden expedition found at Acomal, Quintana Roo. In the earlier and southern efflorescence of architecture the details of mask panels were worked out in stucco as a rule, but later the faces of gods were actually carved into the stone itself. Decorations in intaglio or relief with purely geometric patterns were also much used for façades, particularly in the northern part of the Maya country. The huge house of the governor at Uxmal, Yucatan, three hundred and thirty feet long and the longest building left behind by the Mayas anywhere, is literally covered with such geometric decoration.

On the other hand, the use of stelæ, or monuments, was much commoner in the south than in the north. For a good while the Mayas were in the habit of erecting one of these monuments every twenty years, with inscriptions carved upon it, and it is from these monuments that most of our dates have been derived. Most of the monuments thus far found seem to have been definitely connected with buildings, especially with temples.

In the south, cities were often laid out in a regular plan about an acropolis or raised mound. In the north the planning was more haphazard, but in both areas at times there seems to have been a tendency to lay out cities with a relation to the points of the compass. Never forget that every Maya building of any importance was raised upon some sort of sub-structure, varying in height from six inches to more than a hundred feet. The tallest Maya buildings are those in Tikal, Guatemala, the roofs of some of the temples being about one hundred and eighty feet above the ground. A typical Maya chamber was a plain rectangular room, with very thick walls, few or no windows, and many doors. The interior roof was often roughly arch-shaped, but the Mayas never dis-covered the principle of the true arch with the key-stone. Instead they used the false or corbeled arch, advancing successive courses of stone until the little space left at the top between the walls was bridged by one large stone. In the false arch each stone had to support itself, and this necessitated a great deal of bulk in the walls.

Professor W. H. Holmes estimates that in the palace of the governor at Uxmal there are more than two hundred thousand cubic feet of solid masonry and only about one hundred and ten thousand cubic feet of interior space. And he thinks that if you include the masonry in the substructure of the building, you have forty times as much stonework as interior space. Expert as they were in façade-decoration, the Mayas were not especially advanced in the engineering side of building, and in handling heavy masses of masonry they were distinctly inferior to the Peruvians.

Because they were under the necessity of making their walls very thick, as just explained, their usual method of constructing a building of more than one story was to set each story behind the former one on a solid substructure, giving the entire edifice the appearance of a great flight of steps. At Paalmul, however, I found a two-story building with the second story directly above the first, and other examples of the same thing have been found elsewhere. There is a five-story building at Tikal, Guatemala, and four-story buildings at Sayil, Yucatan, and Palenque, Chiapas. One peculiar feature of Maya architecture which it would not do to omit mentioning was the roof comb. Sometimes this was a mere crest of stonework and stucco, running along the middle of the roof of the building; at other times it was a continuation of the front surface technically known as a "flying

221

façade." It gave space on which to apply the embellishments of their art.

The setback principle resorted to lately in the skyscrapers of New York, in order to permit a little light and air to filter down into the cañons which are the streets of that horrible city, seems to have been invented by the Mayas. And perhaps it was invented out of sheer ignorance of how to avoid it, as in the case of a building of two or three stories, just described.

One of the most interesting structures found in the Maya area is what archæologists call the "ball-court." This consists of a flat court between two high, perpendicular walls, two opposite temples usually filling up the other two ends of the quadrangle. One of the prettiest controversies in archæology has arisen concerning the origin and significance of these ball-courts. The popular theory, which we shall examine in the next chapter, is that the ball-court was brought to Central America by the Toltecs of Mexico, who are believed by some scientists to have conquered the Mayas of Yucatan about 1200 A.D.

Whether the Mayas were conquered by foreigners or fell into civil strife and destroyed themselves, there is no doubt that there were many civil wars toward the end of the Maya supremacy in Central America, and that the story of the rise and downfall of the Maya people is the story of the gradual decline of a

222

healthy and vigorous interest in the arts of peace and the commerce by which they were spread, and the gradual rise of a spirit of imperialism and inter-tribal jealousy leading to the decay and collapse of the glorious civilization which had gone before. Here is an object-lesson that modern nations would do well to take to heart!

# CHAPTER XI

## BASKET-BALL AND THE TOLTECS

BASKET-BALL and archæology may seem to have little in common, but one of the moot points in the history of civilization on this hemisphere before the arrival of the white man concerns an ancient American ball game which was a prototype of basket-ball.

A few tourists with enough originality to care about the remarkable antiquities of America have seen at Chichen Itza the remains of a great ball-court. From one wall there still projects a stone ring, and a similar ring had formerly been fixed in the face of the opposite wall. Each ring served as a goal for a team of Maya ball-players, and the ball was a solid one of native rubber. Scoring was very difficult, for the diameter of the ball nearly equaled that inside the rings—set, by the way, at right angles to the horizontal plane in which the "baskets" of our game are laid. That is to say, in the Indian game the ball had to be pushed through the rings from the side, not dropped through from above as in basket-ball. So difficult was it to force the ball through either ring that the first performance of this feat constituted victory for the side accomplishing it. And we are told that the frenzied "rooters" of those times were wont to shower upon the lucky player who had scored a "basket" their jewels and sometimes their clothing as well!

The Spanish conquerors found the Aztecs playing this game in the highlands of Mexico. The Aztecs called the game *Tlachtli* or *Tlaxtli* (pounounced *tlashtlee*). The following description of the game is left us by Herrera, who accompanied Cortez to the court of Montezuma; but we should note that the game was much more like basket-ball, with which Herrera was, of course, unfamiliar, than like tennis, to which he compares it.

The Emperor took much delight in seeing the game of ball which the Spaniards have since prohibited due to the mischief which often happens at the game. By the Aztecs this game was called *tlachtli*—being like our tennis. The ball was made from the gum of a tree that grows in hot countries, which, after having holes made in it, distills great white drops that soon harden and being worked and molded together, this material turns as black as pitch.

Note that the Spanish conquerors were unfamiliar with rubber, which is one of the many gifts of America to the world.

The balls made thereof, although quite hard and heavy to the hand, did bound and fly as well as our footballs and there was no need to blow them, nor did they use staves. They struck the ball with any part of the body as it happened or as they could most conveniently. Sometimes he lost who touched it with any other part but his hips, which was looked upon among them as very dextrous and for the purpose that the ball might rebound better they fastened a piece of stiff leather to their hips. They might strike the ball every time it rebounded, which it would do several times one after another, in so much that it looked as if it had been alive. They played in parties, so many on each side, for a load of mantles or what the gamesters could afford. They also played for gold or feather work and sometimes they played themselves away. The place where they played was a ground room, long, narrow and high and higher at the sides than at the ends. They kept the walls plastered and smooth, also the floor. On the side walls they fixed certain stones like those used in a mill, with a hole quite through the middle. The hole was just as big as the ball and he who could strike it through thereby won the game, and in token of its being an extraordinary success which rarely happened, he had the right to all the cloaks of all the lookers-on.

It was very pleasant to see that as soon as ever the ball was in the hole, those standing by took to their heels, running away with all their might to save their cloaks, laughing and rejoicing, while others scoured after them to secure their cloaks for the winner, who was obliged to offer some sacrifice to the idol of the Court and to the stone whose hole the ball had passed.

Every Court had a temple day where at midnight

they performed certain ceremonies and enchantments on the two walls and on the middle of the floor, singing certain songs or ballads, after which a priest of the Great Temple went with some of their religious men to bless it. He uttered some words, threw the ball about the court four times (toward the four points of the compass) and then it was consecrated and might be played in, but not before.

The owner of the Court, who was also a lord, never played without making some offering and performing some ceremony to the Idol of the Game, which shows how superstitious they were even in their diversions.

Notice that it was the Aztecs whom the Spaniards first saw playing this game. Scientists have been inclined to believe that the Aztecs got the sport from their predecessors the Toltecs. The latter have been thought to have carried the game to northern Yucatan, the northern part of the area occupied by the Maya civilization, when Toltec mercenaries were imported by the ruler of the city of Mayapan to help in civil war against other Maya cities. That was toward the end of the twelfth century, A.D.

The fact that until recently the ball-courts found in the Maya area were all located in the northern part in conjunction with such other supposedly Toltec features of architecture as flat roofs and stone columns in the shape of rattlesnake rain-gods, has given force to the theory that the ball-court was essentially

227

a Toltec rather than a Maya institution. But a few months before this paragraph was written, Mr. Frans Blom, of Tulane University, reported finding ball-courts in the southern part of the Maya territory, the seat of the so-called Old Empire.

This brings us to one of the greatest puzzles in American pre-history. A few of the questions reflecting the puzzle might be set down as follows: (1) Was there ever such a people as the Toltecs? (2) If there was, were the Mayas older than the Toltecs, and did they influence the Toltecs more than the Toltecs influenced them, or vice versa? (3) Were ball-courts first built by Mayas or by Toltecs?

It is fair to you readers to admit that there are scientists of considerable standing who question whether the Toltecs ever existed at all. On the other side of this controversy there are scientists of equal standing who not only contend that the Toltecs were an actual people, but who can tell you many details about their government, their history, and the personalities of some of their leaders. The Toltec question is inextricably bound up with the question of the identity of Quetzalcoatl, Toltec wind- and rain-god. Now, there is no doubt that this god was the equivalent of the Maya Kukulcan by the very derivation of the two names. (Quetzal and Kukul are both names for the quetzal, which to-day is the national bird of Guatemala; Coatl and Kan are two words for snake.)

Ball court and cast "basket" at Chichen Itza

You may remember that earlier in this book we spoke of how almost everywhere in America the natives had a legend concerning the arrival of a white-clad, bearded man who brought culture from the east. This legend was of incalculable aid to the Spanish conquerors. They were white and bearded, and they reached Mexico in a year Ce Acatl, which means a year of the morning star, associated with Quetzalcoatl. The superstitious natives regarded Cortez as a personification of the ancient rain-god who was supposed to have brought culture to Mexico from the east in the dawn of history. This confusion of identities made possible the conquest of the whole continent by about two hundred white men, the most dramatic conquest in the history of the world.

But now to go back. Archæologists are pretty well agreed that the legend about Quetzalcoatl bringing culture to Mexico from the east refers to the intrusion of Maya culture into Mexico. (Yucatan is east of modern Mexico City.) But archæologists are in disagreement as to whether Quetzalcoatl was really a god or whether he was actually a man who later became a god. *Those scientists who speak with most certainty and definiteness about the Toltecs are inclined to think that Quetzalcoatl once actually lived in this world.*

Dr. Herbert J. Spinden of the Brooklyn Museum, who, like Dr. A. M. Tozzer of Harvard, is a leader in the scientific group which professes to know a good deal about the Toltecs, says:

Quetzalcoatl, perhaps the most delightful figure in ancient American history, was Emperor, artist, scientist, and humanist philosopher. He established orders in knighthood as well as the coronation ceremonies used by the later Mexican chiefs. He developed the various industrial arts and built up a wide trade in cacao and other products. As a patron of the peripatetic merchant he appears under the name of Nacxitl, which means four-way foot. Apotheosis being an idea strongly fixed among the Toltecs, Quetzalcoatl was deified as Tatchel, God of Winds, on account of his support of the Mayan god of rain storms, and for his astronomical work he was further deified as the God of the Planet Venus.

In his preface to my book, "Silver Cities of Yucatan," Dr. Spinden gives further details about Quetzalcoatl as follows:

Quetzalcoatl, Emperor of the Toltecs, and conqueror of the Mayas—priest, scientist and architect in one commanding individual—was a contemporary of Henry II and Richard the Lion Hearted. He died in far off days before a reluctant King John signed the Magna Charta of English liberties. His holdings in Mexico and Central America were several times more extensive than the holdings of those puissant monarchs of the Angevin line in France and the British Isles, his philosophy of life was richer and his contributions to the general history of civilization were greater than theirs. Old stone walls in eastern Yucatan are mute evidence of the commerce, religion and art that Quetzalcoatl built up as the expression of his practical and ideal State. He encouraged trade that reached from Colombia to New Mexico, he preached a faith of abnegation and high ethics which later led speculative churchmen to identify him with St. Thomas, and in sculpture and architecture he formed a new and vital compound of the previous achievements of two distinct peoples, the Toltecs of the arid Mexican highlands and the Mayas of the humid lowlands. We can restate three of Quetzalcoatl's personal triumphs in astronomical science corresponding to the years, 1168, 1195 and 1208. We know that he conquered the great city of Chichen Itza in 1191 and erected therein a lofty temple which still bears his name and a round tower which is still an instrument for exact observation of the sun and moon. We know that Quetzalcoatl set up a benign system of local self government among conquered tribes of Guatemala which made those peoples relate his praises in song and story. We know that after his death he was made a god because during his life he had been "a great republican."

We first hear of the Toltecs through the Aztecs. The Aztecs claimed that they themselves originated in the Chicomoztoc, or Seven Caves. This must not be taken literally, any more than the Garden of Eden story must be taken literally. A belief that they orig-

231

inated underground was fairly general among the natives of North America, and Chicomoztoc was simply a part of this myth. But it seems probable that the Aztecs did originate somewhere north of the Valley of Mexico. When they arrived in that valley they found a nation called Chichimac occupying the country and speaking Nahua. The leaders of this Chichimac nation reported to the Aztecs that when they themselves had come to the Valley of Mexico, they had found there the remains of a culture much higher than their own, and to this culture these Chichimac people gave the name Toltec. This name is derived from the city of Tulan or Tollan, said to have been the heart of the Toltec Empire.

There seems to be little doubt that the Aztecs and Chichimacs were both nomads when they reached the Valley of Mexico, and that their knowledge of arts and crafts was learned largely from agriculturists occupying the valley, who told the invaders that their own culture had been derived from a vanished agricultural people which had preceded them, i.e., the Toltecs. Certainly archæologists have found remains of a culture much higher than that of the Aztecs at the so-called Toltec sites, as these were defined for the Aztecs by their predecessors in the Valley of Mexico. It seems, therefore, that there once existed in the valley a nation with a high degree of culture (which played basket-ball). The only question is whether we shall call this people Toltec or something else. And, as Mr. Thomas Joyce of the British Museum says, "As a mere matter of evidence I cannot see that any name can be given to this pre-Aztec culture other than that of Toltec."

Does it really make much difference whether you think that Quetzalcoatl was a distinguished human being, who carried the Maya culture from Yucatan to upland Mexico, or think that he was a mythical personage invented to explain how the Toltecs got their culture from the Mayas? In any case, when all the evidence is in, there is little doubt left that the Mayas were a far older people than the Toltecs, and that the latter gained much of their culture from the former.

But back of the Toltec culture in the highlands of Mexico were several others, remains of which have recently been dug up. Dr. George Vaillant, a leader in the fascinating work of gaining light on these very early civilizations of Mexico, points out that between the pottery remains of some of these ancient cultures there is more difference than there is, for example, between the pottery of the Toltecs and the pottery of the Aztecs. This suggests that if we are going to regard the Toltecs and the Aztecs as two distinct peoples, it is rather indefinite to stamp everything which antedated the Toltecs as the work of one race called "Archaic," or to apply that term to the makers

233

of all hand-fabricated pottery as distinguished from mold-made pottery.

We are here confronting another great riddle. There is a tremendous need for more excavation of the remains of these earliest Mexican cultures—some of them being as much as twenty feet below the surface.

The average man likes a good mystery. He also likes to know the facts. But he does not like to be told, "It may be this way or it may be that way, we cannot be certain just how it is." Yet this last answer is the only answer the careful scientist can yet give to laymen regarding the Toltecs and their predecessors. We are certain there was in the highlands of Mexico before the time of the Aztecs a people more cultivated than the Aztecs, a people to whom it seems plausible to give the name Toltec. But we can be sure of very few things in their history.

How uncertain we are is well evidenced by the fact that in the excellent little book called "Ancient Civilizations of Mexico and Central America," written by Dr. Herbert J. Spinden and published by the American Museum of Natural History, the chapter on this subject is quite different in the revised edition published in 1928 from the chapter on the same subject in the original edition published in 1917. All this because great changes in our conception of the Toltecs have come about through eleven years' work in research—in which research, by the way, Dr. Spinden was one of the leading participants.

We must take with considerable salt the Annals of Quauhtitlan, an account of Toltec history written after the Spanish conquest, which makes definite statements about such alleged historical events as the foundation of the Toltec Government at Cuxhuacan in 726 A.D., and the overthrow of the Toltec Empire in 1070 A.D. with the collapse of the power of Tula. We can tell more about the Toltecs if we hearken to archæologists than if we listen to the accounts of self-styled historians long since dead.

Apparently the Toltecs had a certain amount of sun-worship in their religious life, to judge by the fact that the sun's disk is found in various sculptures. Toltec art seems to have been much influenced by Maya art, and from the Central Americans these early Mexicans are believed to have derived their idea of the great importance of snake-worship, an idea handed on by the Toltecs to the Aztecs and to even more northern tribes.

The fact is that we get a good deal of our alleged knowledge of the Toltecs by inference from observation of the remains of the Mayas, Aztecs, and other peoples. Judging by such remains it appears that the Toltec power at one time extended from what is now Durango in northern Mexico to Nicaragua. It seems likely, therefore, that the imperialism and love of conquest marking the domination of the Aztecs was exhibited before them by the Toltecs.

Some of the ancient Mexican cities identified as Toltec—besides Tula, already mentioned—were Azcapotzalco, now a suburb of modern Mexico City, from which city pottery fragments, beautiful figurines, and other relics of no mean level of ceramic art have been excavated; Xochicalco, "The House of the Flowers"; San Juan Teotihuacan, and Cholula. "Teotihuacan" means "Where the Gods Dwell."

Many tourists to Mexico City have taken time to make the side excursion to Teotihuacan and have seen the impressive roadway called the Pathway of the Dead, the large Pyramid of the Moon, and the larger Pyramid of the Sun, which has more bulk than the famous pyramid of Cheops, in Egypt. The greatest Toltec pyramid is the one at Cholula, in the neighborhood of modern Puebla. Like the Pyramid of the Sun at Teotihuacan, it is inferior to the more famous work of the Egyptians in height, although its summit was more than two hundred feet above the surrounding level—enough to make it an exceedingly impressive landmark, you may be sure. But the base of this Cholula pyramid averages more than one thousand feet on a side, and the structure has three times the volume of the pyramid of Cheops.

The Mayas made nothing so large as these Toltec pyramids, but their own pyramids were better made,

Three faces, with snouts, of
Kukulcan at Uxmal

Courtesy American Museum of Natural History

Chac-Mool—Maya-Toltec

being of rubble faced with cut stone instead of adobe bricks faced with concrete. The Toltec temples also were inferior in construction to Maya edifices of the same sort, and none of the particular temples which are believed to have topped these pyramids is standing now. But it is thought that the typical Toltec building had a flat ceiling supported by wooden timbers, instead of the vaulted stone roof of the Mayas. In comparing the pyramids of America with those of the eastern hemisphere, we must bear in mind that the Americans always made a pyramid with a large flat top, since its first function was to support a temple. This was not so in Egypt, and is itself sufficient to account for the greater height of the needle-pointed pyramids of the Africans.

Cholula, by the way, was still inhabited when the Spaniards reached Mexico. But most of the remains which archæologists have found in the shadow of the biggest pyramid in the world were left by people long antedating the Aztec civilization overthrown by Cortez.

In conclusion, we may remember the Toltecs as the people who are supposed to have invented pulque, now the national drink of Mexico. We may remember them as the people who built the largest pyramid man has ever made. We may remember them as the people who very likely introduced rubber to the Mayas, rubber which they themselves had probably

237

got from the Olmeca people that inhabited the damp country of southern Vera Cruz and western Tabasco.

And we may remember the Toltecs for their courts on which they played the ancient American game of basket-ball.

Eventually we may find that that game and many other features of culture attending it were neither Toltec nor Maya, but were the product of an older people—one of that group of ancient peoples which we lump together under the name "Archaic."

At present it certainly seems that the Toltecs owed much more to the Mayas than the Mayas owed to the Toltecs. That means that in our present state of knowledge the Toltecs are chiefly important as a link between the Mayas and the Aztecs, and, through the Aztecs, between the Mayas and many of the other American peoples north of Central America. For the time being it is chiefly as the torch-bearers of Maya culture from the Isthmus of Tehuantepec nearly to the Great Lakes that the Toltecs seem to deserve to be remembered.

CHAPTER XII

THE AZTECS: THE RISE OF TEMPORAL POWER

A MONG the higher native cultures flourishing in America before the white man came, to the Aztec alone have the descendants of the first white settlers given anything like the recognition deserved. And in view of the general neglect and ignorance of the American civilizations which far surpassed the Aztecs in original achievement, the reputation the people of Montezuma enjoy seems altogether unjust. Yet it is easy to understand how the Aztecs have attracted so much attention. They were people who loved wealth and display. Imperialistic, warlike, bloody, they expended their tremendous energy, wasted their vast vitality in the pursuit of materialism.

Outwardly religious, the Aztecs lacked true piety. Their religion was the worship of things, their ritual the currying of the favor of the gods of battle in order that the Aztec avarice for more territory might be satisfied. Was it by virtue of the very fact that they were not really religious that they managed to make one important contribution to civilization in America —namely, the development of purely temporal power

239

in government at the expense of that rule of the priest which had characterized the civilization of the Toltecs and the Mayas? With this one exception the culture of the Aztecs was all borrowed from earlier and greater peoples, and with this one exception the chief importance the Aztecs have in history is that they served to pass on to other nations to the north of them the elements of Toltec and Maya civilization, much weakened by Aztec abuse of them. But the exception is important. The development of temporal power, had the conquering white man not brought in the same institution, would have put all America tremendously in the debt of the Aztecs.

The Aztecs have had the benefit of a first-class press-agent. Prescott's "Conquest of Mexico" amazed the world with its recital of splendor at the court of Montezuma. Either when he wrote his "Conquest of Peru" his pen had a little less cunning or perhaps the greater remoteness of Peru detracted somewhat from the interest of that story for readers in the United States and Europe. As for the real leaders of early American civilization, the Mayas, Prescott had scarcely heard of them. Moreover, the Spanish conquerors themselves were by nature much better fitted to appreciate the fire of the Inca Empire and the gaudy splendor of the Aztec Empire than the artistic and scientific glory of the Mayas.

Frankly, Maya achievement in these fields was

over the heads of the cutthroats who clustered around Cortez. The picturesque extravagance of the Peruvian and Mexican courts, the efficiency with which the Incas subjugated neighboring nations, and the wanton cruelty and unnecessary bloodiness of the religion of the Aztec warrior were just the sort of things to appeal to the men who had crossed the Atlantic from the country that had perfected the diabolically brutal machinery of the Inquisition.

The fact that, by their religion, special paradises were reserved for warriors killed in battle and for women dying in childbirth, gives us the clue to the social point of view of the Aztecs. They were essentially imperialistic. The first duty of every man was to be a good soldier, and the first duty of every woman was to produce soldiers. But the very fact that a man was judged and honored according to his fighting ability lent Aztec society a democratic tone. There was no such chance for the courtly fop to keep down the vigorous soldier as there was in the France of Louis XIV or in the England even of Elizabeth. The best asset an Aztec father could give his son was the ability to pull a good bow, to wield a mean *macquauitl*, a wooden broadsword edged with volcanic glass and capable of taking off a man's head with one blow.

The bow is the characteristic weapon of the Aztecs, though no one knows where they got it. As said be-

241

fore, the Aztecs seem to have started somewhere north of the Valley of Mexico and pushed their way southward, conquering with their bows the native Nahua, who used the atlatl, or spear-thrower. After a series of fights, lasting from two to twenty years, they reached Chapultepec about 1325. Neighboring tribes did not like the arrogant manners of the Aztecs and in self-protection the new-comers had to enlist the assistance of the King of Colhuacan. They helped him in his own feud with Xochimilco. (One of the sights now shown to tourists in Mexico City is the Chinampas, or Floating Gardens of Xochimilco.)

Remember that civil war is supposed to have disrupted the Toltec Empire about 1220 A.D., although Cholula is said to have maintained a living sample of Toltec culture until the Spaniards arrived. Hence, irrespective of the fact that it is somewhat difficult to fix dates in Aztec history definitely, there seems little doubt that the Aztecs got the torch of Toltec culture at first hand.

Tenochtitlan, the Aztec capital, was founded in 1364 where Mexico City now stands. But unlike the capital of the modern republic, Tenochtitlan was a sort of Venice, a city built on a network of canals. The center of the old city was a big plaza called the Tecpan, situated where the Zocolo, or main plaza, and the National Palace of Mexico are to-day. The chief temples were all on the Tecpan. It was here that were enacted the bloody scenes of sacrifice which gave Prescott the material for some of his most vivid writing. It was always the object of the Aztec general to capture his enemies alive, rather than to kill them. For a dead enemy could only be given to the vultures, but a live one could be offered to the God of War, Huitzilopochtli. The priest always marched into battle ahead of the Aztec warriors. When prisoners were captured they were handed over to the priest and carried back to the capital to have their hearts torn out of their living bodies, in the ritual of the bloodiest religion that ever flourished on the American continent.

A neighboring tribe, the Tlascalans, obligingly fought a battle with the Aztecs every year to see who could get the most prisoners for sacrifice. The Aztecs seem to have had a rudimentary sense of sportsmanship, because it was their custom to give certain captives a chance of liberty by arming them with toy shields and swords and setting each prisoner to defend himself against an Aztec soldier fully armed. If the captive, by a miracle of energy and skill, could succeed in getting the better of six Aztecs in succession he was set at liberty. But the instant he was wounded the priests dragged him away for sacrifice.

Indeed, so important was this matter of taking prisoners that after the archers, the slingers, and the hurlers of javelins had begun a combat from long distance, or even after the men of arms had used their swords and spears at close quarters, the Aztecs would often "fake" a retreat in the hope of getting the enemy to follow them into a trap. The war customs of the Aztecs were imitated to some extend by tribes in what is now the United States, and this practice of cutting out an enemy's heart as a steaming sacrifice to the God of War was emulated by tribes as far north as Canada.

The warrior who could capture a prisoner was considered of infinitely more use to the State than one who merely killed an enemy. The former was rewarded and the latter was not. Ironically or otherwise, the success of the small band of Spaniards under Cortez in vanquishing a huge host of Aztecs was in no small measure due to this ceremonial manner in which the Aztecs made war. That is to say, many of the Spaniards would have been killed except for the determination of the natives to capture the white men alive.

Some of the lists of the tributes the Aztecs collected from the peoples they conquered in war would bring a warm glow to the heart of a merchant. Vast quantities of cotton goods, cotton clothing, bundles of feathers, sacks of cacao, and tiger skins from one nation; amber and emerald and tons of rubber from another; cacao and gold and cochineal from a third; gold and copper and turquoise from a fourth. An

244

Courtesy American Museum of Natural History

Obsidian mirror with gilded wooden frame, reflecting an effigy vessel
from near Tampico

interesting reflection of the activities of the sanitary engineers of those times lies in the fact that the more impecunious people were allowed to pay their tribute in scorpions, snakes, even lice; that is, those who could not contribute wealth were allowed to destroy nuisances!

The genius for organization, exhibited in the completeness with which the Aztec rulers squeezed the last drop of tribute from conquered tribes, is a national characteristic. In their excellences as in their faults, the Aztecs were the Romans of America. Roughly it might be stated this way: they were weak in creation and strong in organization. They were to the Mayas as the Romans were to the Greeks.

Originally the Aztecs consisted of eight allied and interrelated tribes making up the nation Mexica or Mexici—from which we get our modern "Mexico." The tribes were called Calpulli, which means "Great House." The name was taken from a sort of barracks where the older men met to discuss battles and where the young ones were trained in the art of war. Agricultural land was owned by the Calpulli; the Aztecs no more tolerated private ownership of land than did any other of the great nations of ancient America.

In the matter of land tenure the Aztec Empire suggests the powerful nations of medieval Europe more than it suggests Rome. The Aztec emperor was wont to reward his great captains with large grants of land. They in turn divided it up among their followers according to the military ability of the latter. Thus the basis of land tenure was military service. The power in this way engendered carried over into civil government, and virtually all the important executive positions were held by men who had proved themselves mighty in war.

In envisaging the social life of the Calpulli one gets the pleasantest picture afforded by a contemplation of these "Romans of America." For here was not so much the bloodiness and cruelty of war as its stern, silent discipline. Here was not the barbaric golden splendor of court display, but rather the maintenance of that rude virility which had marked the first Aztecs who entered the Valley of Mexico.

Throughout every phase of Aztec society and through all the years of Aztec history—and it might be said that those years were brief enough, for there were only about two centuries between the arrival in the Valley of Mexico and the overthrow of the empire of Montezuma by the Spaniards—we find running this strange duality. That is to say, a gorgeous barbaric splendor existing side by side with a stern, Cromwellian puritanism. More of the latter trait later.

It may surprise us who are so busy nowadays with the effort to abolish war to learn that one of the most warlike peoples that ever lived, the Aztecs, were very

246

happy. There was virtually no fear of starvation or poverty, the fear that lurks in the breasts of ninety per cent of the citizens of a commercial nation like the United States of America. And is there not a good deal to be said for the form of society in which the individual is sure of a tolerably good living, even though he may be called upon at any moment to give up his life? Primitive emotions die hard, and admiration for the warrior is one of them. In our hearts probably most of us admire a nation of warriors like the Romans or the Aztecs more than we admire a nation of tradesmen like the French, British, or Americans of to-day. Civilized though we call ourselves, we still somehow consider it more admirable to get what we want by force than to get it by stealth and trickery. Down with Rotary and Kiwanis! Up with National Guard and Boy Scouts!

However, it is only fair to admit that the Aztecs, like the Mayas and every great American nation of antiquity, had their Rotary Clubs. That is, they had their societies and guilds. The most important guild was the Pochteca, an organization of traveling men. These peripatetic merchants worshiped Yacatecutli. The ritualism with which he was served sometimes included Coyotlinautl, the god of the guild of feather-workers.

Now, these Pochteca came to have a great deal of importance in Mexico. They basked in the smile of the emperor, and only the sons of business men could become business men without the special permission of the ruler. The merchants were exempt from agricultural labor and from jury duty. The most important feature of the Pochteca, however, was their employment as agents of Aztec imperialism. Just as the British oil-man or rubber-man serves the British flag, so they were spies very useful to the emperor, and for this reason were given special privileges and insignia, such as lip-plugs of gold. These merchants were importers as well as exporters. They carried Aztec influence perhaps as far south as Panama and perhaps as far north as Canada.

Just as Rotary Clubs and Kiwanis Clubs to-day interest themselves in matters of civic improvement, the merchants of ancient Tenochtitlan got behind the movement to build a great aqueduct from the springs of the hills of Chapultepec into the heart of the capital. The water of the lake on which the city was virtually superimposed was not drinkable. The importance of transportation facilities was well understood by these merchants who had to import from long distances the cotton for the consumption of their mills just as the owners of cotton-mills in Massachusetts now have to import their raw material from our Southern States.

It is curious that previous writers about the Aztecs have overlooked a salient fact—that is, that the Az-

tecs were the original puritans of America. Not only
did they kill people for stealing corn; they killed them
for committing adultery and they killed them for getting drunk. The situation in the United States of
America to-day is mild and tolerant compared with
the situation in the empire of the Aztecs in regard
to intoxication. Drowning to death was the penalty
for adultery, but trampling to death was the penalty
for drunkenness.

It was really the Aztecs who made America ripe
for puritanism. The historian Sahagún gives us horrible pages filled with homilies of a moral nature
which Aztec parents inflicted on their children. Any
one who is irked by the repressive atmosphere of a
Sunday afternoon in New England can thank his
God that he was not born under Aztec rule.

As would be characteristic of a puritanical community, we find that even the amusements of the
Aztecs had a religious significance. One has to think
back to the England of Cromwell, the vigorous
Roundhead, to find a parallel of a country in which
there was not a moment's relaxation from the consciousness of the dire way in which man was ruled
by the gods. The Mayas loved their gods, the Aztecs
feared theirs.

It is not a mere accident that the Aztecs, who
were puritans, were also very inferior artists. No
puritan civilization has ever produced great art. On

the other hand, it is nothing unusual for puritans to be good fighters. The English under Cromwell fought well, but they produced no art that was worth an empty oyster-shell. The people of the United States of America, puritans to the core, have produced little art worth a plugged nickel—though they are beginning to improve—yet they have always been good fighters. The fact of the matter is that puritanism is an intellectual concept associated with cleanliness, which is associated with death. Death to bacteria. That is to say, sterility. Art is an emotional thing associated with fertility, which is associated with sensuality, which, in puritanical minds, is associated with dirt. No nation that is not sensual can produce great art. That is where the Anglo-Saxons fall down, and that is where the Aztecs fell down.

Indeed, more than any people in ancient America the Aztecs resembled the people of the United States to-day. They were not great artists at all, but they pretended to be. They kept alive the pottery of Cholula, the textiles of the Toltecs, and the architecture of the Mayas in the same way that we Americans keep alive the artistic impetus of Greece in the columns that you may find before almost any American bank in northern New York or eastern Iowa. Like the English, whom they resemble, both in their puritanism and their genius for organization, the Aztecs were much greater in literature than they were in any other art. Here is something no philosopher has ever been able to account for—namely, the fact that a people afraid to be orgiastic may excel in literature when they cannot excel in any other art. The following poem in free verse from an Aztec writer shows the capacity for deep feeling and the tendency to sadness which many Aztec poets have:

All the earth is a grave, and naught escapes it; nothing is so perfect that it does not fall and disappear. The rivers, brooks, fountains, and waters flow on, and never return to their joyous beginnings; they hasten on to the vast realms of Tlaloc, and the wider they spread between their marges the more rapidly do they mold their own sepulchral urns. That which was yesterday is not to-day; and let not that which is to-day trust to to-morrow.

The caverns of earth are filled with pestilential dust, which once was the bones, the flesh, the bodies of great ones who sat upon thrones, deciding causes, ruling assemblies, governing armies, conquering provinces, possessing treasures, tearing down temples, flattering themselves with pride, majesty, fortune, praise, and dominion. These glories have passed like the dark smoke thrown out by the fires of Popocatepetl, leaving no monuments but the rude skins on which they are written.

251

I have already likened the Aztecs to the Romans, the modern Americans and the British; they might be compared also to the Japanese. Romans, Americans, British, and Japanese all have the sort of pronounced ability for organization which characterized the Aztecs; in addition the Japanese are conspicuous for their tendency to borrow outstanding features of the cultures of other people. This predilection for borrowing was characteristic of the ancient Mexicans. The science and art of the Aztecs—including their astronomical knowledge and their calendarical system—was pretty much borrowed from the Toltecs and Mayas.

One excellence of the Aztecs, however, was featherwork. In the manufacture of mosaics, both of feathers and precious stones, they have hardly been equaled by any other people in the entire world. But it is impossible to rank them higher than third in point of culture among the ancient peoples of America. At very best the Aztecs would come after those foremost Americans, the Mayas, who surpassed them in astronomy, architecture, painting, sculpture, ceramics, textiles, and road-building—to mention only a few points.

Nor could the Aztecs be placed ahead of the people of the Incas. For although the Aztecs had worked out a system of writing which was part hieroglyphic and part pictographic, whereas the Peruvians had no

252

Courtesy American Museum of Natural History

Cast of Mexican calendar stone, the original of which is in the Museum of Mexico City

writing at all, the latter easily surpassed the Mexicans in engineering, medicine, weaving, pottery, and painting. Moreover, in many respects the Aztecs were inferior to the Toltecs, and in some—such as the making of pottery—they must rank after the Pueblo peoples of the southwestern United States. So the best possible ranking the Aztecs can be given among ancient American peoples is third place, and they may eventually be placed fourth or fifth.

Even some of the Aztec gods were borrowed. Such was Xipe, the god connected with sacrifice by flaying, who was borrowed from southern Mexico—probably from tribes in Oaxaca, the State in which are the famous ruins of Mitla, believed by many scientists to have been made by the Zapotecs, one of the Mexican nations which reached a degree of considerable culture, although overshadowed by Aztecs, Toltecs, and Mayas.

Another borrowed god was Quetzalcoatl. This deity, almost identical with the Maya sky god, Kukulcan, as we have seen, reached the Aztecs via the Toltecs.

Altogether the Aztecs had a great many gods, far too many to enumerate here. Of course, a large percentage of them were native deities. The Aztec masses worshiped the Earth Mother and the Sky Father. There was also a belief in a god called Ometeuctli, who was vaguely believed to be the Su-

253

preme Deity. But at the head of what might be called the more "living" gods was Tezcatlipoca. Among such warlike people as the Aztecs, of course, the God of War, Huitzilopochtli, was very powerful. But this bloody deity was no more powerful than Tlaloc, the God of Rain. Tlaloc was supposed to have stolen maize from Quetzalcoatl.

It was believed that Tlaloc lived in his own special heaven in the east, a place called Tlalocan, and that he ruled over the souls of those who had died of dropsy or who had been drowned. He was assisted by a number of minor rain-gods called Tlaloque, who helped distribute rain from magic pitchers and produced thunder by striking the pitchers with rods. It is recorded that the Aztecs sacrificed many children to Tlaloc. And if the poor victims wept on their way to the place of sacrifice, it was considered a good omen. There, again, is the typical cruelty of Aztec civilization.

In the early days, when the Aztecs were migratory tribes, the priests, who often went into battle with the troops, were military and temporal as well as religious leaders. But as the Valley of Mexico was settled and agriculture was developed, with the consequent increase in astronomical ritual, the priests found more and more demand on their energies in the field of ceremonialism alone. So, for the first time in American history, there came to be born purely temporal rulers.

As the priest fell back into his purely sacerdotal duties, these temporal rulers were at first usually chosen from the leading warriors. That is, at first they were usually elected. But as the Aztec tribes became more and more settled the matter of the succession of rulers became increasingly hard to decide. From electing a ruler out of a sort of natural aristocracy it came to be understood that the chieftain's title would pass on to a male in his own family. There was a good deal of variety about this. In the Tezcoco tribe the title usually passed from father to son, but in the Tenochtitlan tribe the son would not inherit the power until all the father's brothers had had their turn at it.

Just as it is impossible to keep all individuals at one level, so is it impossible to keep all tribes or nations. In Aztec history two tribes forged ahead of all the others, the tribes of Tezcoco and Tenochtitlan. Then gradually the last named secured domination even over Tezcoco. Montezuma, or Moctezuma, the Aztec chief who was overthrown by the Spaniard Cortez, and whose fame has been kept alive by the writings of the American historian Prescott, was not in fact the Emperor of the Aztecs as he is generally considered. He was simply the ruler of the tribe of Tenochtitlan, the particular tribe that had secured dominance in the Aztec League of Nations.

In American history the Aztecs will be remembered for three things:

First for the strange combination of luxury and puritanism—a contradictory combination which perhaps no other country but the modern United States has exhibited to such a degree as the Aztecs.

Secondly, for the general "bloodiness" of their civilization—of which the most significant single item was a great fondness for war and a high degree of efficiency in the military art. It is interesting to speculate on what might have happened if the militaristic Aztecs had ever fallen afoul of the militaristic people of the Incas of Peru.

Finally and above all, the Aztecs are memorable for their skill in organization, which was best illustrated by their greatest contribution to the list of original American achievements—namely, the development of purely *temporal* power. While European nations, and particularly the English, were separating Church and State on the eastern side of the Atlantic, the Aztecs were doing the same thing in America.

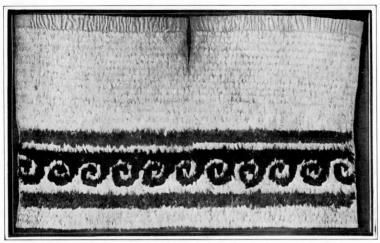

Courtesy American Museum of Natural History

Feather poncho, mostly yellow, with black scroll

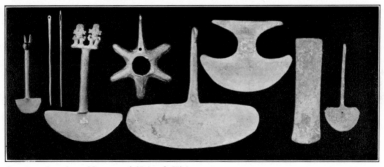

Courtesy American Museum of Natural History

Bronze implements

## CHAPTER XIII

## THE WORLD'S MOST SUCCESSFUL EXPERIMENT IN SOCIALISM

HOW would you like to be born in a country where you had the certainty that you would always have plenty to eat, and the certainty that you would be married at an early age and that your wife and your children also would have plenty to eat?

In the lands we all inhabit to-day a fear of poverty or starvation is never very long absent from the breast of the average man; the question of finding a husband is a matter of frantic concern to most women, and many females wither away in a useless barrenness. But in the country of which I am speaking there is no starvation of any kind, the sexual variety included. In this country there is no poverty whatsoever. On the other hand, there is no wealth except the wealth of the hereditary rulers. Every man is certain of a sufficiency of the necessaries of life, but he may be sure that, irrespective of how original and thoughtful he may be, he may not rise above the level chosen for him at his birth by circumstances. There will be no misfit; the man whom nature has intended to be a cobbler will be a cobbler and the man whom nature has intended to be a musi-

257

cian will be a musician. But it will be impossible for the person of initiative and natural shrewdness to corner any commodity, and make himself wealthy by selling to the nation that which the common effort has created. There will be no place in this country for the heretic or rebel, for all are born with a common aspiration, to serve the State.

This, in short, is Utopia, the Utopia of the Socialist. It is not a dream, however; at least it is not a dream unrealizable. This dream has been realized; the country we are talking about is the Peruvian Empire of the Incas.

But what was the other side of the picture? As just indicated, if no one had to fear the depths, neither could any one aspire to the heights.

From the cradle to the grave the life of the individual was marked out for him; as he was born, so would he die, and he lived his allotted span under the ceaseless supervision of officials. His dress was fixed according to his district; he might not leave his village except at the bidding of the State, and then only for state purposes; he might not even seek a wife outside his own community. An individual of ability might perhaps rise to be one of the subordinate inspectors, but the higher ranks were inexorably closed to him. Even his own family was not entirely under his control, for his daughters, if of exceptional beauty, might be taken by the State to serve in one of the "convents."

Thus, vividly, Thomas Joyce outlines the deadly level dullness of life in the socialistic Empire of Peru. It must have been like living in a jail. A clean, well-ventilated, well-fed jail, but a jail nevertheless.

Trying to visualize what life was like in ancient Peru, I recall some of the words uttered by William James after suffering from the ennui of the community of "uplifters" at Chautauqua. In a revolt from the tameness of that place, the great psychologist exclaimed:

Let me take my chances again in the big outside worldly wilderness with all its sins and sufferings. There are the heights and depths, the precipices and the steep ideals, the gleams of the awful and the infinite; and there is more hope and help a thousand times than in this dead level and quintessence of every mediocrity.

Ancient Peru, of course, did not suffer from the "uninspiring goodness" which Mr. James found at Chautauqua. The deadliness of Peruvian life came from its stifling regimentation. In some respects a pretty fair modern parallel for the land of the Incas was the Prussia of the first decade or so of the twentieth century. Before the World War Prussia had a close regimentation which the people dumbly accepted just as the Peruvians did. Nevertheless both the Prussians and the Peruvians had a capacity for ecstasy which is entirely lacking in the good Chautauquan. Poetry is beyond the possibilities of the type of soul that flourished at the original assemblages at Chautauqua Lake, New York, or thrives in the atmosphere of the modern traveling Chautauqua lecture circuits of Kansas and Nebraska.

But the achievement of poetry and music was not an impossibility to the Prussians, nor was it at all beyond the reach of the Peruvians if we can judge by a few splendid examples of Peruvian poetry handed down, such as the one at the close of this chapter. To repeat, the dullness of life in Peru was the dullness of too much acquiescence, of over-organization, but never the dullness of sterility.

On the whole, it is a pretty safe assumption that at least nine out of ten modern Americans would prefer life in the United States with all its cruelties— with all its unremitting economic struggle and the ever-lurking fear of poverty, with all its heartless repression of normal instincts and its unforgivable waste of human capacities—would prefer life in the United States to life in ancient Peru. For, even though here too we have some of the very regimentation that afflicted the subjects of the Incas, we have no such wholesale restriction of individuality.

But the point to stress now is that Peru proved that socialism will work. Capitalism or some other scheme of social organization may be preferable, but it is ridiculous for advocates of such other systems to argue that socialism is unworkable, for the ancient Peruvians have given us the answer to that. Yet it is difficult to recreate for modern observers a picture of life in the Inca Empire. We have very little material with which to build the picture—just a bit of pigment here and there, recovered for us by the efforts of archæologists and ethnologists.

But there can be no doubt at all about the type of government enforced by the Incas, and there can be no doubt at all that it was successful. Ironically enough, it proved to be the vehicle on which the very sort of imperialism that modern capitalistic government aspires to create was carried eventually from the little nucleus of territory about the capital city of Cuzco over a far-flung empire reaching northern Ecuador at one end and the river Maule, well down into northern Chile, on the other.

The rulers of modern Soviet Russia seem to be trying to build up just such an imperialism of communism as the Inca emperors built. Critics of Russia to-day sometimes say that the Russian scheme of social organization is inimical to creative art. Friends of Russia deny this, and at least they may point to the fact that art flourished in Peru under communism. The Peruvians had no written language, so they left us no bound volumes of history, but the relics found by archæologists are themselves conclusive evidence as to the high quality of the creative ability of the Peruvians in the field of applied esthetics.

The archæologist who works in Peru has great advantages over his fellow laboring in the wet countries of the ancient Mayas. A strip about forty miles deep back from the coast of western South America is intensely dry, and here time has not yet destroyed either the pottery or even the textiles buried in thousands of graves. Peruvian pottery is admirable for loveliness of line, as well as for color of decoration, which is original often to the point of appearing fantastic to modern eyes. The Peruvian weavers sometimes used a fiber made from the maguey plant—a member of the same family that gave the Mexicans their beer, their rope and their dental floss.

The Peruvians also had wool, from the llama, the alpaca, the vicuña—all three members of the camel family. But above all they wove in cotton, of which they had two kinds, a pure white and a golden brown. You would be surprised to realize how much we imitate the designs of the Peruvian weavers in our carpets, pillow-covers, book-covers, wall-papers, and clothing. Here is just another instance of modern America stealing from ancient America without giving credit where credit is due.

Definitions of culture and definitions of civilization are easy to make, but are unsatisfactory to accept. Considering that the Peruvians never invented writing and had no system even for the recording of numbers except an elaborate method of tying knots in cords called *quipus,* objections might be raised to ranking them as a civilized people. But when one reflects upon their genius for government and colonization, and when one goes to a museum and looks upon the miracles they left behind in thread, one wonders if civilization can be defined so narrowly. As Professor L. Leland Locke says, "Here is found the anomaly of a people with a highly complex civilization, particularly in governmental machinery, with a wealth of tradition, with a peculiarly rich and expressive language, but with no system of writing, either hieroglyphic or phonetic."

Yet is this more remarkable than the fact that a people as advanced in most things as the Mayas knew not so simple a device as the wheel?

Speaking of miracles in thread accomplished by the Peruvians, William F. Murphy, in his authoritative treatise "Textile Industry," says: "The perfect thread is not to seek; it has been made."

And such another authority as Dr. Charles W. Mead of the American Museum of Natural History endorses the statement that the subjects of the Incas accomplished "the most extraordinary textile development of a pre-historic people."

Of all the achievements of the Peruvian weavers, the tapestries were perhaps the finest. Such an internationally accepted authority as Mr. M. D. C. Crawford says:

In tapestry Peru reached its highest textile development. The harmony of color, the beauty and fastness of the dyes, and the perfection of the spinning and weaving, place these fabrics in a class by themselves, not only as compared to other textiles of this land, but as regards those of any other people.

The chief social and economic interest in Peru was the textile art, the blanket and clothing business. Not even in Lawrence, Massachusetts, or Paterson, New Jersey, is so high a percentage of the population concerned with the textile industry as was the case throughout the vast Inca Empire.

It is not surprising that a people so expert in weaving should have achieved distinction in the manufacture of feather-work as well. But whereas in feather-work the Peruvians were rivaled by the Mexicans, in the field of metallurgy the subjects of the Incas were supreme throughout America. The Peruvians understood casting, melting, soldering, and gilding, and they worked in gold, copper, lead, and silver. Their mines were rather shallow excavations, and many of them have been found. However, probably much of their gold was obtained from rivers, by

264

the washing process. Rivers were partially dammed up in the dry season to catch the metal brought down by the floods of the rainy season.

Although some copper was manufactured in Mexico and in the Great Lakes district of what is now the United States, most of America was in the stone age when the white men arrived. But the Peruvians were well advanced into the bronze age. Long before Pizarro conquered Peru the subjects of the Incas had learned how to make bronze by mixing tin with copper. Cylindrical pottery furnaces were used for smelting metals, and as many of these were placed on hills to get the benefit of a wind, the scene at night was often picturesque, hilltop signaling to hilltop with sullen fire. When one sees the furnaces of Pittsburgh and Gary, the textile mills of Paterson, Lowell, and Lawrence, one thinks of Peru of the Incas.

Of course it is wrong to speak of the whole nation as Incas. It is just as wrong as it would be to call the people of the United States presidents or senators. The term "Inca" was applied only to the males of the hereditary ruling class of the Peruvian Empire, including the emperor. The subjects of the Incas lived mostly in huts made of cane with roofs of thatch. Sometimes the walls were plastered with mud. In some of the cold parts of the country the ordinary people lived in stone huts, but most of the stone

265

ruins which remain were public buildings or edifices of the rulers.

The Peruvians were expert masons. They were more skilled than the Mayas or Aztecs in handling great blocks of stone and in fitting them together, so cunningly that they have endured to this day. But they were far inferior to the Mayas in the matter of architectural decoration. Dr. Charles W. Mead says of Peruvian architecture:

Its most striking features are simplicity, symmetry, and solidity. The Incas had no knowledge of the true arch with its keystone, and did not use columns. Timber was not available in most localities where their structures were built. When wood was used no mortise joints were made, and as they did not know the use of iron, the beams were tied together by ropes of vegetable fibre. . . . The ancient builders were able to transport bulky masses of pottery and granite, and cut them with the greatest nicety, but the magnificent walls so raised were roofed with sticks and thatched with wreaths of grass.

Because of the frequency of earthquakes in their country, the Peruvians so constructed their buildings that the rooms did not communicate with one another, but opened into courtyards. Many Spanish buildings of much less age have been crumbled by earthquakes which have been survived by the buildings of the Incas. The most striking pieces of Inca construction that remain for our admiration are the roads and the abutments of great bridges consisting of four strong cables made of woven vine over which branches were laid. Such bridges are still being used in Peru; and although they may sound flimsy to us, they are capable of being crossed by loaded mules. In some places the Peruvians used pontoon-bridges made of bundles of reeds, and sometimes voyagers got across the river by means of a big basket suspended from a cable.

Perhaps the Peruvians inherited their ability in architecture and engineering from the mysterious so-called pre-Inca people who preceded them. Some of the remains of the earlier people are called "Megalithic," a word which merely means "big stone." These big-stone remains are found over a wide area, but the most conspicuous examples are at Chavin, Huarez, Quecap, Ollantaytambo, Sacsahuan, and Tiahuanaco. The fortress on the hill at Sacsahuan, which is back of Cuzco, is a good example of this sort of masonry. The stones at the bottom of the structure are much larger than those at the top, but throughout the stones are of varying size. This means that the front of the fortress presents a streaky rather than an even appearance, for the edge of one stone does not fit the edges of those just about it.

Perhaps the most interesting big-stone remains are those at Tiahuanaco, on the edge of Lake Titicaca in

267

Bolivia. Here are rows of huge monoliths of dressed sandstone. One of them, more than twelve feet high, six feet wide, and four feet thick, is believed to weigh more than twenty-six tons. It was suggested that these monoliths which line an inclosure facing the points of the compass resemble the great stone circles found in Europe. The rather superficial resemblance is not important, and more recently it was found that these big monuments were once connected by a wall.

The inclosure was ended with a stairway made of great stones. At one side of the "yard" is the celebrated monolithic gateway of Tiahuanaco, probably the most extraordinary ancient ruin in all America. The central figure which decorates this gateway seems to be human. His head-dress terminates in a series of puma heads. (The puma was apparently a sacred animal to these ancients.) It is impossible to date any of these pre-Inca ruins, but several of them, such as the Tiahuanaco gateway just described, and the famous Chavin stone, present unmistakable resemblances to the art of the Mayas of Central America.

Two other centers of pre-Inca culture—not, however, conspicuous for big-stone remains, but rather for their pottery which has been exhumed from graves—are Trujillo and Nasca, both on the coast of Peru. The Trujillo pottery is marked by a frequent use of realistic forms of animals as well as scenes

268

from the daily life of the people. The lines of the pottery of the Nasca region are inferior, but for coloration no pottery ever made in any part of the world has been so rich as the pottery of the ancient Nascans.

Nothing at all is known about any of the so-called pre-Inca peoples except what has been learned from the relics just described. Apparently the Incas themselves were puzzled by these things, and the archæologists employed by the court of Peru were studying them when the Spanish conquerors arrived.

Largely owing to the fact that the Peruvians had no writing, little is known of their history. Several lists of the reigning Incas were left us by historians who wrote just after the Spanish conquest. Unfortunately there is a most distressing lack of uniformity about these accounts. One of them gives as few as eight Incas and another gives one hundred rulers. It is the consensus of opinion that the last list is too long and that the Inca Empire was probably not founded before the twelfth century A.D. It was perhaps at the height of its glory toward the end of the fifteenth century, and it seems to have been already showing signs of decay when the Spanish conquerors arrived early in the sixteenth century.

The Inca Empire was expanded greatly by a series of conquests until it reached from the river Ancasmayu in northern Ecuador to the river Maule in Chile and included what to-day comprises the countries of Ecuador, Peru, Bolivia, part of Chile, and part of northwest Argentina. Throughout this country the valleys were lush and beautiful and the mountains were peaks of barren beauty.

The Peruvians kept a large standing army ready to jump at any moment to any province that appeared rebellious. The provinces were governed by administrators appointed by the Incas, and all this information has come down to us through prodigious feats of memory of the trained memorizers who kept the history of this great nation and handed it on by word of mouth, much as the fame of this or that sage or warrior was kept alive by the troubadours of early Christian Europe.

No one who sees the remains of the great stone road that ran the entire twenty-two-hundred-mile length of the Inca Empire, no one who sees the crenellated profile of the majestic city of Machu Picchu, can doubt the majesty and glory and grandeur that was Inca. Many things of the empire have not crumbled yet. The splendid buildings, roads, and bridges of the Peruvians reflect an outstanding fact about the social nature of those people—namely, they were essentially organizers. Viewed from a materialistic basis, there was much less inefficiency and waste in the Government of the Incas than in any Government of our times.

Recognizing what we often forget in these days

of great centralization of population in cities, that
the land is the source of all wealth, the Peruvians
divided their land into three parts. One was allotted
to the Inca, another to the Sun (that is, the Church),
and the third was for the support of the populace.
All land, however, was worked by the people. It was
characteristic of a certain humanitarian strain prevailing in the Inca civilization that after the land of
the Church had been cultivated, the soil devoted to
the support of the cripples, widows, orphans, and soldiers abroad on military service was next attended
to. When the people had seen to the planting of their
own crops, then, and not till then, were they required
to tend the fields of their powerful ruler, the Inca,
who was supposed to be the Son of the Sun.

From about the twelfth century, when the Inca
Empire really got under way, until it was given its
death-blow by the soldiers of Spain, the chief concern
was the conquest of neighboring nations. The Peruvians were not only excellent soldiers; they possessed
the skill in colonization which perhaps only the Romans and the British have equaled. The Peruvians
understood very well the art of playing off one neighboring nation against the other. And when they had
conquered both, they were wont to tranship large sec-
tions of the population of one conquered nation into
the territory of another, using the mutual suspicion
of naturally hostile peoples to aid the Inca sword in

keeping order. Other large bodies of the newly won subjects of the Sun were habitually put to work building roads connecting their own unfortunate land with the capital of the conquerors, so that the latter might quickly throw in fresh troops at the first sign of rebellion.

For the most part, however, the actual administration of government in a conquered colony was extremely wise. Wherever possible the Incas seem to have allowed the subjugated people to keep a great many of their own laws and customs. Very often there was to the natives little indication that they had been conquered, except the necessity of paying taxes to Cuzco. One other penalty, however, was always attached to losing a war with Peru, and that was that the defeated nation had to adopt the religion of the Incas. For in Peru, as in every other ancient American nation, except the Aztec Empire in its latest days, Church and State were one and identical.

Just as the interested observer of the course of Peruvian history may be inclining toward the conclusion that one important cause of the great success of the Incas in warfare against neighboring nations sprang from the unity of Peruvian life that was achieved by its communistic organization, he comes up against the striking fact that the only neighboring nation that the Peruvians did not conquer was a people which believed in the importance of individual

272

freedom with a passionate devotion not even exceeded by the Anglo-Saxon. This people was the Araucanian nation.

The Araucanians lived just south of the river Maule, in north-central Chile. It is significant that even in its heyday the Inca Empire never succeeded in thrusting its southern border beyond the river Maule. These Araucanians, by the way, had the distinction of being the only American nation that came into frequent contact with the invading Spaniard without losing its independence. Other American peoples, such as the Taironas of the Sierra Nevada de Santa Marta region of Colombia, were not conquered by the Spaniards, but after taking one despairing look at the dangerous mountain passes of the Tairona country the Spaniards seem to have abandoned the job, and contented themselves with calling the Taironas Sodomists.

The Araucanians, however, were constantly at war with the Spaniards for more than a hundred years, and got distinctly the better of the argument. After the expulsion of Spanish rule from South America, the Araucanians voluntarily merged themselves with the new nation of Chile. Although at no time in their history were they in the first rank of peoples, from a cultural standpoint, they have won a small immortality for themselves by virtue of the fact that they were devils for fighting.

Now, although the communal form of organization of the Peruvians can hardly be overemphasized, within certain limits they did allow the individual a considerable degree of choice. It was impossible for any one to rise from the rower ranks to the higher, and most of each man's and each woman's life was spent in service to the State. Moreover, all industry was organized by crafts for the common good. But, as we have seen, the aptitudes of the individual were carefully studied, and to a large extent a man was allowed to choose what craft or profession he would practise. Of course any one is more likely to excel at work he likes than at work that is repugnant to him, and to the fact that the Peruvians were allowed a certain degree of choice of the means by which they would gain their livelihood may perhaps be attributed the fact that they seem to have been a rather inventive people.

It is not surprising that the Peruvians never achieved the proficiency in astronomy of the Mayas, for the Mayas were essentially a trading nation, and traders and sea-goers have ever needed more of astronomy than men who pursue all life's conquests on land. Medicine, however, has always been a handmaiden of the military art. Whatever may be said of warfare, it gives a great deal of practice to the surgeon. Hence it is no wonder that the Peruvians were the best surgeons in ancient America, and possibly the best surgeons of the entire world of their time.

Coca, from which we get cocaine, was widely used as a local anesthetic in operations. Indeed, it seems probable that the surgeons of Peru were the first surgeons in the world to employ anesthetics. So many bags filled with dried coca leaves have been found around the necks of mummies in graves unearthed by archæologists that there is no doubt the chewing of coca leaves was widespread. There is no evidence that the universal practice of taking this drug in mild doses had any harmful effect on the people of the great empire of the Incas, and we of the United States to-day, who are so suspicious of all the products nature has given to man to ease his painful way through this weary world, may sometimes wonder if we have not gone too far in our suspicious attitude toward all natural stimulants and anodynes.

Peruvian physicians made wide use of physics and of the practice of bleeding. Snuff was considered a very helpful treatment for colds, and the sap of the Molle tree was employed to heal cuts. Archæologists have found so many pottery figurines in human form with one or both feet amputated and the skin drawn over the stump after the manner of modern operations that there can be no doubt that the ancient surgeon was skilful with the knife. The operation seems to have been particularly common along the coast, perhaps due to the fact that a sand-flea of that region, which burrows into the human foot to deposit its egg, often produces blood-poisoning, necessitating amputation.

But the most spectacular accomplishment of the Peruvian surgeon of which we have any evidence was his skill in trepanning, or cutting out a piece of the skull. Copper-headed clubs and slings for throwing stones were used so much in battle that fractures of the skull were frequent. Even so, it is difficult to account for the fact that of two hundred and seventy-three of the skulls examined by Dr. MacCurdy of Yale, seventeen per cent had been trepanned, and one had been cut open five times! Unless the cemeteries from which these skulls were taken were adjacent to some ancient military hospital, it may be concluded that the practice of trepanning the skull had some sort of religious significance, and was sometimes resorted to when not necessary for physical reasons. Unfortunately, as the Spanish conquest wiped out the last of the professional memorizers—"human files"—through whom the Inca Government kept its records, we can only speculate as to the reason for the prevalence of this spectacular operation of trepanning. Nevertheless we must join our surgeons in marveling at the skill with which it was done— sometimes with knives of copper, no doubt, but often with knives of stone.

276

Courtesy American Museum of Natural History

## Peruvian mummies

Courtesy American Museum of Natural History

## Trepanned skulls unearthed in Peru

As just noted, the Peruvians were far inferior to the Mayas in astronomy. Nevertheless they had made a good deal of progress, and had their own kind of observatory. To check on the arrival of the solstices they had set up on each side of Cuzco eight stone columns arranged in two rows, so that they might easily note the relative position of the sun and its rising and setting. Other stone pillars—or the line followed by the shadows cast from them—told the Peruvians when the equinoxes had arrived.

Most writers about the land of the Incas make a great deal of the importance of sun-worship in Peru. Now, sun-worship probably had no very important place anywhere in South America before the foundation of the Inca Empire, and even the Incas used a calendar based on the moon before they began to attach great importance to the sun. Along the coast the inhabitants made a great deal of the cult of the sea. Moreover, it should be remembered that sun-worship is just another side of rain-worship—both being adoration of the gods of fertility.

Finally, the chief god of the Incas was Uiracocha, the deity allied to Pachacamac, who was recognized as the Creator in the coastal district. As Uiracocha was considered the Creator of the Universe, he was given credit for being the parent of lightning, rain, and thunder, as well as of the sun and moon. The fact that the sun was worshiped by the people of the bleak

277

mountain uplands, where the cold may be very sharp at night and early morning, no more shows any connection between Peru and Egypt than the fact that the sea was worshiped by the fishermen of the west coast of South America argues that they must have exchanged ideas with the high civilization of the Isles of Greece.

Pretty certainly the importance of sun-worship among the Peruvians as a whole was exaggerated for us by the early Spanish explorers, whose avaricious desires were inflamed by the sight of all the gold used in the temples of the sun. Undoubtedly the Peruvians had an intricate and highly developed system of philosophy, and a very elaborate religious ritual. Until we know more about such things it gives a very lopsided picture of Peru for us to represent the Peruvians as people who were primarily engaged in falling on their knees and adoring the "Great Eye of Heaven." The most important feature of Peru— the feature that makes the Inca Empire memorable among the nations of man since the start of history —was the widespread and highly successful organization of the whole empire on a basis of State socialism.

The relation of the Inca Empire to the other great nations of America of that time still lies mainly in the field of speculation. No one can doubt that there were many contacts between the Mayas and the Toltecs, between the Toltecs and the Aztecs, and—through the Toltecs and Aztecs—between the Mayas and people far north of where to-day stands Mexico City. But some scientists do say flatly that they see nothing to indicate that the Incas were at all aware of the other high American civilizations flourishing in Central America and Mexico.

To the writer, this view seems far too conservative. Resemblances between Peruvian and Mexican pottery, similarities between the sculpture of the famous Tiahuanaco gateway and the Chavin stone on the one hand and the characteristic architectural sculpture of the Mayas on the other, seem to combine and dovetail, suggesting that the early South Americans had some contact with the high culture flourishing far to the north of them. Unless turquoise deposits shall be discovered in South America we shall have to assume that the artists who made the lovely turquoise inlays of Peru got their azure mineral from the nearest outcropping at present known, which is at Santa Fé, New Mexico, some twenty-eight hundred miles away. At the very least a most persuasive case can be made out for the statement that the culture of all Peru seems marked by a common American character.

Indeed, it is not stretching the matter too far to see in the great Inca god Uiracocha another representation of the same omnipotent being known to the Mayas as Kukulcan, and worshiped by the Toltecs

279

as Quetzalcoatl. What a pity that the rich literature learned by heart by the trained memorizers of the Incas has been lost to us! However, the following gift to world culture which has survived the general destruction shows that the bards of the Incas were not far behind the poetic high priests of the Mayas in the fine expression of the awe and wonderment the sensitive human being must feel as he contemplates the great forces of nature.

### AN INCA HYMN

O Uiracocha! Lord of the universe,
Whether thou art male,
Whether thou art female,
Lord of reproduction,
Whatsoever thou mayest be,
O Lord of divination,
Where art thou?
Thou mayest be above,
Thou mayest be below,
Or perhaps around
Thy splendid throne and scepter.
O hear me!
From the sky above,
In which thou mayest be,
Creator of the world,
Maker of all men,
Lord of all Lords.
My eyes fail me
For longing to see thee;

Courtesy American Museum of Natural History

Feather head-dress—Chimbote, Peru

Courtesy American Museum of Natural History

Pan-pipe—Peru

For the sole desire to know thee.
Might I behold thee,
Might I know thee,
Might I consider thee,
Might I understand thee.
O look down upon me,
For thou knowest me.
The sun—the moon—
The day—the night—
Spring—winter
Are not ordained in vain
By thee, O Uiracocha!
They all travel
To the assigned place;
They all arrive
At their destined end,
Whithersoever thou pleasest.
Thy royal scepter thou holdest.
O hear me!
O choose me!
Let it not be
That I should tire,
That I should die.

CHAPTER XIV

PACIFISTS OF THE PUEBLOS

THERE is more unexplored land left in South America than in any other continent, and it is quite possible that in the future archæologists will find in the southern continent the vestiges of several great nations of antiquity concerning which we now know nothing. It is logical to expect that worthwhile results will reward the investigator who follows up the great raised roadways in western Venezuela left behind by a people believed to have been called Timote or the explorer who penetrates the heart of the Santa Marta Mountains of Colombia, where the Tairona nation—unconquered by the Spaniards and believed to have manufactured the best goldwork of ancient America—is supposed to have had its capital.

It is conceivable that somewhere under the jungle of South America will be found the remains of a civilization higher than any of the early cultures of which we are now aware. In the meantime the Mayas of Central America, the people ruled by the Incas of Peru, and the Toltec-Aztec people of ancient Mexico occupy the topmost three rungs of the ladder of old American civilization, and hold these rungs in the order named. A little below these three nations in the scale of culture, but nevertheless holding a pretty high position, are the Pueblos of our own Southwest.

As we have already seen, if America has any right to call herself "the cradle of the human race" it is probably through this southwestern area that her claim may be substantiated. It is from this region that the oldest traces of man in America have come —the fine darts that were shot into bison, of extinct species, at Folsom at least fifteen thousand years ago, the bone of a man who hunted the little ground-sloth in a cave in Bishop's Cap Mountain fifty thousand years ago, the men who shot the dart-points found lodged in a gravel-bank which was the surface stratum of the earth not less than three hundred and fifty thousand years ago. Also, from not very far from this part of the western hemisphere (Wyoming), came the little "half-ape" Tarsius, the ancestor of those anthropoid apes from which evolutionists believe man to be descended.

These southwestern States are blessed with one of the most splendid climates in the world. A considerable altitude, with a great deal of sun and very little dampness, has permitted the artifacts of ancient man to be preserved as they have been preserved in no other part of America except the dry coastal

283

desert of Peru. Now that the ingenuity and patience of Dr. A. E. Douglass of the University of Arizona has perfected a means of reading the later history of the peoples of the Southwest by counting the rings in the timbers used to support the roofs of the Pueblo villages, we can begin to expect a day in the not distant future when the chronology of the Southwest from the present time back to a date in the very early history of America may be worked out with dependable accuracy.

At present we are fairly sure of a number of national developments in the Southwest which preceded the Pueblos, whose communal life is still carried on in the ancient way, thanks to the encouragement of scientists and despite the opposition of ignorant bureaucrats in the United States Government.

There is good reason to believe that the ancestors of the modern Pueblos were the cliff-dwellers. "Pueblo," of course, is the Spanish word for "village." The name Pueblos is commonly applied to those natives who lived in compact villages of adobe buildings arranged around a ceremonial center. Now, such modern inhabited villages as the pueblo of Taos or the pueblo of San Ildefonso or of such ruined community houses as Aztec or as Pueblo Bonito—which has more than five hundred rooms—such pueblos, in short, as are found standing out in the open throughout the valleys and hillsides of New

Mexico, Arizona, and adjacent territory, are the immediate physical descendants of the older pueblos which were built in caves for protection against the nomadic tribes which were ever at war against the sedentary agricultural people of the villages.

Many tourists are familiar with two good examples of these cliff cities—namely, Spruce Tree Ruin and the near-by ruins on Mesa Verde, well named Cliff Palace. Both of these amazing structures are built up between the dry floor and the rock roof of a cave. Both of them contain the characteristic kiva, or subterranean ceremonial chamber of the modern Pueblos and both of them bristle with the picturesque turrets under escarpments that lend to the ancient cliff settlements something of the appearance of the crumbling castles on the Rhine.

One of the chief characteristics of the people who inhabit pueblos to-day is their aversion to war. And this seems to have been a characteristic of their ancestors who lived in the cliffs, for the bones of many of the latter which have been found show that they were shot by arrows fired from behind *and from below.*

Farther back in time than the cliff-dwellers were the cave-dwellers. There is much fascinating exploration to be done in the many caves of the Southwest, some of them so huge that the word "cave" is inadequate—a new word ought to be invented. For example, the famous Carlsbad Cavern has already been explored more than thirty-two miles underground, and there is no telling how much farther its ramifications run. Such a place is no cave in the ordinary sense; it is an underground city—indeed, an underground world!

The word "cave-dweller" is too vague to be of much use. Indications are that a number of cultures filtered into the Southwest from outside. Perhaps these invasions will never be adequately traced, but in the meantime scientists tentatively describe three populations which preceded the Pueblo people as Basket-makers, Post-Basket-makers, and Pre-Pueblos. First were the Basket-makers, whose remains were discovered by S. J. Guernsey, Havard anthropologist and artist, a few years ago. Apparently they lived in flimsy structures which have long since disappeared, but they used the sandy floors of large dry caves to store their crops and to bury their dead, and most of what we know about these people has been gained by excavation in such places. The Basket-makers did not have the bow and arrow. They hunted and fought with darts four or five feet long, thrown by the device called atlatl. This is a characteristic arm of the early Mexicans and its use by the Basket-makers is an interesting suggestion of how Toltec influence spread northward across the Rio Grande in remote times. As the Toltecs were the torch-bearers

of Maya culture, here then is also an interesting indication that the Basket-makers, who lived perhaps as
long ago as two thousand years before Christ, were
the beneficiaries of some of the culture which had
been developed in Central America.

The Basket-makers had no cotton and did very little weaving with the loom, but they were skilful in
making bags of woven twine which they ornamented
elaborately. Their name has been given them from
the fact that they manufactured a great deal of coiled
basket-work, ranging from trays, through bowls and
jars, to panniers. The most characteristic thing about
the Basket-makers is that they had no pottery at all.
The Pueblo peoples, on the other hand, produced
great pottery in the past; indeed, thanks to the encouragement of ethnologists, they are making a very
fair grade of ceramics to this day.

Now, the Pueblos are a round-headed people who
deform their skulls in infancy by flattening them behind with a cradle board. The Basket-makers, on the
other hand, were a long-headed people who, quite
content with the skulls God gave them, practised no
such gruesome deformation. It is obvious that the
Pueblos are a different racial stock from the Basket-
makers; no one knows whether both races invaded the
Southwest from some other quarter or whether one
or both were indigenous to the New Mexico-Arizona
region. And probably no one ever will know. But

there is unmistakable evidence that the Basket-makers lived before the Pueblos. And recently there has been found reason to think that although the two were distinct races, the Pueblos inherited some of the culture of the former. It is believed this was handed down through two intermediate peoples: first, the Post-Basket-makers, who had long, undeformed heads like the Basket-makers, and who began the manufacture of a crude type of pottery; secondly, the Pre-Pueblos, whose round heads were artificially flattened behind like the Pueblos and in whose hands pottery became much more developed than it had been.

If the use of the spear-thrower by the Basket-makers suggests a contact with the Toltecs, there are even more features of Pueblo civilization which show analogies to the culture of Old Mexico. Pottery of Toltec type has been found at Pueblo Bonito. The use of turquoise, the worship of the turkey—which was domesticated—cremation, and, above all, this practice of head-deformation are Toltec customs, as they were Maya customs before that. Probably there was more than one invasion which brought these things up from Mexico. It must be remembered that the Pueblos are to this day a number of different tribes; indeed, as many as five distinct languages are spoken in the Pueblo area.

From the very beginning there have been fights in the Southwest between the farmers and the hunters

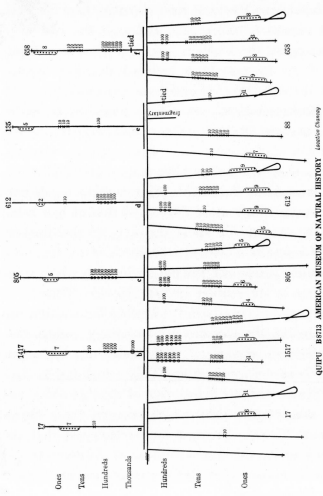

**QUIPU B8713 AMERICAN MUSEUM OF NATURAL HISTORY** *Location Chancay*

*The pendant strands are grouped in fours, each group being tied with a top strand. The top strand SUMS the numbers on the four pendent strands.*

⬭ *indicates Ones, each dot is a single one. Each ✕ indicates a Ten.* ⊙ *indicates a Hundred.* ⊚ *indicates a Thousand.*

Courtesy American Museum of Natural History

Arrangement and numerical significance of the knots used by the Peruvians in counting

—that is, between the Pueblos or their sedentary agricultural predecessors and such wild nomadic tribes as the Navajos and Apaches. The horizons of Southwestern scenery are generally walled by mountains —natural back drops for something to happen against. And something was usually happening! It is a tribute to the spirit of coöperation pervading the Pueblo people and to their intense national vitality that they were able to keep their culture alive in the face of repeated onslaughts by wild nomads who preferred living by robbery to making the effort to produce agricultural food in the dry sandy soil of the Southwest.

The feats of irrigation which the Pueblos accomplished, while not so stupendous as those of the Incas, have nevertheless aroused the admiration and envy of modern engineers. A typical example is the ancient city of Los Muertos, whose many irrigation canals were estimated by Mr. F. W. Hodge, formerly director of the United States Bureau of Ethnology, to have watered as much as two hundred thousand acres.

Two of the outstanding architectural features of the Pueblos were the development of the kiva, a circular subterranean chamber for religious meetings, and the construction of huge massed terraces which supported each entire village. In these terraces is shown the same setback principle used in the Maya pyramidal temple. Just how the Maya influence reached the Pueblos is a question. Probably the greater part of it was transmitted through the Toltecs of upland Mexico, but it is quite possible that some of it seeped over westward from the moundbuilders of the Mississippi Valley, who, as we shall see in the next chapter, show such marked cultural resemblances to the great builders of Central America as to give much strength to the theory that Maya trading canoes once traveled farther up the Mississippi than where the city of New Orleans now stands. Like the Pueblos, the Mayas domesticated turkeys, and like them, too, they flattened their heads, although it is true that the Maya cranium was flattened in front and the Pueblo behind.

In the matter of careful city-planning and grouping about a ceremonial center, the Pueblo settlements surpass most of the cities of the Central Americans. And even the biggest Maya building—monastery, palace, or what not—never had so many rooms as the communal structure at Pueblo Bonito, with its eight hundred chambers.

Of course the manufacture of basketry and pottery were the chief industries of the Pueblos, the baskets being made by the men and the pots by the women. The art of weaving also was highly developed, the materials used including cotton, woven rabbit skins, buffalo skins, and turkey feathers. Big flocks of turkeys were kept to supply the material for ceremonial robes of feathers.

To-day there is a tariff line between the United States and Mexico along that same Rio Grande whose head-waters were a center for life in the ancient villages of adobe. In those times there was also a sharp demarcation of industry near this region, at least so far as metal was concerned. The copper which spread eastward from the mines in the vicinity of Lake Superior seems not to have been sold much to the Pueblos; they bought most of their copper from the Toltecs and Aztecs, who understood better how to work it than did the natives of the Great Lakes region.

Although the nomadic tribes of the Southwest were generally at war with the Pueblos, there were nomadic peoples of the plains farther north which made periodic trips to the Southwest in order to exchange their skins of buffalo and deer for maize and for the robes of cotton manufactured in the communal villages. The Pueblos did a good deal of hunting on their own account, however, and characteristically they did it in the communal manner, whole tribes taking part in the hunt. Some of the tribes around the Rio Grande took fish from that river, but others, like the Zuñi, had a taboo against fish. There was no taboo against bathing, however, and in general the Pueblos have always been a very cleanly people.

There is truth in the old saying that cleanliness is next to godliness; almost without exception the native American tribes civilized enough to eat maize flour have been cleanly in personal habits.

Women have much influence among the Pueblos, relationships being counted chiefly through the female line. Society is divided up among clans—that is, among people related through their mothers. The government cannot be called matriarchal, however, for the actual administration is in the hands of a male governor and a male council. The governor is elected by the people, and the council is also chosen in a democratic way, although in some pueblos its members hold office for life, while in others they are elected annually. In addition to the governor there is another important officer, the war chief. He is appointed annually by the cacique, a religious officer, with the consent of the council. In the old days of raids by the Navajos and Apaches, the war chief had charge of the defense of the pueblos. To-day he concerns himself with such communal enterprises as hunting and digging irrigation ditches.

It cannot be too much emphasized that the Pueblos have always been pacifists, seeking only to be let alone to develop their original ideas of civilization in their own way. Perhaps this is one reason why they often chose such remote and barren locations for their villages. We know from the accounts of the Spaniards that when the Europeans attacked the Pueblos the latter ran up ladders to the tops of their houses and pulled the ladders after them. Whenever there was time before an attack, the children, women, and old men were sent away to mountains and caves. Those villages which were so fortunate as to possess water supplies were able to withstand sieges for many months. While the Pueblos never went so far as to practise turning the other cheek, there was about their tenacious pursuit of peace something Tolstoyan.

The democracy of Pueblo life is almost as marked a trait as its pacifism. It would be difficult to name another people in the history of the entire human race so democratic as these red men of butte and mesa. Individualism is not rampant at all, although individual excellence is rewarded by distinction in social and religious standing. But there is neither extreme wealth nor extreme poverty among these pacifists of the terraced villages. Each family, no matter how distinguished its head may be in social, religious, or political life, occupies the same sort of house, eats the same sort of food, wears the same sort of clothing. Snobbery is something the Pueblo cannot comprehend. And so is fawning self-abasement.

We citizens of the United States who profess to be concerned with "making the world safe for democracy" could do much to further that program by keeping the modern Pueblo villages intact—protecting

293

their social life against the encroachments of the white man, as living laboratories of pure democracy. It is to the everlasting credit of the Puéblos that their civilization has never been so weak as to need the services of a dictator. Misguided attempts of the Indian Bureau at Washington to "Americanize" (God save the mark!) the modern Pueblos should be resisted by every white American who is concerned to see that civilization on this earth shall be saved from the Lenins and the Mussolinis.

The Mayas gave the world a demonstration of what heights in science and art may be attained by an intensely religious spirit directed by an intelligent aristocracy. The Peruvians of the Incas gave the world a demonstration of how huge a material prosperity may be attained where energetic and loyal masses accept socialism imposed by an intelligent autocracy. The Aztecs, separating Church from State, gave America its first demonstration of the feasibility of secular as opposed to religious rule. But perhaps the contribution of the Pueblos to the development of government and the science of social management is greater than any of these; at any rate, perhaps no other nation since families first began to form into larger social units has ever so nearly attained Utopia. Dr. A. V. Kidder well says of the Pueblos:

There can be little doubt that had they been al-allowed to work out their own salvation, they would eventually have overcome their difficulties, and might well have built up a civilization of a sort not yet attempted by any group of men. It is the tragedy of native American history that so much human effort has come to naught, and that so many hopeful experiments in life and in living were cut short by the devastating blight of the white man's arrival.

Harassed as the Pueblos were by raids and invasions of the less cultured nomadic peoples of the plains, it is not strange that Pueblo character turned inward upon itself and developed ritualism to a high degree. By the way, as between the tribes of pueblo and tribes of plains there is a most interesting contrast in point of view toward religion—the institution which "is one of the ways man has made himself most miserable," as Dr. Ruth Benedict of Columbia University has facetiously remarked. The tribes of the plains, who are the familiar "Indians" of our early Colonial stories and legends, do not believe that you can work up religious experience by ritual. They seek communion with the Great Spirit through ecstasy and visions. The Pueblos, on the other hand, shun ecstasy and cultivate self-control with all the puritanical perseverance of a Cotton Mather. Ritual is the thing, and hence the priesthood is extremely important. On the whole the gods are not regarded with much fear or awe. They, in a way not easy to explain to a white man, are regarded to a great degree as the souls of the dead, who come to earth now and then to bring the living the great boon of rain. The living receive them as honored guests.

It is not strange that the concept of rain-worship, which perhaps first reached the Southwest from its fountainhead in Central America, should take on a new emotional intensity in a region of almost perpetual sunshine. Although in some modern pueblos the ritual of Roman Catholicism has heavily overlaid the ancient ceremonialism, enough of the latter remains to show us that among all these tribes of arid desert and sandy mountain the deities of the rain are and have always been of paramount importance. The Maya-Toltec conception of the serpent in association with life-giving water still lives in Arizona and New Mexico, and no more interesting ancient ceremony may be seen in performance anywhere in the world than that witnessed by the occasional tourist who is so lucky as to be present at one of the rain- or snake-dances of the aborigines of our Southwest.

The wooden slabs on which are painted cloud symbols or ears of maize, and which the women carry during ceremonies to gain heavenly help for the crops of the Pueblos, the live rattlesnakes that the priests of the Hopi pass from hand to hand in the snake-dance, the horned serpent of painted deerskin used by the Zuñi—what are these but reminders that the cult of the great Maya god Kukulcan is not yet

Courtesy American Museum of Natural History

Messhomomah, one of seven Aztec or Moqui Palian cities of the Arizona desert

wholly dead on this earth? Yea, of the fifteen sets of priests of the Pueblos, what is this first and most sacred set of four priests but a modern survival of the gods of the four points of the compass, the Chacs, who directed the rain ceremonies in ancient Yucatan?

Let not devotion to our own gods blind us to the beauty of the worship of the ancient gods of America. Hark to the rain-priests of the Pueblos, as they pray aloud:

### 1

Come you, ascend the ladder; all come in; all sit
    down.
We were poor; we were poor; we were poor; we were
    poor; we were poor; we were poor,
When we came to this world through the poor place,
Where the body of water dried for our passing.
Banked-up clouds cover the earth.
All come, all come, all come, all come, with your
    showers.
Descend to the base of the ladder, and stand still;
Bring your showers and great rains.
All come, all come, all ascend, all come in, all sit
    down.

### 2

I throw out to you my sacred meal that you may all
    come.
Hold your gaming-stick; throw it forward. All come,
That the seeds may be strong and come up,
That all the plants may come up and be strong.

Come you, that all trees and seeds may come up and be strong.

### 3

Cover my earth-mother, four times with many flowers.
Let the heavens be covered with the banked-up clouds,
Let the earth be covered with fog; cover the earth with rains.
Great waters, rains cover the earth. Lightning cover the earth.
Let thunder be heard over the six regions of the earth.

### 4

Rain-makers come out from all roads, that great rivers may cover the earth;
That stones may be uprooted and moved by the torrents.
Great Rain-makers come out from all the roads;
Carry the sands of our earth-mother of the place.
Cover the earth with her heart, that all seeds may develop;
That my children may have all things to eat and be happy;
That we may have all kinds of seeds and all things good;
That we may inhale the sacred breath of life.
Send us the good south winds;
Send us your breath over the lakes, that our great world
May be made beautiful, and our people may live.

# CHAPTER XV

## RAIN IN THE NORTH

THIS is a rain-prayer of the Navajos, who since the white man gave them sheep and goats have made their living largely by herding the animals which give them the wool to make the famous Navajo blankets that are sold to American tourists:

Tsegihi.
House made of the dawn.
House made of evening light.
House made of the dark cloud.
House made of male rain.
House made of dark mist.
House made of female rain.
House made of pollen.
House made of grasshoppers.
Dark cloud is at the door.
The outward trail is dark cloud.
The zigzag lightning stands high up on it.
Male deity!
Your offering I make.
I have prepared a smoke for you.
Restore my feet for me.
Restore my legs for me.
Restore my body for me.
Restore my mind for me.

Restore my voice for me.
This very day take out your spell for me.
Your spell remove for me.
You have taken it away for me.
Far off it has gone.
Happily I recover.
Happily my interior becomes cool.
Happily I go forth.
My interior feeling cold, may I walk.
No longer sore, may I walk.
Impervious to pain, may I walk.
With lively feelings may I walk.
As it used to be long ago, may I walk.
Happily may I walk.
Happily with abundant dark clouds, may I walk.
Happily with abundant showers, may I walk.
Happily with abundant plants, may I walk.
Happily on a trail of pollen, may I walk.
Happily may I walk,
Being as it used to be long ago, may I walk.
May it be beautiful before me.
May it be beautiful behind me.
May it be beautiful below me.
May it be beautiful above me.
May it be beautiful all around me.
In beauty it is finished.
In beauty it is finished.

A pastoral people needs rain to produce pasturage
for its flocks almost as much as an agricultural people
like the Pueblos needs rain for its crops. Even when
the Navajos were mere savage raiders without flocks,

they appreciated the importance of rain for the several tribes they attacked and robbed. So the worship of rain-gods in ancient America was not confined to the higher nations which practised agriculture and built with stone and adobe.

From the northern frontier of the Pueblos to the southern frontier of the Eskimos there are no stone ruins to indicate that man ever reached a very high state of development in this wide territory. The area includes most of what is the United States to-day, and the fact just noted is perhaps some excuse for the tendency on the part of modern "Americans" to underestimate the importance of the nations which lived in this hemisphere before the coming of the Spaniards and the English.

But every State in the United States has its aboriginal relics of one kind or another. Some are merely the sites of old villages—invisible to every one but a trained archæologist—in which excavation would reveal arrow-heads or scrapers or bone needles or bits of old pottery. However, two thirds of our States have much more conspicuous monuments of the past than these. That is, they have relics of those mysterious people who, for lack of a better name, we have called mound-builders. Two thirds of the States of the Union have some of these mounds, many of them being in fantastic shapes such as the form of snakes, buffaloes, or what not. One county in Illinois alone

301

has six hundred and fifty-five mounds. It is characteristic of our disregard for antiquity that all but fifty of these mounds have been dug into and most of them looted. As Dr. Fay-Cooper Cole of the National Research Council says, "It is as if a valuable illustrated historic book of six hundred and fifty-five pages placed on reference in a county court house or public library had been rifled by the public until all but fifty pages had been torn out."

Mounds have been plowed over by farmers, dynamited by vandals, records of early America destroyed which can never be replaced. The utter irresponsibility of most of the people of the United States toward relics of the sort which Greeks or French or Italians or British would instinctively venerate was well illustrated in 1928, when a town in central Illinois planned a picnic and advertised that part of the festivities would include the opening of "an Indian mound." Fortunately, an archæologist who happened to see the advertisement intervened in time to prevent the devastation from taking place. He learned to his horror that the plan was to blow up the mound with a stick of dynamite, "to see what it contained"!

For the most part our people exhibit more respect for hot-dog stands than for such antiquities as aboriginal mounds. We are just beginning to learn that these mounds are a great natural resource which should be conserved as carefully as our forests and deposits of mineral wealth. We are just beginning to learn that mounds should never be opened except by trained archæologists who are prepared to report everything as they find it—that is, to transcribe each page of local history into the larger book of all America instead of tearing the page out piecemeal or defacing it.

The pyramidal mound as a foundation for building extends from the Great Lakes in North America to the mouth of the Amazon in South America. But there are more of these mounds about the valleys of the Mississippi and Ohio than anywhere else. The man or woman who cannot afford to take the train to Mexico or the steamer to Yucatan, Guatemala, or Peru, who cannot even afford the trip to Arizona or New Mexico, can get some feeling of direct contact with the great fountainhead of ancient American culture by driving his or her flivver to the nearest aboriginal mound and reflecting that it is now generally supposed that the mound-builders were not a separate race from the red men found here by the first whites, but were the direct ancestors of the former, and by reflecting that the view is growing in scientific circles that the settlements of the mound-builders were the northernmost outposts of the glory that was Maya and the grandeur that was Aztec.

Even practices suggestive of the civilization of the Incas existed north of what is now the Mexican border. The Natchez tribe of the lower Mississippi built temples to the sun and believed in the relationship between their rulers and the Monarch of the Heavens which suggests the sun cult of old Peru. This Natchez people had a caste system very similar to that of the Aztecs. There is a great deal of persuasiveness in the statement of Dr. Paul Radin that "the Natchez simply obtained it from the same source as did the Aztecs and their Nahuatl predecessors—from the Toltecs."

Instead of the basket-ball of the Mayas and Toltecs, the ritualistic game of the Natchez was that which is played in our colleges to-day under the name of lacrosse. Many considerations lend force to Dr. Radin's contention that the mound-builders of our Middle West inherited much of their culture from the Toltecs and Mayas—some of it directly and some of it via the Natchez, who had been reached by Maya trading canoes coming up the Mississippi. The chief consideration tending to this conclusion is the dictate of common sense. But, as remarked before, that, with all too many scientists, is the last consideration to have weight.

Many of the copper objects found in the mounds came from the great mining district around Lake Superior, but some copper as well as some shell ornaments have been found bearing designs that are unmistakably Mexican and others that are unmistak-

Courtesy American Museum of Natural History

Navajo weaver using the batten—Arizona

ably Maya. Recently the sacred serpent so identified with rain-worship in Yucatan has been found on pottery unearthed from a mound on the Illinois River.

And why not? How silly to argue that great national developments like those in Peru, Central America, and upland Mexico should exist contemporaneously without knowing anything of one another! Human nature was the same then as it is to-day; one of its fundamental traits was curiosity and another was the instinct for adventure. Man had just as much wanderlust then as he has now, and if his facilities for transportation were not so highly developed, they were nevertheless adequate to make voyages and treks of thousands of miles nothing to marvel at.

It has been suggested that some such trek (from Siberia) or some such voyage (from the South Sea Islands) has been responsible for the presence even till to-day on the northwest coast of North America of a group of tribes presenting certain culture traits which seem to set them markedly apart from the other peoples of North and South America.

These tribes—Tlingit, Haida, Tsimshian, Kwakiutl, Bella Coola, Coast Salish, Nootka, Chinook, Kalapooian, Waiilatpuan, Chimakuan, etc.—are as a whole characterized by an extraordinary development of capitalism and a caste system conspicuous for a notable degree of snobbery with a high valuation on names and for a ritual for the ostentatious

305

public exchange of property, called the "potlatch." These North Pacific coast people as a whole are famous for their wood-carving, and some of their characteristic tall carved totem-poles are available for study in certain of our museums.

Alleged connections between these people and Siberians or Polynesians or Melanesians have not yet been proved. They remain perhaps the greatest puzzle in American ethnology.

But to go back to archæology—that is, to the past as contrasted with the present—we modern Americans, awakening to the importance of the antiquities in our two continents and to the necessity of preserving them as a veritable book of record from the spoliation of curio-hunters and amateur archæologists, have a rare sport at our very door in the opportunity to study these things with intelligent respect. In a month of hard motoring a man could touch most of the high spots of ancient culture north of the Pueblo region, and he would find that as a rule these high spots are the ones in which have been found tangible vestiges of the influence of those great Central Americans who seem to have provided a large share of the vital spark for every important blooming of culture north of Panama and for a good many south of it.

For instance, in tracing out the history of some of the famous plains tribes which figure most promi-

306

nently in native American resistance to the "winning of the West" by our own forefathers—the Arapaho, Blackfoot, Cheyenne, Comanche, Iowa, Kansa, Missouri, Omaha, Pawnee, and others, it will be found that one of the most illustrious was the Pawnee, which of this entire group was the one that seems to have been reached by the largest number of influences from Mexico and Central America. The Pawnees had the human sacrifice of the Aztecs, Toltecs, and Mayas, as well as a yearly cycle of ceremonies relating to the growing of maize.

Swinging eastward, our motorist might find at Etowah, Georgia, archæologists digging up ornaments of gold and copper decorated in a manner quite plainly Mexican. Keeping on northward, he would cross the territory of the Sioux and Algonquian peoples, famous in the annals of our own colonial times for the trouble they made the first white settlers, and both of them—but especially the Sioux—somewhat affected by a dilution of the great Central American influence that reached them via the Pawnee.

Then in New York State and vicinity our wanderer will find living descendants of a people perhaps as ferocious in war as even the Aztecs and the Peruvians. The reference is, of course, to the famous Five Nations of the Iroquois. The Iroquois, who by the way, gave women more privileges than the wives and settlers of our own white ancestors enjoyed, had many features in their social and religious life which seem to have had a Southern origin. Probably some of these reached them by way of the mound-builders, although the blow-gun of South America probably reached the Iroquois via the Atlantic coast, where other tribes used it.

These early New Yorkers lived in long wooden houses of a shape similar to some of the long stone "palaces" of Yucatan, and they surrounded their villages with wooden stockades just as some Maya cities on the eastern coast of Yucatan—Tuluum, Xelha, and Xkaret—were surrounded by stone walls. There is reason to believe that the high position given to women, and the special importance attached to a rite called the condolence ceremony—used when a chief died—were inherited or derived by the Iroquois from the Toltecs of Mexico. The maize festival of these New Yorkers looks Mexican or Maya, too. Indeed, although we think of the Iroquois as primarily warriors, the most important thing in their culture was their agriculture, which was built up around the maize, beans, and squashes of the Mayas, Aztecs, and Toltecs.

By this time, if our motor tourist has any imagination at all, he will feel that what Lincoln said of Gettysburg should be true of the many other spots in America which have much older historical associations. Mankind will never forget what was done at

Gettysburg, and mankind should never forget what was done in every State of the Union and in Canada by those foster-ancestors of ours, the first Americans.

If the amateur student of ancient history wishes to pursue his investigations further, he will not find that many tangible traces of Maya or Mexican influence have yet been discovered north of the Iroquois country, but he will learn that rain-worship was observed over virtually the whole of the continent. Even the Eskimo of the far north, whose relation to the other American nations is very doubtful, worshiped the life-giving rain. There is evidence in the following Eskimo poem, as beautiful in spirit and phrasing as the Navajo prayer to rain-gods with which this chapter began:

I look toward the south, to great Mount Koonak,
To great Mount Koonak, there to the south;
I watch the clouds that gather round him;
I contemplate their shining brightness;
They spread abroad upon great Koonak;
They climb up his seaward flanks;
See how they shift and change;
Watch them there to the south;
How the one makes beautiful the other;
How they mount his southern slopes,
Hiding him from the stormy sea,
Each lending beauty to the other.

309

## CHAPTER XVI

## NOT TOO LATE TO DISCOVER AMERICA

IT IS one thing to show the average cultivated man or woman that ancient America had a high civilization. It is another thing to get him and her to entertain the thought that this civilization was possibly indigenous, developed here without any help from other continents. In fact, so deep-seated is the pro-European, pro-Asiatic bias which our Plymouth Rock, Mount of Olives background has carved into our very souls that the chief concern of many laymen, once they have acquired a smattering of information about Maya and Inca and Aztec, is to decide to what particular part of the European-Asiatic world they shall attribute the seed that blossomed into Aztec and Inca and Maya.

Nor is it enough for them to choose among the Chinese, Sumerians, Phenicians, or Egyptians. It has become a favorite pastime with amateur archæologists, and even with pseudo-professional archæologists, to create lucubrations ranging from an imposing hundred-thousand-word volume down to a "two-stick" letter to the newspapers "proving" that red-skinned humanity in America would never have got

310

more than one jump above the anthropoid stage but for the benison of light shed upon our two fortunate continents by the lost tribes of Israel, the lost continent of Atlantis, or—even lovelier conception—the lost continent of Mu (spelled that way, but pronounced as a cow would utter it).

Though it may seem undignified for a writer who is striving humbly but earnestly to adhere to the truth as closely as his abilities permit, even to mention such whimsies and pipe-dreams as these theories relating ancient America to Atlantis and Mu, they nevertheless should be mentioned if only because they indicate the ineradicable tendency of the human soul to cultivate romantic error at the cost of sober truth; the inherent predilection of the human spirit never to array itself in black or white when pink or lavender is available. The only difference between the theorist who fills the Sunday supplements of the yellow journal with "evidence" that ancient Yucatan was the child of Atlantis and the "scientist" with a string of learned degrees after his name who has written half a dozen volumes to air his hallucination that all human culture is inherited from the banks of the Nile is a difference in degree, not in kind.

W. J. Perry, G. Elliott Smith and W. H. R. Rivers, with their hard-ridden heliolithic theory—based on the obscenity that man has been inventive only once, and then in Egypt—are only more *plaus-*

311

*ible* than Colonel Churchward, sponsor of the continent of Mu theory, not more *intelligent*. They are sounder in their premises, but every bit as weak in their reasoning. No one can deny that four and five thousand years ago a nation was building pyramids and worshiping the sun on the banks of the Nile, whereas one may certainly question whether several thousand years ago there was a spectacular human culture on a continent which has since sunk beneath the Pacific Ocean. But if there *was* such a continent, it is more logical to argue that America derived the benefit of culture from it than to contend that every manifestation of intelligent activity exhibited by man was an inheritance of the product of the cerebration of the Egyptian priests.

All this sort of argument concerns a matter called diffusion by the medicine-men of the modern era whom we dub scientists and heed with all the confidence that our ancestors put in prophets. As a matter of fact, this question of diffusion is ceasing to be taken very heatedly even by the scientists themselves. The diffusionists are a comparatively small element in the anthropological world, but they make up in noise what they lack in numbers. Their opponents belong to what is called the evolutionary school. Inasmuch as every layman in smoking-car or country club who ever speculates upon the origin of culture in ancient America falls—although he does not realize it—into either the diffusionist or the evolutionist school, it may not be amiss to analyze these two tendencies.

Roughly speaking, the diffusionist believes that man is an imitative animal, the evolutionist believes that man is an inventive animal. The diffusionist thinks that any given trait of culture is invented only once and spreads throughout the world by imitation. The evolutionist contends that man is much the same creature wherever he is found, and that if he has the brains to create something in one part of the world, the chances are he may have the brains to create it independently in another.

Now, although evolutionists outnumber diffusionists in the ranks of the scientists, among laymen probably the diffusionists predominate. This is because among the masses of human beings comparatively few are able to think—a reflection that would seem to tend to bolster up the whole original conception of diffusion! But while admitting that the mass of human beings are unable to think, the evolutionists still contend that there are leaders endowed with inventive mentality among *all* peoples. The fact to be noticed here, however, is that the man in the street is generally a diffusionist; that is to say, to stick to our American field, once he has become cognizant of the splendor of the ancient American scene he seems to feel it can be accounted for only by the assump-

313

tion that ancient Americans imported their culture from some other continent.

It satisfies the average man to believe that culture had one origin, just as it satisfies him to believe that there is only one true god and Allah is his Prophet. No sooner has the average man visited a few ruined cities in Central America or Peru or read a few books about them than he begins to talk loudly about resemblances he notices between them and the ruins of Egypt, China, or what have you. And this is the average man of cultivation, not merely the average man of the Tennessee which made it a crime to suggest to school-children that man might have been descended from "lower" animals, nor the average man of the Utah which soberly believes that all learning was found on certain gold plates the existence of which was revealed to Joseph Smith.

The method by which the typical lay diffusionist proceeds is simplicity itself, his argument is as simple as the familiar contention that all cats are black at night. To take a concrete example, as soon as he notices that both Egypt and Peru had pyramids and sun-worship, he rushes out to aver that Peru was settled by Egyptians. There are two great chances for error in this line of reasoning. The first is the one stressed by the anti-diffusionists or evolutionists and summed up in their contention that it is quite possible that different races occupying widely separated areas of the globe might react to similar conditions by inventing similar institutions. The second waives this point and embraces the proposition that even granting for the sake of argument that the common possession of pyramids and sun-worship shows there was once contact between Peru and Egypt, why must we assume immediately that Peru was settled from Egypt rather than that Egypt was settled from Peru?

Here, of course, we run right up against the American hemispheric inferiority complex again. Our ancestors crossed the ocean in the *Mayflower,* we were brought up in a religion centering about certain events which once occurred in Palestine, therefore everything worth while in human development must have come from the other side of the Atlantic.

Is it logical to contend that man in only one small area of the world's surface has had the ability to invent, that man elsewhere has had the ability only to remember and imitate? Is it not more logical, is it not more in conformity with what we know of human nature to maintain that man everywhere is largely the creature of environment and that where environments are similar two groups of human beings with no means of communication will react similarly to their environment? For example, given a hot climate and a plentiful supply of pliable wild grass, is it not logical to expect two tribes, thousands of miles from

each other, independently to arrive at the invention of
the straw hat? Is not that point of view just as logical as to contend, as the diffusionists do, that one of
those tribes *must* have acquired the straw hat by some
actual contact with the other tribe?

On the basis of logic it seems to this writer that
the evolutionists have distinctly the better of the diffusionists, and particularly so far as America is concerned. Most of the American institutions which happen to resemble Asiatic or African or European institutions and which are used by the diffusionists as
proof that America got her culture from abroad—
most of these are not fundamentals in ancient American life, they are the oddities, the unusual things,
the what scientists call *curiosæ*.

Such things, for example, as sun-worship and pyramids. Mere animals—dogs, cats—indeed, mere plants,
such as sunflowers, are sun-worshipers by their in-
stinctive conduct. Is there anything, then, so original
and esoteric in human obeisance to the great planet
whose warmth and light makes life possible on this
terrestrial sphere? As for the pyramids, what is a
pyramid anyway but a glorified ant-heap? Most of
the designs and forms in modern textiles, sculpture,
painting, and architecture have reached us from
primitive man, who originated them by imitating
nature.

So far as America is concerned, the weight of evidence unmistakably indicates that our two western continents built up their own culture without help from the other hemisphere. This is indicated by what America did not have, as well as by what she did have. The wheel seems to have been unknown in the West. If there had been a cultural contact with Asia or Europe, would not so common a mechanical device of the eastern hemisphere as the wheel have been brought to America? Even the diseases of America were distinct. Research seems to indicate that syphilis and possibly yellow fever were American diseases, unknown in Europe before the white men brought across the Atlantic to the red men the great blessings of malaria, typhoid, cholera, measles, smallpox.

Thus the very diseases of America, the fact that no conspicuous disease of parasitic nature was common to both hemispheres, may be added to the list of evidences against diffusion along with the complete independence of American languages and American agriculture. To seize upon a few *curiosæ* like sun-worship and pyramids as proof that America got her culture from Egypt or China or what not, in the face of the overwhelming evidence to the contrary contained in the complete independence of such vastly more fundamental and important matters as language and agriculture seems very flimsy arguing indeed!

One who truly appreciates the magnificent cultural

achievements of the Americans is inclined to resent almost as a personal insult the implication that would rob America of the credit for such things. What sense is there in contending that the weaving of Peru and the astronomy of Central America, for example— both of which surpassed any weaving or astronomy current in Europe, Asia, or Africa at the time Columbus crossed the ocean—were derived by imitation of the inferior weavers and astronomers of those eastern continents? The *reductio ad absurdum* of this theory that America got her culture from the East was found in the contention that examples of ancient Peruvian clothing indicating a high degree of skill in the weaver's art must have been put upon the Peruvian corpses by Europeans performing their ghoulish work after the Spanish conquest!

However, it is not the purpose of this writer to enter the diffusion controversy at any length; nor would an extensive treatment of such an academic, philosophic discussion have any place in this book. But it is the writer's purpose to leave his readers with a plea that they try to maintain an open mind. Let us have fair play. Even if the independence of American agriculture and language still leaves you unconvinced that there was no important cultural contact between the western continents and the eastern ones, at least try to give America what the man in the street calls "an even break" in this matter of transmission of culture. Granting cultural contact for the sake of argument, what fairness is there in this everlasting assumption that America was the child and Europe the parent, America the receiver and Europe the donor?

The late Augustus Le Plongeon was a writer whose theories must be taken with a great deal of salt, yet some of them have a very salutary effect as publicity to combat the errors of conventionally minded scientists with European hemispheric superiority complexes. Thus, when Le Plongeon contended elaborately that Egypt had received its civilization through emigrants from the Maya cities of Central America he was greeted with loud laughter by the savants of the world, but the fact remains that his contention was just about as logical as the contention of Elliott Smith and Perry and Rivers that Central America received its culture from Egypt.

The force of ocean currents is often cited by romancers building up theories about early voyages that "diffused" culture from one continent to another. In line with which, observe the fact that a Maya trading canoe cast loose upon the Gulf Stream would reach Norway far sooner than Pacific ocean currents would bring Egyptian cargo-boats to the coast of Peru or Guatemala.

After lingering in Scandinavia to build the megalithic (big-stone) structures whose remains are found there to-day, those Mayas or other early American emigrants might have proceeded along the coasts of Holland, France, Portugal, Spain, and Italy, sampling wines, cheeses and olives, before striking across the Mediterranean to Egypt in a voyage which would be mere child's play for men capable of driving their sailing-canoes between Yucatan and the mouth of the Mississippi.

Rubbish? Of course. The same sort of rubbish we hear from the small but determined group of erudite but unintelligent men who maintain vociferously that America and all the rest of the world got the flame of knowledge from a tiny spark created in Egypt. These men deserve mention here only because they are so much more noisy than sober experts like Mr. Flinders Petrie, the most distinguished British Egyptologist, Professor J. L. Myers of Oxford, and Sir Arthur Evans, who have only subdued, scornful chuckles for the suggestion that Egypt is the mother of all culture. That brilliant anthropologist Bronislaw Malinowski asks:

Are we to suppose that the use of fire for warmth and cooking, of water for drinking and irrigation, or air for breathing is each a cultural invention once made in Egypt and thence diffused? The question might appear absurd had it not been seriously put forward that the use of water for irrigation, of large stones for building, of gold for practical and decorative uses, is due to one single influence diffused all over the world.

The same authority utters the last word on this diffusion controversy as follows:

Diffusion is but a modified invention, exactly as every invention is a partial borrowing. . . . No culture is a simple copy of any other. No historian of present day European culture would dare assign it to any one original source. . . . Every cultural achievement is due to a process or growth in which diffusion and invention have equal shares. As independent entities, neither invention nor diffusion ever takes place in the sense that you could either spontaneously generate an idea or pour it out from one head into another. Diffusion and invention are always mixed, always inseparable. . . . In the case of every modern invention, we know that it is invariably made and remade time after time in different places, by different men along slightly different roads, independently of one another. Thus the invention of the wireless can be treated as a single and singular event and ascribed to one man or another only after its nature has been completely misconceived. . . . The compass, the art of writing, chemistry, the calendar—all were independently invented, as is known to archæologists. Paper was made of papyrus in Egypt, of rags in China, of another material in Mexico. It is identical only in its function. The technique of production, the material or way of using it, had to be independently invented. . . . Diffusion

321

never takes place: it is always a re-adaptation, a truly creative process. . . . Civilization is fortunately not a disease—not always at least—and the immunity of most people to culture is notorious; *culture is not contagious!* It has neither been invented nor diffused, but imposed by the natural conditions which drive man upon the path of progress with inexorable determinism.

These words might well be borne in mind by some scientists who deny indignantly that there was any contact between the Americas and other continents before the arrival of Columbus, and yet who contend just as vigorously that the wide use of maize, of a certain type of loom, and of tripod support for pottery vessels in America indicates that there was a good deal of "diffusion" in their own continents. The fact is that there may have been and probably were long trade voyages up and down the coasts of our continents thousands of years ago.

Moreover, it is even possible that the Atlantic and Pacific were crossed several times *in both directions* long before Columbus was born, perhaps long before the invention of writing. But it would be absurd to pretend we know this, and even more absurd to pretend—as some "scientists" do—that we know in which direction these oceans were crossed first. A conservative but constructive summing up of the "diffusionist-evolutionist" controversy has recently been given by

Professor Boas to his most advanced students at Columbia University in approximately these words: "The postulate that diffusion has occurred among neighboring groups is readily acceptable, but is doubtful over long distances. On the other hand, we have found that wide apart separate invention is possible."

All that we can do is to try to keep an open mind. And this certainly involves discarding the Biblical interpretation of American history which would identify Quetzalcoatl with St. Thomas, would see in the American aborigines the ten lost tribes of Israel, and would, in fact, account for everything significant in America before 1492 by an ingenious process of hunting out parallels and analogues in Biblical lands or elsewhere on the other side of the Atlantic.

But alas, there has been "diffusion" with a vengeance since Columbus rowed ashore to San Salvador that October morning nearly four hundred and forty years ago! The tragedy is that most of the best points in old American civilization have been ruined by that intrusion of a mechanistic, capitalistic European civilization on the artistic, communistic civilization of America. It is fascinating to speculate as to what might have happened in America if the white man had never come. Would the extending empires of the Aztecs and the Incas have met in Central America and fought for the dominance of the whole West?

323

Would the victor—perhaps settling down to a sedentary and reflective existence—have breathed new life into the artistic and scientific conceptions of the Mayas and carried them forward to even greater glory? And would the Pueblos in their protected villages of New Mexico and Arizona have worked out a scheme of life more nearly resembling Utopia than anything man has yet achieved?

We shall never know the answer. American culture was paralyzed by the European conquest, even though the death-blow was not finally given until the Spaniards extinguished the last stronghold of the independent Maya princes and priests at Tayasal on Flores Island in Lake Peten, Guatemala, in 1697.

Yet that expression "death-blow" is not entirely accurate. The metaphor of paralysis is better. American culture was paralyzed by the conquest, not entirely killed. A little life is maintained in the body yet, but it is life which looks backward, which takes from the past; not the truly creative life of a vital people. American culture is like a great tree whose trunk is virtually dead, but whose branches still put out a few feeble leaves. The botanist who inspects these leaves can see what the whole structure was like in its prime, even though he cannot expect of it any further noteworthy growth. In South America there are still tribes of red men who keep up many of the customs that were scattered far and wide by the imperialistic drive of the Inca Empire. In the inaccessible mountains of northwestern Panama the unconquered Guaymis still maintain many of the culture traits of the Aztecs, including the use of the spear-thrower or atlatl which the Guaymis call *natlatai.*

Mr. Hyatt Verrill, who has visited the Guaymis, says that "in their dialect the Guaymis are distinctly Aztecan, and over forty per cent of the words in their language are almost pure Nahuatl" (the language of ancient Mexico).

In the mountains of Guatemala, Mr. Oliver La Farge has found the Jacaltecas maintaining many of the ancient ceremonial officials of the Mayas for the observance of rites which neither the Spaniards nor the modern Guatemaltecans have succeeded in stamping out. Every year the Jacaltecas elect "Prayer-makers" or Chaks whose functions are very similar to the rain-priests of old. This tribe of red men also elects Captains of Dancers, which have charge of the sacred wooden drum "nose of the village." The Watch Winaq (Good Men), of whom there are eight at Jacaltenango, are self-electing, hold office for life, and "know a good deal of the secret, old knowledge," Mr. La Farge tells me. In their prayers they call on the Days, such as Eight Ahau, and particularly on Year-bearers. It is they who on the Year-bearer Day sacrifice a turkey and burn its blood, the same ceremony that was described by Bishop Landa and that may be seen in the old Maya book called the Dresden Codex.

The Year-bearer is the day on which the year begins, according to the old Maya calendar. This day changes, there being altogether four Year-bearers. It must be remembered that the Mayas believed the days were really gods who once lived on earth, "which," says Mr. La Farge, "helps to explain why the Old People worshipped them so much. The ordinary Indian, as in olden times, knows little of all this, but just does what the soothsayer tells him to."

These last words of Mr. La Farge suggest that investigators of the mathematics and calendarical lore of the old Mayas may err if they concentrate their attention on purely matter-of-fact interpretations of such things. The implications of magic in the Maya calendar and inscriptions were probably far-reaching, as has been suggested by Dr. Ruth Benedict, who, as an authority on the religions of primitive peoples, especially those north of Central America, is well qualified to make such a suggestion to special students of the Mayas.

What a thrill there is in finding that all the applied cruelty of the Spanish conquest, all the regimentation and repression of mestizo government since the Spaniards were driven out of America have not succeeded in entirely killing the old customs, so that even

326

the ancient calendar of the best astronomers of the entire world in 1492 is secretly observed to-day by red men keeping their stores in villages tucked away in the mountains of Guatemala!

Similarly I have seen the modern Mayas of Yucatan, Quintano Roo, and British Honduras burning copal to ancient gods of the rain in their wayside shrines, have heard them tell how they still have "maize masses," that both the white man's Christ and the red man's Kukulcan may bless the earth with the friendly showers which mean bountiful crops of the good yellow maize of the ancients.

It is not too late to discover America.

327

# BIBLIOGRAPHY

Bandelier, Adolph F. *Social Organization and Mode of Government of the Ancient Mexicans.* Twelfth Annual Report, Peabody Museum of Harvard University, Cambridge, Mass., 1879.

Benedict, Ruth Fulton. *The Concept of the Guardian Spirit in North America.* American Anthropological Association, Menasha, Wis., 1923.

Bennett, Robert R. *The Ancient Maya Causeway in Yucatan.* Reprinted from Indian Notes, Vol. VII, No. 3, Museum of the American Indian, Heye Foundation, New York, 1930.

Beyer, Hermann. *The Analysis of the Maya Hieroglyphs.* Late E. J. Brill, Ltd., Leyden, 1930.

Blom, Frans, and La Farge, Oliver. *Tribes and Temples.* Department of Middle American Research, Tulane University, New Orleans, 1926.

Boas, Franz. *The Mind of Primitive Man.* Macmillan, New York, 1927. *Primitive Art.* Aschehoug & Co., Oslo, 1927. *The Central Eskimo.* Sixth Annual Report, Bureau of Ethnology, 1888.

Brinton, D. G. *The Maya Chronicles.* Library of

American Aboriginal Literature, Vol. I, Philadelphia, 1882. *The American Race.* David McKay, Philadelphia, 1891.

Carrier, Lyman. *Beginnings of Agriculture in America.* McGraw-Hill Book Co., New York, 1923.

Churchward, James. *The Children of Mu.* Ives Washburn, New York, 1931.

Cogolludo, D. L. *Historia de Yucatan.* Madrid, 1688; Mérida, 1868.

Gann, T. W. F. *The Maya Indians of Southern Yucatan and Northern British Honduras.* Bureau of American Ethnology, Bulletin 64. Smithsonian Institution, Washington, D.C., 1918. *Ancient Cities and Modern Tribes.* Scribner's, 1926.

Gann, T. W. F., and Thompson, Eric. *The History of the Maya.* Scribner's, 1931.

Guernsey, S. J. *Basket-Maker Caves of Northeastern Arizona.* Report on the Explorations, 1916-17, by S. J. Guernsey and A. V. Kidder, Harvard University Museum, Cambridge, Mass., 1921.

Joyce, Thomas. *South American Archæology.* Macmillan & Co., Ltd., London, 1912. *Mexican Archæology.* Putnam, New York, 1914; Lee Warner, London. *Central American and West Indian Archæology.* P. L. Warner, London, 1916.

Kidder, A. V. *An Introduction to the Study of Southwestern Archæology.* Yale University Press, New Haven, 1924.

Kidder, A. V., and Ricketson, Oliver. *An Archæological Reconnaissance by Air in Central America.* "Geographical Review," April, 1930.

LaFarge, Oliver. *Adaptations of Christianity among the Jacalteca Indians of Guatemala.* "Thought; A Quarterly of the Sciences and Letters," American Press, New York.

Lothrop, S. K. *Tulum, an Archæological Study of the East Coast of Yucatan.* Carnegie Institution of Washington, 1924. *Pottery Types and Their Sequence in El Salvador.* Indian Notes and Monographs, Vol. I, No. 4, Museum of the American Indian, New York. *Further Notes on Indian Ceremonies in Guatemala.* Indian Notes, Vol. VI, No. 1. Museum of the American Indian, New York.

Madeira, Percy C., Jr. *An Aerial Exploration of Central America.* Bulletin of the Geographical Society of Philadelphia, April, 1931.

Mason, Gregory. *Silver Cities of Yucatan.* Putnam, New York, 1927. *Pottery and Other Artifacts from Caves in British Honduras and Guatemala.* Indian Notes and Monographs, Museum of the American Indian, New York.

Mason, J. Alden. *The Language of the Salinam Indians.* University of California Press,

331

1918. *A Preliminary Sketch of the Yaqui Language*. University of California Press, 1923.

Mead, C. W. *Old Civilizations of Inca Land*. American Museum of Natural History, New York, 1924.

Means, Philip Ainsworth. *History of the Spanish Conquest of Yucatan and of the Itzas*. Peabody Museum of American Archæology and Ethnology, Harvard University, 1917. *Study of Ancient Andean Social Institutions*. Connecticut Academy of Arts and Sciences, 1925. *Survey of Ancient Peruvian Art*. Yale University Press.

Morley, Sylvanus G. *Introduction to the Study of Maya Hieroglyphs*. Bureau of American Ethnology, Bulletin 57, Washington, D.C., 1915. *The Inscriptions at Copan*. Carnegie Institution, Publication No. 219, Washington, D.C., 1920.

Nuttall, Zelia. *The Astronomical Methods of the Ancient Mexicans*. Boas Anniversary Volume, New York.

Radin, Paul. *The Story of the American Indian*. Boni & Liveright, New York, 1927.

Saville, Marshall H. *Bibliographic Notes on Uxmal, Yucatan*. Indian Notes and Monographs, Vol. IX, No. 2, Museum of the American Indian, New York, 1921. *Reports*

*on the Maya Indians of Yucatan,* by Santiago
Mendez, Pedro Sanchez de Aguilar, and
Francisco Hernandez (Marshall H. Saville,
Editor). Indian Notes and Monographs,
Vol. IX, No. 3, Museum of the American
Indian, New York.

Spinden, H. J. *A Study of Maya Art; Its Subject
Matter and Historical Development.* Memoirs
of the Peabody Museum, Vol. VI, Cambridge,
Mass., 1913. *Ancient Civilizations of Mexico
and Central America.* Handbook Series No. 3,
American Museum of Natural History, New
York, 1922. *Reduction of Maya Dates.*
Papers of the Peabody Museum of American
Archæology and Ethnology, Vol. VI, No. 4,
Cambridge, Mass., 1926.

Stephens, J. L. *Central America, Chiapas, and Yucatan.* Harper, New York, 1841. *Incidents
of Travel in Yucatan.* New York, 1843.

Teeple, John E. *Maya Astronomy.* Carnegie Institution of Washington, Publication No. 403,
1930.

Thompson, J. Eric. *A Correlation of Maya and
European Calendars.* Anthropological Series,
Vol. XVII, No. 1, Field Museum of Natural
History, Chicago, 1927. *Civilization of the
Mayas.* Field Museum of Natural History,
Chicago, 1927. *Ethnology of the Mayas of
Central and Southern British Honduras.*

Anthropological Series, Vol. XVII, No. 2, Field Museum of Natural History, Chicago, 1930.

Tozzer, Alfred M. *A Comparative Study of the Mayas and the Lancandones*. Macmillan, New York, 1907.

Vaillant, George. *Excavations at Zacatenco*. American Museum of Natural History, New York, 1930.

Verrill, Hyatt. *Old Civilizations of the New World*. Bobbs-Merrill, Indianapolis, 1929.

Willard, T. A. *The City of the Sacred Well*. Century Co., New York, 1926.

Wissler, Clark. *The American Indian; An Introduction to the Anthropology of the New World*. Oxford University Press, 1922.

NOTE: Many valuable handbooks on the subject of the aborigines of the Americas have been published from time to time by the American Museum of Natural History, New York City.

# INDEX

Acomal, Quintana Roo, 219
Agave fiber, 110
Agricultural methods of prehistoric Americans, 34, 111 *et seq.*
Agricultural products originating in America, 129
Ahaukan Mai, Maya high Priest, 165
Ahkin Mai, Maya high priest, 165
Ahpuch, Maya god, 144
Allouez, Father, 83
American antiquities, 9 *et seq.*
American civilization, theories of origin, 319 *et seq.*
American prehistoric culture, end of, 324
Americans, Asiatic origin theory, 29
Anesthetics of ancient Peruvians, 275
Animals, domestic, of primitive Americans, 56, 113
Apache Indians, 289
Aqueducts, of the Aztecs, 248; prehistoric, 119
Arapaho Indians, 307
Araucanian nation, 273
"Archaic" art, 76-78
"Archaic" people, 75 *et seq.*
Architecture, of the Incas, 266; of the Iroquois, 308; of the Mayas, 218 *et seq.*; of the Pueblos, 289
Art and literature of the Aztecs, 250
Artifacts, European, 24; found at Bishop's Cap Mountain, 22, 283; found at Folsom, New Mex., 23; found at Frederick, Okla., 21; found at Las Vegas, Nev., 23; found at Vero, Florida, 21
Art, Mayan, 179 *et seq.*
Art of the "Archaic" era, 72-75
Asiatic origin of Americans, theory of, 29

Astronomical observatories of Maya, 156
Atlantis legend, 311
Atlatl, Pueblo weapon, 286
Ax, primitive American, 58
Azcapotzalso, Toltec city, 236
Aztecs, 225 *et seq.;* aqueduct building, 248; conquer the Nahuas, 242; culture, religion and power, 239-256; gods, 253; guilds and societies, 247; legend of origin, 231 *et seq.;* literature and art, 250; moral code, 249; priests of 254; social life, 246; tribes of, 245, 255; war tactics, 244

Bacabs, Maya gods, 146
Ball-court, Maya, 224
Balsam of Peru, 102
Baptismal rites, Maya, 174
"Basket-makers," the, 75, 286, 287
Beans, native American, 89
Beer, primitive American, 98
Bella Coola, Indians, 305
Benedict, Ruth, 295, 326
Berries, native American, 82
Beverages of prehistoric Americana, 97
Bishop's Cap Mountain artifacts, 22, 283
Blackfoot Indians, 307
Blom, Frans, 157, 228
Boas, Dr. Franz, 29
Bonacca Island, 197
Books, Mayan, 48
Bronze, ancient Peruvian, 196; early use of, in America, 47
Brown, Barnum, 23
Burial mounds, 53

Calendar of ancient Peruvians, 277; of the Jacaltecas Indians, 326; of the Mayas, 13, 48, 160-163

335

# INDEX

Calpulli, Aztec tribes, 245
Cara nation, 65
Carlsbad Cavern, 286
Carrier, Lyman, 38, 104, 115
Cartier, Jacques, 84
Cascara sagrada, 99
Cauac, Maya god, 146
"Cave-dwellers" of the Southwest, 285
Cereals, native American, 84
Chac-Mool, Maya god, 146
Chacs, Maya gods, 146
Chacs, the Maya priests, 166
Champollion's deciphering of Rosetta Stone, 17
Chanchan, city of, 65
Chapultepec, 242
Chavin de Huantar monolith, 71
Chavin, Peru, 267
Cheyenne Indians, 307
Chibchas, the, 65, 76, 197
Chicha beer, 98
Chichen Itza, 111, 137, 146, 156, 158, 182, 187, 194, 208, 212, 219, 224, 231
Chichimac nation, 232
Chicle, 102
Chicomoztoc, Maya city, 135
Chilam Balam, 135, 136
Chilans, the, Maya priests, 165
Children, parental regard for, 59
Chimakuan Indians, 305
Chimney, primitive, 53
Chinampos, or Floating Gardens of Xochimilco, 242
Chincook Indians, 305
Chocolate, 99
Cholula, Toltec city, 236, 237, 242
Cholula, Toltec pyramid at, 12, 236
Churchward, Colonel James, 312
Cities, agricultural, of Maya, 120
Cliff cities of the Pueblos, 285
"Cliff-dwellers," the, 284 et seq.
Cloth, early materials used, 54
Clothing, primitive American, 54
Coast Salish Indians, 305
Coba, 208
Coca, 99
Cocaine, 99
Codices, Mayan, 48
Cofan, Maya city, 211
Cogolludo, Spanish historian, 168

Cole, Dr. Fay-Cooper, 302
Colhuacan, King of, 242
Colombia, 282
Colon, Ferdinand, 107
Columbus, Christopher, 3, 4, 5, 37, 154, 197, 323
Comanche Indians, 307
Commerce, of prehistoric America, 193 et seq.
Communal ownership of land, 61
"Conquest of Peru"—Prescott, 240
Cook, Captain, 200
Cook, Harold J., 21
Cook, Dr. O. F., 38, 39, 40, 41, 82, 117, 120
Copal, 102
Copan observatory, 157
Copan, Maya city, 156, 158
Copper, primitive American use of, 47, 194, 195
Copper work, Incas, 265
Córdoba, Hermandez de, 107
Corn, antiquity of, 35, 42-45
Cotton, primitive use of, 55, 108 et seq.
Cozumel Island, 171
Creation, Usher's theory of, 17, 18
Cuicuilco, Mayan city, 124; ancient building at, 30
Cultural affinities, 69-80
Cultural divisions of primitive Americans, 64 et seq.
Cultural unity of primitive America, 46-63
Cummings, Dean Byron, 30
Cuxhuacan, Toltec city, 235
Cuzco, Peru, 267

De Candolle, Alphonse, 37, 38
De la Vega, Garcilasso, 148
De Landa, Bishop Diego, 48, 120, 151, 165, 172
De Leon, Pedro de Cieza, 94
Diaz, Bernal, 212
Diaz, Juan, 138
Diffusionist theory, 313
Divorce, primitive, 58
Domestic animals of early Americans, 113
Douglas, Dr., 284
Dresden Codex, the, 163

# INDEX

340

# INDEX

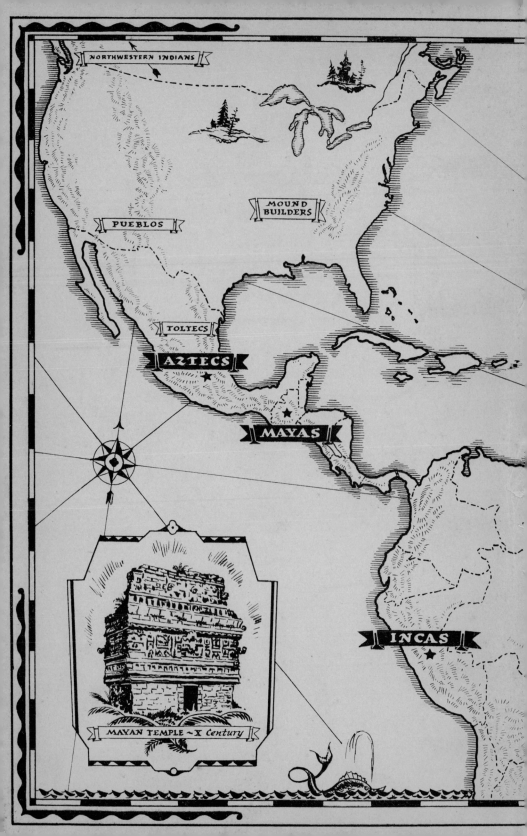

NORTHWESTERN INDIANS

MOUND BUILDERS

PUEBLOS

TOLTECS

AZTECS

MAYAS

INCAS

MAYAN TEMPLE ~ X Century